IMPROVING B▪A▪N▪K PROFITS

The Cost Control Approach to Increasing Income

3rd Edition

PAUL F. JANNOTT

BANKERS PUBLISHING COMPANY
PROBUS PUBLISHING COMPANY
Chicago, Illinois
Cambridge, England

ISBN 1-55738-334-0

Printed in the United States of America

BB

1 2 3 4 5 6 7 8 9 0

Table of Contents

Preface

There are certain areas in South Africa where diamonds can be found on the ground. One has to know what diamonds look like in their natural state, but they are there in all different weights and shapes for those who wish to look for them. This book contains acres of diamonds for those bankers who are serious about profit improvement. These ways to improve bank profits are ready for use in any bank. They were collected and tested in a twenty-year period of managing the day-to-day operations of large and small urban and suburban banks located in the eastern and midwestern sections of the country. To my knowledge, this book was the first of its kind published—a collection of original information on the subject of profit improvement, rather than a composite of other published material.

The ways of improving a bank's profits that are presented in the chapters that follow relate to the operations functions of a bank rather than to the loan and investment functions. Consequently, this is not a book about asset and liability management; it is about the ways—affecting both income and expense items—that a bank immediately can use to improve substantially its bottom line. Chapter 1 shows how to organize a campaign for profit improvement within a bank to maximize results. The other chapters list over 200 ways to reduce costs and improve profits.

Three new chapters were added to this edition relating to management concepts for improving profits. Each chapter contains several new ways directly to improve a bank's profits. In addition, several chapters were revised and expanded. Special note should be made of the added material in Chapter 11, "Reduced Interest Expense," which will be extremely helpful when interest rates increase.

Today, a multitude of forces have a negative effect on bank profits: the constant erosion of demand deposits, periods of low loan demand, state-imposed installment loan usury rates, added federal regulations, increased FDIC insurance, increased competition for deposits from large retail chains, insurance companies, and brokerage firms, escalating labor costs, and increased customer awareness of investment interest rates. A banker need only reflect briefly on these forces to become motivated to use every way possible to offset these negative effects on profitability. This book is dedicated to those motivated bankers.

PART ONE

TO BEGIN

Chapter 1

The Profit Improvement Campaign

COMMITMENT

If your bank has assets of $100 million and earns $1 million per year you should have no problem increasing your earnings per year by $150,000 to $250,000 by using the methods described in this book. But the size of your bank doesn't matter. Any bank can increase its profits by 15% to 25% per year. And some banks may even increase their profits by 30%. I've done it myself using these methods. It doesn't take a lot of work on senior management's part. But it does take commitment and dedication to get the job done. This book covers many operational subjects—clerical staffing, a variety of personnel related expenses, fee incomes, cash and cash items, and 19 different operating expense categories. To address each of these areas takes time. It is a major project that requires the backing of senior management and the determination to investigate each area to achieve the maximum results. This is a senior management project.

ORGANIZE THE PROFIT IMPROVEMENT CAMPAIGN

There are two ways to organize a campaign for profit improvement—the senior officer committee approach and the single senior officer approach. Either approach requires the support from the chairman of the board and/or the president of the bank and requires cooperation from each *senior* officer in the bank. The senior officer committee approach in most banks is the best way to organize this profit improvement campaign because all the senior officers will be directly involved from the beginning and throughout the campaign, will support one another, and will be able to make decisions in the meeting. There is no need to discuss an idea later with anyone outside the committee to obtain their approval because all the important officers will be at the meeting.

The first thought when formulating an organizational structure for a project such as this is how to get all officers and managers, if not all employees, involved. My advice is to organize only the senior officers towards this goal and eventually their efforts will filter down through the ranks. Other officers and managers will get involved because the members of the committee on occasion will be asking these officers to do some of the research that may be required to obtain sufficient information before the committee can make a decision on a subject. But to try to get everybody involved from the beginning becomes organizationally cumbersome and will dilute the direct involvement of the senior officers. In the beginning this committee will not need ideas solicited from a number of sources. This book will provide the committee with enough ways to increase profits to keep them active for several months. After exploring these areas other officers can become involved more formally, if desired, by organizing subcommittees.

The second way to organize a campaign for profit improvement is for the president to assign a senior officer to the project and give him or her this book with the admonition to get the job done. And this approach is effective particularly in smaller banks, as long as the right senior officer is selected. The subject matter of this book is oriented to the day-to-day practical operations of a bank. And so the person in charge of this campaign should have expert knowledge in the operations part of banking and should be senior enough to make convincing recommendations directly to the president upon which immediate decisions *to act* will be made. Also, since most of these decisions will involve the operations part of the bank the implementation of these decisions will be mainly the responsibility of the senior officer in charge of operations. It would seem appropriate and most effective, therefore, that this officer be in charge of the campaign.

If the committee approach is used, as recommended for larger banks where the organizational structure of the bank is more complex, the following areas of the bank should be represented by the senior officer in charge of that area:

Accounting
Auditing
Branch administration
Central operations
Data processing
Investments
Loans
Marketing
Personnel
Retail banking

Several of these functions may be under the jurisdiction of one senior officer (such as branch administration, central operations, retail banking and data processing, or accounting and investments) and only the senior officer in charge of these multiple functions should be on the committee. It is necessary to have all this representation on the committee for two reasons. First, because some of the areas covered by the committee directly affect all parts of the bank. For example, chapter 3 explains how to reduce staffing, overtime, and fringe benefits for all employees in the bank, not just operations employees. Fee incomes involve all fees—deposit and loan oriented fees—and most of the expense items covered relate to all areas of the bank. The second reason for this all inclusive representation is that this committee need not address only the areas mentioned in this book but should be encouraged to develop other ways to increase income—perhaps some related to loan interest rates or the investment of bank assets. Once the ball is rolling and everybody participates, the bottom line results could go way beyond original predictions.

If the committee approach is used, there should, of course, be a chairman. The chairman could be the president, the executive vice president or the senior operations officer. If the president would prefer to be an inactive member of the committee, in order not to influence the committee's recommendations, then a logical choice is the senior officer in charge of the most functions in the bank who will be in charge of implementing most of the decisions.

The chairman of this committee will be responsible for obtaining results in the shortest possible time. First of all, it is important to set some kind of goal. A 15% increase in annual profits is certainly realistic. A 20% increase is ambitious but attainable. Whatever the goal is, however, it should be translated to dollar amounts. So if you currently earn $1,000,000 and you wish to set the goal at 20%, then the goal should be quoted as a $200,000 increase in profits. There is more motivation attached to reaching a dollar goal than a percentage goal. Senior officers should be members of this committee because they are more naturally motivated to obtain results because of their positions in the bank and direct impact on profits. As actions are taken, projected annual increases in profits should be made and reported to everyone on the committee. It is important that committee members know how they are progressing towards the attainment of the goal. This progress report can consist of merely a one or two line description of the item with a projected annualized dollar profit increase notation. The following is a sample of this report.

PROFIT IMPROVEMENT COMMITTEE
Report of Accomplishments 2/1/XX to 3/31/XX

Accomplished profit improvement item	*Projected annualized profit increase*
Increased money order fee by $.25	$9,325.00
Eliminated overtime in check file area	$3,100.00
Instituted the presorting of outgoing mail	$5,350.00
Reduced average cash in bank by $75,000 @ 10%	$7,500.00
Discontinued maintenance contract on three stored manual teller machines	$875.00
Total	$26,150.00

The above sample report shows what has been done for the two month period (2-1-XX to 3-31-XX). It is assumed that the committee was formed on 2-1-XX. As new items are accomplished they are added to this list and a new total is tabulated. Future reports, therefore, always start from the beginning (2-1-XX). The list at the end of the twelve months might be two pages long, and total thousands of dollars but it is an ongoing record of what has been accomplished for all to see. Only items decided upon and *instituted* should be reported. Items discussed are not accomplishments. Implementation of items discussed is the key. The chairman of the committee must end discussions after all members are heard, ask for a consensus decision, assign the implementation to someone, be certain that the item has been implemented, and then put it on the report. The chairman need not, in fact should not, wait until the whole amount of an item has been saved (for example, over a twelve-month period) or even part of it. Listing a conservative projected annualized figure is sufficient. Getting accomplishments reported on paper as soon as possible is important because it motivates committee members. There is something formal and rewarding about published results. A double check on whether or not the projected annual savings amount was close to the real annual savings can and should be made after the twelve-month period has expired.

How often are the profit improvement committee meetings scheduled? During the beginning months you should find that every two weeks will work out well because there will be a lot of items to discuss and decide upon. As the list of potential items for discussion gets smaller the meeting times will be less frequent. This book offers approximately 185 potential items for discussion, so the committee should be meeting often for several months!

It is important that the chairman of the committee have an agenda for each meeting that has been typed and sent to each committee member, along with any pertinent research, in advance of the meeting. Agenda items should be decided upon after sufficient discussion. It is not as important that all the agenda items be covered, as it is that each item discussed be brought to a conclusion. The minutes of each meeting can be simple. A mere listing of the items discussed with conclusions is all that is required. This will aid in following up on items that were deferred.

HOW TO USE THIS BOOK TO MAXIMIZE RESULTS

The best way to start this campaign (whether conducted by one person or a committee) is to begin with the simple items that require little research and offer sizeable immediate dollar results; and then to tackle the more complex items. For motivation purposes it is important for all concerned to experience tangible results at the beginning of the campaign.

This book has been divided into seven parts:

Part One — To Begin (consisting of this chapter on organizing the profit improvement campaign)

Part Two — Reduce Personnel Expenses

Part Three	Increase Fee Incomes
Part Four	Cash and Cash Items
Part Five	Reduce Other Major Expenses
Part Six	Reduce Operating Losses
Part Seven	Management Concepts for Improving Profits

The chapters within each part relate to the subject matter of that part. Some general relationships, although not vital, exist between the chapters within each part, but there are no relationships between chapters of any one part to any other. As a practical matter, each chapter is basically self-contained. The information in one chapter does not lead to, or act as a base for, succeeding chapters. When reference is made to a certain chapter, unless otherwise noted, it is not necessary to reread preceding chapters.

It is recommended, however, that before even starting this project, you read the whole book to comprehend its scope and to designate for future quick reference those items that are critical for your bank to investigate. For instance there may be something major going on in your bank right now, relating in some way to profit improvement, that would be of help to you, now, before you even start the campaign. A classic example of this would be if you are now accepting quotes for an outside data processing service. Chapter 10 "A Review of Data Processing Costs," identifies several ways to negotiate these quoted fees. And the savings in fees, upon negotiation, could be astronomical. But you wouldn't know this if you hadn't read that chapter. So, you are urged to read the whole book before starting the campaign.

Start first with the simple, but dollar rewarding items, and then lead into the more complex items. Investigate first the six ways to increase NSF and overdraft charges (Chapter 5) and the ten important fee incomes often overlooked (Chapter 6). There are thousands of dollars of increased income possible from these sixteen items and all that is required to start this income is a very small amount of market research, which can be done in a few hours, and a decision. A few profit improvement committee meetings should be all that are needed to accomplish this and you will be off and running with an active campaign and you will have immediate profit results to be tabulated and reported.

The next step is to start assigning the subject matter covered in the other chapters to members of the committee in relation to their area(s) of expertise. The subject matter for these assignments could be divided into the following categories:

1. Reducing Teller Staffing (Chapter 2)
2. Reducing Other Personnel Related Expenses (Chapter 3)
3. Checking Account Service Charges (Chapter 4)
4. A Review of All Fee Incomes (Chapter 7)
5. Reducing Cash (Chapter 8)
6. Reducing Float and Correspondent Bank Costs (Chapter 9)
7. Reducing Interest Expense (Chapter 11)
8. Profit Improvement in Purchasing (Chapter 12)
9. Postage and Telephone Expenses (Chapter 13)
10. Other Expenses (Chapter 14)

The subjects of data processing costs (Chapter 10) and three major operating losses (Chapter 15) should be reviewed by the chairman of the committee to determine if there is an urgent need to address any of these subjects. Because of the nature of the material presented in these two chapters, the degree of urgency will vary from bank to bank. The subject matter presented in the last three chapters of the book, which relates to profit improvement concepts, should be reviewed and discussed by the committee as a whole to determine how these concepts can be used in the bank's campaign to obtain maximum results in improving profits. With regard to the ten subjects listed, however, they all should be assigned as soon as possible.

As an aid in assigning these subjects, it is important to take into consideration that the subjects of teller staffing (Chapter 2), checking account service charges (Chapter 4) and reducing cash (Chapter 8) require the development of basic statistical data, and even though this data is obtained from within the bank, the clerical tabulations required take time to compute. Consequently the committee member(s) to whom these subjects are assigned should have some clerical help available to them. The subject of reducing float and correspondent bank costs (Chapter 9) should be assigned to a committee member who is very familiar with this complex subject. Many of the ten subjects, however, can be assigned to committee members, with the understanding that parts of these subjects can be studied by junior officers and their findings reported to the senior officer committee member. In many banks depending on the size of the committee, most if not all of the subjects can be assigned at once, with agreed upon completion dates for reporting back to the committee.

DEVELOP STATISTICAL DATA

The proper use of statistics in any management function, but particularly in a profit improvement environment, provides the manager with the tools to uncover sources of profit improvement and to determine correct conclusions for a course of action. Since statistics are in effect a bridge between the past and the future they can serve as a road map for future actions.

For those subjects that require the development of statistical data, detailed examples of reports are presented with descriptions. It should be noted that the statistical formats used are basically simple, but because they are not familiar to the reader the explanation has to be detailed.

An effort was made throughout the book not to create complexity out of basically simple data and concepts, so no mathematical formulas were used in developing sample statistical data. In using those chapters that require the development of statistics, you will obtain most of the data from within your bank because the historical method was used (comparing a bank's own data from the past with the present and future) in developing the subject matter for the chapters. As an aid to this comparison, percentages of total figures were used because in real practice this was found to be very useful in developing quick, easy to comprehend comparisons.

STATISTICAL DATA SOURCES

For profit improvement purposes there are two important statistical data sources—computer reports and monthly bills. Computer reports are valuable for basic volume information—i.e., number of accounts by category, transaction volumes, and for certain general income and expense statistics such as the monthly income earned from certain service charges and the monthly expense for those expense items under investigation. For more specific information regarding large categories of expenses such as data processing, telecommunications, forms, energy costs, and maintenance contracts a review of the monthly bills is important. These larger expense items have to be broken down into their components to be reviewed effectively for profit improvement, and only the monthly bills can provide this detailed information.

As you will see in some of the following chapters, there are other sources of statistical data that will have to be used, such as certain personnel statistics, cash usage statistics, and internal loss statistics, that cannot usually be obtained readily from bills or computer reports. These statistics can usually be obtained from monthly or quarterly departmental reports already being compiled and published for departmental use.

FORMATTING STATISTICAL DATA

Throughout the chapters in this book, there are specific examples of how to format statistical data depending on the item being researched. In general, however, compiling historical data for an item is important for two reasons—it shows past performance which is a key to identifying profit improvement ideas, and is a tool to track future performance after profit improvements are made. Once the format is determined, it can be used for gathering data about the past and for tracking the future. For these purposes, the typical periods of time used for past and future statistics are the month, the quarter, and the year. Monthly statistics will produce quarterly and annual statistics through simple addition. Also, as a general statement, comparing quarters of a year with each other and with those of prior years can be important. When developing these formats it is best to start simply, however. When showing statistical data choosing line items is important, particularly when analyzing a major expense category. Also, when showing statistics it is best to show the periods of time used across the top of the report from left to right, and the line items in the first column from top to bottom.

These formatting suggestions are better explained by reviewing the following example. Let us assume that the profit improvement committee wishes to review the bank's data processing costs which are incurred from an outside data processing firm the bank uses to do all of its basic data processing. Up to this point it has been noticed that the monthly bill seems to be getting larger and larger. Figure 1–1 shows a sample report of this expense for the first six months of the year. The information was extracted from the paid monthly bills received from this outside firm. Note that the months are shown across the top and the line items from these bills are identified along the side in the first left column. Six months of bills is a sufficient time frame to analyze to show trends and/or identify specific items within the bills to investigate further. Eventually, of course, this report should be enlarged to show all twelve months of the year and the four quarter totals, and then ideally at the end of the year a separate report should be produced to show a comparison of this years' quarterly totals with last years' quarterly totals.

In choosing line items to show on the report for this expense the tendency will be to get too elaborate. Data processing bills are often highly detailed, and show many sub items. It is best to show major categories only. Always start with a simple, easily-read format. One can further analyze a major category in more detail later. Also, note that the labels used for each line item are easily understood by any banker reading the report. Anyone developing a report like this should be careful to translate data processing or other highly technical terms shown on the bills to more easily understood terms.

From reviewing Figure 1–1 the format of this report easily identifies several areas that should be investigated for potential profit improvement. This subject will be covered more fully, however, later in the book in a separate chapter dealing with data processing expenses.

USING PERSONAL COMPUTERS TO DEVELOP STATISTICAL DATA

A personal computer was used to develop the report shown in Figure 1–1. The PC is a useful tool because it saves typing time in formatting, and it will automatically compute column totals, line totals, quarter totals, and percentage increases or decreases. Also, the PC will allow one to easily experiment and change formats (such as from monthly columns to quarterly and/or annual columns) while still retaining in memory monthly statistics for future reference and reporting. To produce the quarterly totals and percentage changes shown in the far right hand columns of Figure 1–1 only required the PC operator to issue a simple command.

Any of the reports shown in this book can be produced without the use of a PC. The PC merely saves clerical time. The human imagination has to be used in selecting the formats to be produced. Because the PC can produce these formats easily, however, there is no reason to complicate the printed report with too many statistics. The report should be presented as simply as possible so it will be easily read and understood.

STATISTICAL DATA FROM OUTSIDE SOURCES

Bankers often like to compare their bank's performance in certain financial areas with the performance of other banks. Statistical data for all banks is available to any bank. There are a number of private firms that

Figure 1–1 Data Services Monthly Billing Report

Processing categories	*Jan 'XX*	*Feb 'XX*	*Mar 'XX*	*Apr 'XX*	*May 'XX*	*Jun 'XX*	*1st Qtr curr. yr*	*2nd Qtr curr. yr*	*% Diff*
DDA & Sav Accts.	6,739	6,324	7,254	7,184	7,353	7,479	20,317	22,016	+8%
Installment Loans	1,111	1,104	1,288	1,151	1,141	1,129	3,503	3,421	−2%
Mortgage Loans	201	169	189	188	189	217	559	594	+6%
Commercial Loans	487	487	546	539	538	538	1,520	1,615	+6%
Automated Clearing House	124	79	103	115	105	105	306	325	+6%
ATM's	1,299	1,244	1,322	1,317	1,350	1,373	3,865	4,040	+5%
Central Information File	468	450	472	461	763	772	1,390	1,996	+44%
General Ledger Accounting	870	840	890	919	901	913	2,600	2,733	+5%
Account Reconciliation	552	601	503	472	561	470	1,656	1,503	−9%
Microfiche	264	158	189	185	203	192	611	580	−5%
Misc. Charges	320	280	430	720	300	270	1,030	1,290	+25%
Telephone Communications	502	502	672	672	672	672	1,676	2,016	+20%
Grand Total	$12,937	$12,238	$13,858	$13,923	$14,076	$14,130	39,033	42,129	+8%

specialize in providing this data. All of them however, receive their basic information from the same source the Federal Deposit Insurance Corporation, which publishes each year a variety of financial data related to banks. For those bankers who find this method of comparison a valuable tool, it is recommended that they obtain this data free from the FDIC in Washington.

The information about outside sources for bank statistical data is helpful when a bank wishes to compare its performance with other banks. Such a comparison is helpful in pointing out areas of weakness. Your profit improvement committee may wish to research these sources to determine which ones it may wish to use. But even when you make profit-related comparisons with other banks, and you find that you compare favorably, you should not become complacent. This book was not written exclusively for poor earning banks. Its contents are applicable for all banks. In fact, many of the ways described to increase profits were used in banks that were already very profitable. These ways only made them more profitable. In writing this book the assumption is that all banks can increase their profits by using these methods and it doesn't matter how profitable they already are, how they compare with other banks, how big they are, or how small they are.

SUMMARY

To maximize a bank's profit improvement effort a commitment to accomplish results on the part of a bank's senior officers is required. And senior officers should be involved in the whole project. This project or campaign should be organized, ideally around a committee of senior officers, with a chairman to direct the committee's efforts. All senior officers involved in this campaign should be thoroughly familiar with the contents of this book. Goals should be defined and progress should be reported in writing. The committee as a whole should start with simple, but dollar rewarding projects. Projects should then be assigned to committee members using the book as a guide in the assignment and execution of these projects.

The use of statistics, in a profit improvement environment, provides profit-oriented management with a bridge between past performance and future profit increases. The statistical formats used in this hook are basically very simple but they are explained in detail to familiarize the reader with their exact content.

There are basically two important sources of statistical data for profit improvement purpose computer reports and monthly bills. Historical statistical data is needed to record past performance or expenses in order to identify potential profit increase areas, and then, after improvements have been established, to track future performance.

Statistical data should be presented in a simple format with the periods of time involved shown across the top of the page and with the line item categories listed in the left hand column. Line item categories should be shown in easily understood terms.

Personal computers are a help in producing statistical reports because their use reduces clerical time in formatting the report, automatically produces simple arithmetic calculations (i.e., column totals, line totals, percentage increases/decreases), and stores statistics in memory for future use. Even though the PC is a useful tool in providing statistical reports, reports should be formatted simply so that they can be understood easily by those reviewing the report.

For those bankers who wish to compare their performance in a number of financial areas with other banks, there are outside sources of statistical data available. These sources are referenced in this chapter. This book, however, assumes that all banks can profit substantially from addressing the subjects described in this book no matter how their profits compare to those of other banks.

PART TWO

Reduce Personnel Expenses

Chapter 2

How to Reduce Teller Staffing Effectively

Whenever a bank looks toward controlling and reducing salary expense all thoughts usually focus first on the teller function. The tellers comprise the largest number of employees in a bank who perform basically the same function, and so examining teller staffing requirements first is very logical and practical. For most bankers, however, determining proper teller staffing levels is often a frustrating experience. This frustration is caused by the number of variables associated with this vital banking function. One has to anticipate the number of customers who may arrive at the teller windows during each business day, the types of transactions the customers bring to the tellers, the average time for each type of transaction, and the effect that lunch hours and coffee breaks have on staffing requirements.

The typical approach to analyzing teller staffing requirements is to start a bank-wide counting exercise, which is usually done manually, and to amass a library of statistics on the number of transactions by type, per quarter hour, and by location. A set of complicated formulas is then applied to these statistics to arrive at optimum levels of staffing for each hour of each day of the week in each location. When first examining and contemplating this approach, it all appears very scientific, practical and logical, and it is. *But* because it is complicated and laborious, only extremely motivated bankers even attempt the project and few of these ever complete it. The result is frustration and a return to the eyeballing, seat-of-the-pants approach. Of course many of the giant urban banks do successfully staff their teller function by using this scientific approach, with the aid of a specialized staff of trained employees whose main function is to monitor the staffing of the hundreds of tellers employed by these large banks. But how can small and medium-size banks resolve their "gut" and often accurate uneasy feeling that, on some days, or in some locations, or both, there are too many tellers on duty, and that there is no real control of any sort in this area of expense.

What will be presented in this chapter is a more practical and simple approach to the problem of controlling and reducing teller staffing. This approach is based more on logic and psychology than on statistical mathematics. It is not, however, a theory, but rather a proven method that I have used and know to be very effective. The foundation of this approach is to keep a simple record of the number of tellers on duty, by day, by location and to maintain and promulgate this record on a continuous basis. In this approach, a history of teller staffing leads directly into where and when overstaffing occurred in the past and therefore, where and when to avoid it in the future.

The first step in this approach is to tabulate the number of teller workdays (or parts of a workday) now being used to perform the teller function in each location per week. The workday time frame, rather than a finer time frame such as a work hour is used to keep the tabulations simple; also, a historical record of workdays rather than work hours is easier to comprehend and analyze for staff reductions. This tabulation of workdays is done through the use of a simple report that is completed each week in each branch, and then forwarded to a central location. At this central location, a clerk spends a few minutes each week transferring summary information from these reports to a hand written ongoing spread sheet which shows total teller workdays used per location for the week, week by week. Then from reviewing the history shown on this spread sheet and relating it to some very basic transaction data, the logical process begins, which in turn leads quickly to the identification of the areas of obvious overstaffing, and finally to an actual reduction in staff.

What now follows is a detailed description of each step in this approach. Note that in this description, the examples and explanations that are given assume that a bank has a branch system. This approach to reducing teller staffing can also be effective in a unit bank, as is mentioned later in the chapter. In addition, it will become obvious from reviewing the information that follows that each branch employs part-time tellers. As will be shown, the employment of a mix of part-time and full-time tellers is a major factor in reducing teller salary expense.

TABULATE TELLER WORKDAYS

Figure 2–1 is a sample format that can be used by each branch each week to tabulate the number of actual days worked by the tellers. The following is an explanation of the instructions printed on the bottom of Figure 2–1.

1. This is an obvious instruction. It is important to identify who is working on what days, and whether these tellers are classified as full-time or part-time. In adapting this form to your own bank, be sure to draw enough lines for the number of full-time and part-time tellers in your largest branch plus a few extra for additional tellers that may be assigned to that branch on a temporary basis. Those in the branches who complete this form will typically put the names of their permanent tellers on the form once, and then in subsequent weeks duplicate the form to avoid writing in these names each week. In this instance, only the names of the tellers that are assigned from time to time to the branch on a temporary basis are written on the form during the week they work in that branch.
2. This is, of course, the main instruction for this report. Each 1 entered records a teller workday used to staff the branch for that day. There is no real distinction made for reporting purposes between a full day worked by a full-time teller or a full day worked by a part-time teller.
3. This particular instruction is important, as will be seen when we discuss reducing teller staffing, because it gives credit to a manager who might not need a part-time teller all day and either sends the teller home early when the lobby is not busy, or schedules part-time tellers for part of a day (or days) during the week. How these parts of a day are divided into quarters will depend on a teller's normal workday. For instance, if tellers in a branch are normally scheduled to work from 9:00 a.m. (a half

Figure 2–1 Teller Workdays Report

TELLER WORKDAYS REPORT
WEEK ENDING ____________
BRANCH ____________

Full-Time Tellers (names)	*MON.*	*TUES.*	*WED.*	*THURS.*	*FRI.*	*TOTAL*
Part-Time Tellers (names)						
TOTAL DAYS WORKED						

PREPARED BY ____________

INSTRUCTIONS

1. In the first column, list the names of the full-time and part-time tellers, that worked in your branch during the week.
2. For each full day a full-time or part-time teller worked, put a 1 in the appropriate box.
3. If a part-time teller works less than a normal teller's full day, put ¼, ½, or ¾ in the box depending on how much less the part-time teller works.
4. In the appropriate day boxes, indicate if any teller was absent "A," on vacation "V," on a scheduled day off "DO," or is on a leave of absence "LA."
5. If a branch borrowed help from another branch, or if a branch used their own part-time tellers on additional days during the week, put a "TA" (for temporary assistance) in the appropriate day boxes along with 1, ¾, ½, or ¼.
6. Complete the Total column and the Total Days Worked line. The grand total of days worked during the week shown in the bottom right hand box should cross foot. Do not add "A," "V," "DO," or "LA" days.
7. If you have any questions call ____________

hour before the branch opens) to approximately 5:00 p.m. (the branch closes at 4:30 p.m. and so a half hour is added for balancing purposes), then this eight-hour normal day is easily divided into four two-hour segments. So if a part-time teller works up to two hours, a ¼ of a day is recorded, more than two hours up to four hours could equal ½ of a day, more than four hours up to six hours could equal ¾ of a day. Although this approach is based on workdays rather than work hours, accounting for quarter days will not only refine these statistics, but more importantly will also motivate managers to make better use of their part-time teller staff because their efforts are being recorded. This instruction only relates to part-time tellers since these tellers are usually paid on an hours-worked basis. It is assumed that full-time tellers are paid on a salary basis, and if they work less than a normal day, there would be no savings in salary expense effected.

4. The purpose of this instruction is to record, for possible future reference, the reasons why additional help was needed in a branch on particular days. Accounting for the reasons why tellers are absent does not add to the actual number of teller workdays. The additional help assigned to cover these absences, however, is recorded. Another benefit derived from recording these absences is that it would explain why if on a particular day or days, a branch showed a lower than normal count of teller workdays—the answer to this lower count would be that tellers were absent but no replacements were assigned. Since the overall purpose of this whole ongoing recordkeeping project is to control and reduce teller salary expense, one could argue that a distinction should be made between a part-time teller who was absent for whom a replacement was not assigned and who was not paid for the absence, and a full-time teller who under the same circumstance was paid for the absence. The main purpose of this recordkeeping is to provide a bank with an average of the workdays used to staff a branch over a period of time—and not to complicate this project with the minor accounting of whether or not a teller was or was not paid for a particular absence. This argument will become clearer later in this chapter.
5. This instruction will record any additional temporary workdays used to staff a branch.

6. This instruction is self-explanatory.
7. Even though this form should be explained in detail to those who will be completing it, questions will arise, and it is best to include the name of a person who can be called to answer these questions.

DEVELOP A HISTORICAL RECORD OF TELLER WORKDAYS

Figure 2–2 is a completed sample worksheet that can be used to summarize the total teller workdays used by each branch each week for a series of weeks. The branch names across the top of this worksheet should be put in "size of branch" order starting with the largest branch in the first left hand branch column. The size of the branch should be determined typically by the total number of deposit accounts maintained by the branch, but if these totals are similar among two or more branches, the number of checking accounts should be the deciding factor. Figure 2–2 shows the teller workdays used for each branch for a series of nine weeks which is more than sufficient to determine an average. Note that two first weeks of the month are included—one is the first week of the quarter (week ending 4/8/xx).

Figure 2–3 shows the same teller information that was shown in Figure 2–2, but at the bottom some basic account information is included. This account information is matched with the teller days worked statistics in the sense that all the statistics shown relate to the same hypothetical bank—a bank with a total of 34,431 deposit accounts (9,912 checking accounts and 24,519 savings accounts) that uses on average 158 teller days per week to service its customers. Also, a "% of total bank" column was added which will provide a basic tool with which to make some preliminary determinations.

It should be noted here that all the statistics shown in this chapter were extrapolated from a real bank's analysis. Various methods were used to disguise the real bank's identity. These methods, however, in no way altered any of the ratios presented. In other words none of the ratios were altered to prove any theories. The logic used in analyzing these ratios was applied to real statistics.

In analyzing the statistics presented in Figure 2–3, obvious questions arise about the staffing in at least some of the branch offices. From reviewing the teller workdays used by each branch each week (as shown on the top section of Figure 2–3) there appears to be inconsistency in staffing for like weeks within most of the branches. Why, for example

Figure 2–2 Weekly Teller Workdays Summary Report

Work weeks ending	Main Office # of Work-Days	North Branch # of Work-Days	West Branch # of Work-Days	East Branch # of Work-Days	South Branch # of Work-Days	Bank Totals # of Work-Days
2/25/xx	49½	55¼	22	14¼	12½	153½
3/4/xx	50¾	63¼	24¾	14¾	13	166½
3/11/xx	53½	59¼	23	14¼	12¼	162¼
3/18/xx	53¾	54¾	26	14¼	13	161¾
3/25/xx	47½	56½	24	12	12½	152½
4/1/xx	49¼	62¾	24	13	13½	162½
4/8/xx	46	59	24¾	14¼	11½	155½
4/15/xx	49	57	21½	12	12	151½
4/22/xx	51½	57	21¼	13½	12½	155¾
Average	50	58¼	23½	13½	12½	158

Figure 2–3 Weekly Teller Workdays Summary Report Combined With Basic Account Information

Work Weeks Ending	Main Office # of Work-Days	Main Office % of Bank Total	North Branch # of Work-Days	North Branch % of Bank Total	West Branch # of Work-Days	West Branch % of Bank Total	East Branch # of Work-Days	East Branch % of Bank Total	South Branch # of Work-Days	South Branch % of Bank Total	Bank Totals # of Work-Days
2/25/xx	49½		55¼		22		14¼		12½		153½
3/4/xx	50¾		63¼		24¾		14¾		13		166½
3/11/xx	53½		59¼		23		14¼		12¼		162¼
3/18/xx	53¾		54¾		26		14¼		13		161¾
3/25/xx	47½		56½		24		12		12½		152½
4/1/xx	49¼		62¾		24		13		13½		162½
4/8/xx	46		59		24¾		14¼		11½		155½
4/15/xx	49		57		21½		12		12		151½
4/22/xx	51½		57		21¼		13½		12½		155¾
Average	50	31.6	58¼	36.7	23½	14.9	13½	8.5	12½	7.9	158
Accounting Information											
# of personal DDA accts.	3,537	42.1	1,903	22.6	1,272	15.1	987	11.7	710	8.4	8,409
# of commercial DDA accts.	571	38.0	450	29.9	233	15.5	124	8.3	125	8.3	1,503
Total of DDA accts.	4,108	41.4	2,353	23.7	1,505	15.2	1,111	11.2	835	8.4	9,912
# of savings accounts (passbook & statement)	7,810	31.8	9,626	39.2	2,861	11.7	2,270	9.3	1,952	8.0	24,519
Grand total # of accounts	11,918	34.6	11,979	34.8	4,366	12.7	3,381	9.8	2,787	8.1	34,431

did the Main Office use 53¾ teller workdays to staff that office during the week ending March 18, 19xx, but only 46 teller workdays during the first week in April (week ending April 8, 19xx)? And the first week in April was the first week in the quarter. What should be the normal staffing for this office for the first week in the month? When comparing the staffing used for any of the like weeks in March versus April, inconsistencies appear in each of the branches. These inconsistencies are perhaps more dramatic in the larger offices because of the size of the teller staff in these offices, but they still exist in all the offices.

When comparing the percentage of total figures for teller workdays used on average for the nine-week period for each branch, to the percentage of total figures shown for the number of accounts maintained by each branch, it is important to focus on the total number of DDA accounts serviced. DDA accounts traditionally generate considerably more teller transactions than savings accounts. Why does the Main Office on average use 31.6% of the total teller workdays to service 41.4% of the total number of DDA accounts in the bank whereas the North Branch uses on average 36.7% of the total teller workdays to service only 23.7% of the total DDA accounts in the bank? It would appear that the North Branch is overstaffed or the Main Office is understaffed or that the North Branch services a considerable number of Main Office's DDA customers in addition to all of their own customers. It would be hard for senior management in a bank to believe that a branch manager would keep his or her branch understaffed, because of all the flak from customers and management this would produce. Without definite staffing guidelines managers will generally tend to overstaff their branches either on a permanent basis or on an occasional basis. It would not be rare, however, to find one out of five managers who staff a branch at an optimum most of the time. With regard to the hypothesis that one branch may service a high percentage of another branch's customers, there is no way of proving this unless a survey is made. I suspect, however, that this overlapping of customers, particularly between branches that are far enough apart geographically, is not significant enough to warrant using it as an excuse for overstaffing.

To illustrate more graphically the variances in staffing between the branches in relation to the number of DDA accounts a simple ratio of the number of DDA accounts per total weekly teller workdays used could be calculated for each branch. For example, in the Main Office which has 4,108 DDA accounts and uses on average 50 teller workdays per week, the ratio is 82 to 1 (4,108 ÷ 50). This ratio for each branch is as follows:

Main Office	*North Branch*	*West Branch*	*East Branch*	*South Branch*	*Total Bank*
82:1	40:1	64:1	82:1	67:1	63:1

To finalize our review of the statistics shown in Figure 2–3, and considering all the observations and comments mentioned above, it would be logical to suspect that the North Branch is grossly overstaffed, that the West Branch and the South Branch are at least marginally overstaffed, and that the Main Office and the East Branch are optimally staffed. If you were the officer in charge of branch administration in this bank and visited the branches often, you probably suspected most of the above already but *now*, having analyzed the above basic statistics, you would be more convinced and therefore more motivated to do something about it.

To return to our original analysis of the weekly statistics as shown in Figure 2-3, even though we strongly suspect overstaffing in varying degrees in three of the five offices, we do not have sufficient information to define the degree of overstaffing that is occurring in each of these three branches. Also, we should not develop norms based just on the number of DDA accounts in each branch because too many transaction variables are possible. This leads us to the next step in our approach.

DETERMINE TRANSACTION VOLUMES

Any worthwhile analysis of teller staffing should include some basic transaction statistics. Unfortunately many banks have approached this task with great ideals of counting everything for long periods of time, and amassing mountains of statistics which are so cumbersome to analyze that they inevitably end up unused in the basement. What is suggested in this section is a very basic approach that will provide reasonable data that are easy to compile and compare with teller workday statistics.

First of all when counting teller transactions I suspect that in most banks using teller machine tapes is not practical, because either too much time is required to translate the symbols on the tape or because tellers have their own ways of using a teller machine which either will add to or subtract from actual counts. So unless your bank has highly sophisticated teller machines or a sophisticated computerized proof system, you will have to count the transactions by hand, but only for a two-week period. And the fewer the number of employees involved in the counting process the better. Also, tellers should not be involved in counting *their own* transactions. No matter how much you explain to them that all you want to know is how many transactions are processed by the branch each day, they still think you're checking on their personal efficiency. This in turn only leads to possible morale problems and/or fudging.

As to which two weeks' transactions to count, it is suggested that a week with normal volume and a week with heavy volume be chosen. And the weeks chosen should be within the same time period used to *first* tabulate teller workday statistics (for example, the nine-week period shown in Figure 2–2). You want to know how many cashed checks, checking deposits, savings transactions, and miscellaneous transactions are processed by each branch each working day. Counting these transactions has to be done before the transactions reach the proof function in order to tabulate these transactions by type and by branch. Depending on

Figure 2–4 Transaction Worksheet

TRANSACTION WORKSHEET
DAY ____________
DATE ____________
BRANCH ____________
EMPLOYEE ____________

	Cashed Checks	*Checking Deposits*	*Savings Transactions*	*Misc. Transactions*
TOTAL				

Figure 2–5 Summary Transaction Worksheet for the Week Ending 3/25/xx—Branch: Main Office

Date	*Cashed Checks*	*Checking Deposits*	*Savings Transactions*	*Miscellaneous Transactions*	*Total*
Monday 3/21/xx	315	451	187	178	1131
Tuesday 3/22/xx	293	336	148	164	941
Wednesday 3/23/xx	335	368	151	150	1004
Thursday 3/24/xx	443	423	162	162	1190
Friday 3/25/xx	841	925	305	443	2514
Week's Total	2227	2503	953	1097	6780

whether your proof function is centralized or performed in some degree in the branch, the counting either would have to be done in the branch (if any part of the proof function is done in a branch) or could be done at a central location (if the proof function is done centrally). This counting function is easier to control if done centrally. In any event a simple worksheet can be used to tabulate the transactions by type by branch by day. Figure 2–4 is a sample of this worksheet—one is used for each employee doing the counting and for each day for each branch. Each branch's transactions have to be kept separate for each day's activity. When designing a worksheet like this, one is tempted to count every conceivable type of transaction in case there is a need for this information in the future. This temptation, therefore, leads to showing transaction categories such as checking deposits with and without less cash, savings deposits with and without less cash, straight cash deposits, deposits without cash (by type of account), and different types of miscellaneous transactions (E bond sales and redemption, money order purchases, loan payments, or utility payments). This information might be very interesting but I doubt that it would ever be used, and tabulating this information by too many categories could be confusing. So unless you suspect that a particular branch processes a preponderance of a particular type of transaction, in relation to the other branches, that is not categorized in Figure 2–4, it is recommended that only the major categories shown in Figure 2–4 be used. But remember that *all* transactions must be counted and put into the correct category. Savings deposits and withdrawals, for example, are put into the "savings transactions" category, and if the transaction is not savings related, a cashed check, or a checking deposit, it is put into the miscellaneous category.

How big is this counting project and does it slow down the proof operation? Hand counting the transactions for a normal volume five-day work week for the number of accounts shown in Figure 2–3 (9,912 DDA accounts and 24,519 savings accounts) for five branches actually took a total of 48 hours over a five-day period. In order not to hold up the proof operation several people were assigned to count the work as soon as it came into the centralized proof department each day, before it was processed in the proof machine. These people counted only for three or four hours each day and this time was interrupted because the work from all the branches came in three deliveries throughout the afternoon and early evening. The total hours spent, however, for all employees involved for the whole week was only 48 hours. Management trainees and off duty part-time tellers were used. Each employee had his or her own worksheet properly labeled with the date and branch. Tick marks were used to tabulate the counting on the worksheets and only one branch's transactions were put on each worksheet (there was no mixing of branches on a single worksheet). At the end of each day's counting all the worksheets were collected and filed by day by branch. At the end of the week a summary sheet for each branch showing the total count of each type of transaction for each day was prepared for each branch. Figure 2–5 is a completed summary worksheet for the Main Office covering the week ending 3/25/xx (a workweek with normal volume). This summary worksheet was prepared for each branch. Then a master recap of teller transactions by type, by day, by branch was prepared for the whole bank, as shown completed in Figure 2–6.

To make all the statistics gathered so far in this project simpler to analyze, a final branch summary report was prepared which showed only totals of teller workdays used, total transactions for the week by type, and total number of accounts. This final branch summary report is shown in Figure 2–7.

Figure 2–6 Recap of Teller Transactions Week Ending March 25, 19xx

Day and Date	Type of Transaction	Main Office # of Transactions	North Branch # of Transactions	West Branch # of Transactions	East Branch # of Transactions	South Branch # of Transactions	Bank Totals # of Transactions
M	Cashed Checks	315	264	168	71	54	872
O	Checking Deposits	451	205	167	109	66	998
N	Total	766	469	335	180	120	1870
	Savings Transactions	187	216	86	48	68	605
	Misc. Transactions	178	356	63	47	63	707
3/21	Grand Total	1131	1041	484	275	251	3182
T	Cashed Checks	293	227	120	91	81	812
U	Checking Deposits	336	186	141	88	75	826
E S	Total	629	413	261	179	156	1638
	Savings Transactions	148	150	74	50	44	466
	Misc. Transactions	164	479	68	64	24	799
3/22	Grand Total	941	1042	403	293	224	2903
W	Cashed Checks	335	216	117	144	70	882
E D	Checking Deposits	368	191	116	131	63	869
	Total	703	407	233	275	133	1751
	Savings Transactions	151	151	64	47	42	455
	Misc. Transactions	150	336	75	52	26	639
3/23	Grand Total	1004	894	372	374	201	2845

Figure 2–6 Recap of Teller Transactions (continued)

THURS	Cashed Checks	443	322	195	107	103	1170
	Checking Deposits	423	189	140	120	68	940
	Total	866	511	335	227	171	2110
	Savings Transactions	162	150	58	40	51	461
	Misc. Transactions	162	297	59	70	23	611
3/24	Grand Total	1190	958	452	337	245	3182
FRI	Cashed Checks	841	598	358	291	243	2331
	Checking Deposits	925	310	322	191	196	1944
	Total	1766	908	680	482	439	4275
	Savings Transactions	305	272	145	90	77	889
	Misc. Transactions	443	376	157	129	90	1195
3/25	Grand Total	2514	1556	982	701	606	6359
WEEKS TOTAL	Cashed Checks	2227	1627	958	704	551	6067
	Checking Deposits	2503	1081	886	639	468	5577
	Total	4730	2708	1844	1343	1019	11644
	Savings Transactions	953	939	427	275	282	2876
	Misc. Transactions	1097	1844	422	362	226	3951
	Grand Total	6780	5491	2693	1980	1527	18471

Figure 2–7 Final Branch Summary Report

	Main Office	% of Bank Total	North Branch	% of Bank Total	West Branch	% of Bank Total	East Branch	% of Bank Total	South Branch	% of Bank Total	Bank Totals
Average Number of Teller Workdays Used During Nine Week Period (per figure 3)	50	31.6	58¼	36.7	23½	14.9	13½	8.5	12½	7.9	158
Total Transactions for the Week Ending 3/25/xx (per figure 6)											
Cashed Checks	2227		1627		958		704		551		6067
Checking Deposits	2503		1081		886		639		468		5577
Total	4730	40.6	2708	23.3	1844	15.8	1343	11.5	1019	8.8	11644
Savings Transactions	953		939		427		275		282		2876
Misc. Transactions	1097		1844		422		362		226		3951
Grand Total	6780	36.7	5491	29.7	2693	14.6	1980	10.7	1527	8.3	18471
Account Information (per figure 3)											
# of DDA Accts.	4108	41.4	2353	23.7	1505	15.2	1111	11.2	835	8.4	9912
# of Savings Accts.	7810		9626		2861		2270		1952		24519
Grand Total	11918		11979		4366		3381		2787		34431
Optimum Staffing Requirements:											
Using Main Office as Model	50		40½		20		14½		11¼		136¼
Using East Branch as Model	46¼		37½		18½		13½		10½		126¼

DETERMINE OPTIMUM TELLER STAFFING LEVELS

From the final branch summary report (Figure 2–7) we can now determine what the optimum teller staffing levels should be for a week with normal teller transaction volume. First of all note that the percentage of bank total for total checking type transactions (cashed checks and checking deposits) for each branch is almost the same as the percentage of bank total for the number of DDA accounts serviced by each branch. For example, the Main Office processed 40.6% of the bank's DDA type transactions for the week and the Main Office has 41.4% of the number of DDA accounts in the bank. This verifies that the number of checks cashed by tellers is related to the number of checking accounts serviced by the branch rather than to the number of savings accounts serviced and therefore should be grouped with checking deposit activity to show overall DDA activity. Note also, that even though all the branches have more savings accounts than checking accounts, and in the North Branch the ratio is an extreme 4 to 1 in favor of savings accounts (2,353 checking accounts as compared to 9,626 savings accounts), the savings type transactions totals are a small part of each branch's total activity for this normal volume week. These statistics give weight to the point made earlier in the chapter that activity in a branch is related more to the number of checking accounts serviced by a branch than to the number of savings accounts serviced.

The whole premise on which this approach to teller staffing is based is that some of the branch managers do a better job in staffing their branch than others, and that once those branches are identified, they can be used as a model for those branches that are overstaffed. And we can determine by using simple mathematics, the extent of the overstaffing in those branches that compare unfavorably to the model branch or branches. With the statistics shown in Figure 2–7, we can identify the model branch or branches simply by comparing the percentage of bank total for the number of teller workdays used on average, to the percentage of bank total for the number of transactions processed. These percent comparisons are shown for each branch (as per Figure 2–7).

	Main Office	*North Branch*	*West Branch*	*East Branch*	*South Branch*
Workdays Used	31.6%	36.7%	14.9%	8.5%	7.9%
Transactions	36.7%	29.7%	14.6%	10.7%	8.3%

The above percentages show that either the Main Office or the East Branch should be our model branch because in both of these branches the percentage of total workdays used is lower in relation to the percentage of transactions processed. But which branch should we use as the model? If we use the Main Office, the base number of teller workdays is 50 because that is how many workdays the Main Office used on average for the nine-week period (see the first figure in the Main Office column in Figure 2–7). To determine the optimum staffing levels based on the Main Office's statistics divide each branch's percentage of bank total figure for the total transactions by Main Office's percent of total transactions and multiply the result by 50. Thus the optimum staffing level for the North Branch, for example, is 40½ teller workdays per week (29.7 ÷ 36.7 = .809 × 50 = 40.45 or rounded to 40½). Using the Main Office as the model branch the optimum staffing levels for each branch per week would be as follows:

Main Office	*North Branch*	*West Branch*	*East Branch*	*South Branch*	*Bank Total*
50	40½	20	14½	11¼	136¼

If we use the East Branch as the model branch then 13½ is the base number of teller workdays (see the first figure in the East Branch column in Figure 2–7) and each branch's percentage of bank total figure for total transactions is divided by 10.7 (East Branch's percentage figure of bank total transactions) and then multiplied by 13½. The optimum staffing level for each branch using East Branch statistics as the model would be:

Main Office	*North Branch*	*West Branch*	*East Branch*	*South Branch*	*Bank Total*
46¼	37½	18½	13½	10½	126¼

Note that after these optimums are computed they should be included as part of the final Branch Summary Report for easy reference (see bottom of Figure 2–7). The difference in total teller workdays required between using the Main Office and the East Branch as a model is a total of ten workdays per week (136¼ minus 12¼) for the whole bank. From knowing the general traffic conditions in each branch (whether customers are waiting in lines for teller service longer in the East

Branch compared to the Main Office) one can decide whether or not to use East Branch as the model for all offices. If the Main Office was used as the model the average total optimum workdays required per week for the whole bank would be 136¼ workdays, which is a decrease of 21¾ workdays per week on average from the 158 workdays now being used. This is a decrease of 16%. If the average teller was making $5.00 an hour for seven hours a day the savings would be $35.00 per teller workday, times 21¾ workdays per week, times 52 weeks or $39,585 per year. By using the East Branch as the model the annual savings would be an additional $18,200 per year or a total savings of $57,785 annually.

Up to this point we have determined optimum teller staffing requirements on normal volume statistics. Earlier we mentioned that two weeks of teller transactions should be counted. The second week should be a heavy volume week. Traditionally in banking, the first week in the month is a heavy volume week, but the first week in the quarter month could be heavier. Most banks post interest to savings accounts during this week; this increases the number of transactions and generates more traffic in lobbies. Since in our example the North Branch is more overstaffed than the other branches, but also since the North Branch has a larger number of savings accounts it would be logical to select the first week of the quarter for the heavy volume week. Once these transactions are counted you may find that the North Branch's percentage of total of the bank's transactions is much higher during this heavy volume week and you should make allowances in the optimum staffing for this branch during this type of week. In fact, separate optimum staffing requirements could be developed for heavy volume weeks for any branch that shows a significant increase in transactions during the heavy volume week. This separate optimum staffing could be done in the same manner as described before or by merely increasing the normal volume week's requirements by the same percentage as the percentage increase in transactions between the normal volume week and the heavy volume week, as determined for each branch. It should be noted here, that in any branch where significant volume increases occur between the two weeks counted, a review of the weekly Teller Workdays Summary Report (Figure 2–2) should be made to determine if that branch used a significantly higher number of workdays during the heavy week. This high number of workdays used could have distorted the average workdays used for the nine-week period. If this distortion is suspected, the average for the branch affected could be adjusted by dropping out those high number of workdays used for those weeks. Of course, any significantly higher or lower number of workdays used during a week for a particular branch, regardless of the volume, could have the same distortion effect on the average for the nine-week period. In any event, if for any reason the weekly Teller Workdays Summary Report is changed to adjust for distortions, the changes should be carried through to all totals on the report and to the percents of workdays used computations as shown in Figures 2–3 and 2–7. These changes, of course, could very well change the optimums developed.

IMPLEMENT OPTIMUM STAFFING REQUIREMENTS

Up to this point the branch managers are only aware that some research is being done with regard to teller staffing as evidenced by the tabulating of teller workdays currently being used and by the counting of transactions; no results of this research have been announced to any of the branch managers.

The first step in this implementation is to inform the branch managers, in a meeting, of the results of the research that have been made. Include a full explanation of each report that was generated and the logic and mathematics that were used to develop the optimums. If you find in your own survey that a particular branch is grossly overstaffed, care should be taken not to embarrass the manager of that branch in front of his or her peers. You could have a private meeting with that manager before the branch managers' meeting and make that manager aware of the results of the research in advance. Then the manager would not be shocked during the meeting. Also, it should be explained to the manager at the private meeting, as well as to all the managers in the main managers' meeting, that there are several reasons for overstaffing. Overstaffing is not always the result of poor management; it is often due to other factors beyond the direct control of the manager. These factors will be discussed later in this chapter. It should also be explained at the general managers' meeting that the main purpose of the meeting is not to "point fingers," but to explain what has been researched so far, and that adjustments to staff in a particular branch will be discussed in more detail, privately, with the managers involved.

It should also be explained at the managers' meeting that the optimum staffing levels shown on the reports are an attempt to develop goals where none have existed before. These goals should be adjusted for those branches that are now exceeding the optimums. In addition, the managers should be informed that, from now on, the Weekly Teller Workdays Summary Report (Figure 2–2), which will include the optimums (goals) developed, will be published each week and sent to the managers so that they can accurately monitor their effort in conforming to these goals. This report will be cumulative in the sense that each week's workday figures will be added to the previous report on the next line and the whole report will be reproduced. This will continue until the whole page is filled. Thus on one sheet of paper a history of teller workdays used week after week for several months will be developed for constant reference.

Time should also be spent at the manager's meeting explaining the relationship between the weekly teller workdays summary report (Figure 2–2) and the recap of teller transactions (Figure 2–6). Since all the branches show inconsistencies in staffing from week to week regardless of optimums, a review of teller transactions will help any manager stabilize his or her staffing and possibly reduce the staff to even below the established optimums. For example, the optimum for a particular branch may be 11 teller workdays per week and the average over several weeks is 11 workdays used per week but for this average a succession of 9, 10, 11, 12, 13, 10, 9, 11, 13, etc., weekly totals were used. In an effort to reduce some of the 12 and 13 workdays used per week a review of the transaction counts for that branch might show that some of the old standards (such as Mondays and Fridays being always heavy volume days during the week) may not be true. In fact, there may be no appreciable difference in the number of transactions processed between Mondays, Tuesdays, or Thursdays during the week—in which case a workday or two could possibly be eliminated on most Mondays.

So far in the process of implementing optimums for branches some corrective forces have been automatically put in place to reduce the staffing in those branches where overstaffing is apparent. All of these forces revolve around management psychology. Goals (optimums) have been set based on statistics, and goals are motivators. Because of the effort put into the research the managers now know their senior management is determined to stop wasting money on overstaffing. The ongoing reporting to all managers of every branch's optimum and workdays used is a motivator because the managers can now see a history of their own efforts and also can compare themselves with the results of other branch managers' efforts.

IDENTIFY AND OVERCOME OBSTACLES TO IMPLEMENTING STAFF REDUCTIONS

Although some corrective forces have been put into place to reduce teller staffing, there may often be obstacles that will hinder staff reductions particularly in those branches where gross overstaffing is apparent. When counseling the managers of overstaffed branches about achieving their designated optimums it will become apparent, at least to some extent, whether or not these obstacles are the fault of the manager. We shall now explore the obstacles that can hinder efforts to reduce teller staffing. Parenthetically, the knowledge of these obstacles and what to do about them could help any bank run a more efficient teller operation whether or not any of the methodology, so far described in this chapter, was applied.

Part-time versus full-time teller staffing. The sample statistics used throughout the chapter assume the use of some part-time teller staff. It is important that any bank which is serious about reducing teller staffing, should consider the use of part-time tellers in its offices. A rule of thumb ratio of part-time to full-time tellers in each location is one to one—one part-time teller for each full-time teller. It may not be practical to follow this exact ratio, particularly in smaller branch offices, but this ratio is very workable and gives managers the most staffing options if followed in those branches that have the use of four or more teller stations. In fact the larger the office the more important this 50:50 ratio becomes.

To be specific, however, about the importance of a workable ratio for a large branch, we shall use the statistics developed earlier for the North Branch, which is a large branch in this bank and according to these statistics is grossly overstaffed. We know from the Weekly Workdays Summary Report (Figure 2–2) that, on average, the North Branch uses 59¼ teller workdays to staff the branch per week. If we use the Main Office as a staffing model, the conservative optimum staffing requirements for the North Branch during a normal volume week would be 40½ teller workdays. How then can staff reductions be accomplished in the shortest amount of time with the least personnel problems? If this branch was staffed with ten full-time tellers and two part-time tellers, the ten full-time tellers would account for 50 teller workdays (5 days per week × 10 tellers) and two part-time tellers would on average account for the remaining 8¼ days (58¼ – 50). Unless a bank was willing to dismiss some of its full-time tellers, and most banks are not, the only way to reduce staff immediately is to reduce the number of days the part-time tellers work during the week. Even if they didn't work at all the reduction in teller days worked would only amount to 8¼ days per week and the branch would still be overstaffed by 9½ workdays per week. If, however, the North Branch was staffed with 8 full-time tellers and 6 part-time tellers, then the full-time teller staff only accounts for 40 teller workdays during the week and the part-time staff accounts for, on average, the remaining 18¼ (58¼ – 40) work-days. On average, therefore, each part-time teller works three days per week (18¼ ÷ 6). By reducing the number of days each part-time teller works per week on average from three days to one day we could immediately save twelve teller days per week (2 days × 6 part-time tellers).

The above figures indirectly show the flexibility in staffing that can be obtained with the proper mix of full-time and part-time tellers. These figures, however, also point out the problems a manager could have in reducing staff immediately if the preponderance of tellers in the branch were full-time. Immediate substantial reductions would be impossible until some of the full-time tellers left the bank through attrition or were transferred to other branches or departments as openings occurred. Only time and awareness that this branch must reduce its full-time teller staff as the opportunities arise, will cure the overstaffing.

Also by maintaining a proper mix of part-time and full-time tellers in a branch you will be able to staff more accurately if your survey of transactions during a suspected heavy volume week shows a substantial increase in the number of transactions over a normal week, or shows abnormal volume during a particular day or days during the week. Obviously a staff of part-time tellers would enable a branch to service its customers inexpensively during these heavy volume situations. It should be noted that a major cause of overstaffing in any teller area is often caused by heavy volume days during a week or for a specific week during the month or a quarter and the tendency to staff up all month for one very heavy week during the month; or to staff up for several days during a week when there are only one or two days during the week involved. Managers will often do this because the heavy volume periods are so very busy that they will overstaff to insure themselves against being that busy. Another reason overstaffing occurs is that heavy volume periods are sometimes incorrectly identified. Only by surveying volumes using the methods described in this chapter will the real heavy volume periods be determined. Don't be surprised when you survey the volume in some of your locations for a labeled heavy volume time (first week of the month, or first week in the quarter) and find that there is no appreciable

Figure 2–8 Recap of Teller Transactions Week Ending March 25, 19xx North Branch (Staff Determinations)

Date	Day	Type of Transactions	Number of Transactions	% Of Week's Total Transactions	# Of Teller Days Required	Number of Transactions Adjusted*	% Of Week's Total Transactions Adjusted	# Of Teller Days Required Adjusted*
3/21/XX	Monday	Cashed Checks	264					
		Checking Deposits	205					
		Total	469					
		Savings Trans.	216					
		Misc. Transactions	356					
		Grand Total	1041	19%	7¾	1041	20.3%	8¼
3/22/XX	Tuesday	Cashed Checks	227					
		Checking Deposits	186					
		Total	413					
		Savings Trans.	150					
		Misc. Trans.	479					
		Grand Total	1042	19%	7¾	1042	20.3%	8¼
3/23/XX	Wednesday	Cashed Checks	216					
		Checking Deposits	191					
		Total	407					
		Savings Trans.	151					
		Misc. Trans.	336					
		Grand Total	894	16.3%	6½	894	17.4%	7

Figure 2–8 Recap of Teller Transactions (Staff Determinations) (continued)

3/24/XX	Thursday	Cashed Checks	322					
		Checking Deposits	189					
		Total	511					
		Savings Trans.	150					
		Misc. Trans.	297					
		Grand Total	958	17.4%	7	958	18.6%	7½
3/25/XX	Friday	Cashed Checks	598					
		Checking Deposits	310					
		Total	908					
		Savings Trans.	272					
		Misc. Trans.	376					
		Grand Total	1556	28.3%	11½	1210*	23.5%	9½
Week's Total		Cashed Checks	1627					
		Checking Deposits	1081					
		Total	2708					
		Saving Trans.	939					
		Misc. Trans.	1844					
		Grand Total	5491		40½	5145*		40½

* Fridays Transactions and Week's Total Transactions Count Each Reduced by 346 to Compensate for the Two Hour Longer Friday Workday. See Text for Explanation.

difference in volume during those periods than there is during the normal volume weeks surveyed. Also don't be surprised if your survey of transactions during either a normal volume week or a heavy volume week, shows that Mondays and Fridays are no busier than Tuesdays and Thursdays in some of the branches. This leads to the next possible obstacle in reducing teller staff.

Determine staff requirements for the days in the week. Managers should be instructed how to use the volume statistics developed to determine the staffing levels for each day of the week. Using our sample volume statistics developed in Figure 2–6 and continuing to use the North Branch for example purposes, we can isolate volumes for the North Branch only, in the format shown in Figure 2–8, "Recap of Teller Transactions—Week Ending March 25, 19xx North Branch" and use this information. The number of transactions shown for each day in Figure 2–8 were merely copied from Figure 2–6. The "% of Weeks Total Transactions" column in Figure 2–8 was computed by dividing the number of transactions for each day by the total number of transactions for the week. For example on Monday 3/21/xx the North Branch had 1041 total transactions or 19% of the week's total of 5,491 transactions. The next column, which shows the number of teller days required, was computed by using the same percentage figure for the number of transactions for a day and multiplying it by the optimum number of days required for a normal volume week—40½ as computed earlier. This is based on the logic that if, for example the North Branch processes 19% of its weekly transactions on Monday, then it should use 19% of its optimum weekly teller days requirement of 40½ teller days to staff the branch on Mondays—and therefore, staff the branch with 7¾ teller workdays (.19 × 40½). The last three columns are to be used if the branch is open substantially longer on a certain day of the week. The three columns for the North Branch were computed on the assumption that the branch is open two hours longer (from 9:00 a.m. to 6:00 p.m. rather than from 9:00 a.m. to 4:00 p.m.) on Fridays than on the other days of the week. In order to conservatively compensate for this variation in opened hours on Friday the transaction counts for Friday were reduced as follows. Since our statistics per Figure 2–8 show that on Friday a grand total of 1,556 transactions are processed during the nine hours the branch is open, then 173 transactions are processed per hour or 346 transactions for the two hour period. If we reduce the total transactions for Friday and for the week by 346 transactions, we would in effect adjust Friday's transaction count to be more comparable to the other days in the week when the branch is open only seven hours. These adjustments are made on the assumption that since our statistics are based on days worked rather than hours worked, the assigned tellers would each still work the same one workday whether or not the Friday workday was seven or nine hours long. From reviewing the adjusted columns and comparing them to the unadjusted ones, we see that the net effect of these adjustments is to reduce the teller days required for Fridays and correspondingly increase the number of teller days required for the other days in the week. Note, however, that the total number of teller days required for the week (40½) remains unchanged. It should also be noted that some care should be taken when making adjustments for longer work hours for a particular day. A branch, for instance, might be open for two additional hours but the number of customers serviced during this period is much lower during one or two of these hours than the rest of the day, and only a one-hour adjustment or no adjustment is required.

The examples used so far in this chapter are related to banks with branch systems. How effective, however, is this approach to reducing teller staffing in a unit bank? Since this approach is based on the comparison of staff between branches, a unit bank would not have any other offices with which to compare. Many of these banks, however, have affiliations with other banks through common ownership, or local bank organizations, and this approach could be used between any group of banks that are willing to participate. There could be some pitfalls due to differences in teller operating procedures between banks. These differences could distort the teller days used statistics particularly as they relate to the number of transactions processed. But still this approach would be useful in a general way to identify those banks within the group that scored higher than others in workdays used. This in turn could lead to identifying the reasons why excessive staffing exists in these banks. The following section will identify some of these reasons, which could be present in any bank, whether or not it is part of a branch system.

FACTORS THAT INFLUENCE TELLER STAFFING REQUIREMENTS

1. *Teller Management.* There is a direct relationship between the quality of management provided for tellers and tellers' efficiency in performing their jobs. There should be adequate supervision of the tellers. Often the

management of tellers is relegated to the head teller who is swamped with his or her own work and gives little attention to the day-to-day needs of tellers. As a general rule there should be a full-time supervisor for every twelve to fifteen tellers. In small offices where there are only a few tellers on duty, the assistant manager or manager of the office can perform this function along with his or her other duties. With larger teller staffs it is important to have supervisory help available to answer questions, approve larger transactions, and to handle unusual or difficult customer situations. Otherwise tellers will wander around the branch looking for help and waste valuable time that could be used to service more customers. If adequate supervision is not available to help the tellers, the tellers will soon learn that management is not really concerned with servicing customers and their motivation to wait on customers will erode. The result may be that they will take every opportunity to be away from their windows to do miscellaneous chores, visit with one another, or take longer coffee and lunch breaks. This leads to unnecessarily increasing staffing levels to compensate for the time wasted.

It is important that those who supervise tellers know the teller function well, be able to get along with both the tellers and the customers, be customer service oriented, and have some basic training in supervising people.

2. *Teller Limits.* Examine your teller limits for check cashing, savings withdrawals, and signature verification. Are they high enough to permit tellers to perform most transactions without supervisory approval? A lot of teller time can be wasted if tellers are required to seek approvals on routine-type transactions. Just because you experience a $50 or $100 loss a couple of times a year on a routine type of transaction is no reason to put stringent limits on tellers for these transactions. The time wasted on seeking approvals could amount to thousands of dollars per year because the transactions involved are so numerous. When setting limits for tellers, set them by type of transaction, not by having one amount for all types of transactions. Check cashing limits can be set by the type of check (on us, not on us, well-known payroll) and by type of customer (well-known, not well-known). Savings withdrawals can be divided into those presented with a passbook and those presented without a passbook.

Signature verification is a teller time consumer. There is no quick way for most banks to check a signature. Going to a signature card or even to microfiche is time consuming for most banks. Tellers are typically trained to check signatures on everything even when the amounts of the items are small. No bank is going to go broke, if an occasional $10, $25, or even a $50 "on us" check or savings withdrawal has an incorrect signature on it. Besides, professional crooks will not expose themselves to possible apprehension for a small amount (usually for not less than $200). Banks can no longer afford the luxury of checking out everything on small items. It costs too much in time which translates directly to teller salary expense.

Consider assigning limits according to the experience level of the teller. Seasoned tellers could have higher limits than those who are relatively new to teller work. Tellers with higher limits could be designated as senior tellers with the authority to approve items for tellers with lower limits.

3. *Sufficient Look-Up Equipment.* How far do tellers have to walk to look up signatures? If your cards are not on microfiche, one centralized signature card file could create thousands of unnecessary steps for tellers. By using microfiche the whole file can be inexpensively duplicated and made easily available with a fiche viewer and fiche signature card file for every two tellers. Whether phones, fiche or CRTs are used to obtain account information such as balances, account numbers, number and type of accounts maintained by a customer, there should be enough of them to prevent excessive walking to them or waiting to use them. Walking and waiting are time consumers that result in poor customer service and increased staffing requirements.

4. *Time Consuming Teller Transactions.* There are a number of teller-type transactions that traditionally take more time to perform than the normal check cashing, withdrawal and deposit transactions. They are land contract payments, collection items, large cash commercial deposits, updating savings account passbooks, and lottery sales. Should these functions be done by specialized tellers or other personnel in the office? Passbook up-dating, for example, could easily be done by someone other than a teller. The teller would merely give the customer a receipt for the passbook, or if the customer refused to leave the passbook at the bank the teller could take a photocopy of that part of the passbook which is to be updated, and assure the customer that the necessary research would be done and that the passbook would be updated the next time the customer brings the passbook to the bank.

5. *Single Purpose versus Universal Tellers.* Many years ago banks developed the universal teller concept in an effort to provide better customer service. The concept is still sound but it may not be the most efficient type of service in all situations. Variations of the universal teller

concept could be more practical under certain circumstances. Consider establishing check-cashing-only windows with "check-cashing-only" signs, on busy check cashing days. Also, I know of one bank that has twenty teller windows in one office—ten are universal and ten are used for checking-type transactions only—check cashing, checking deposits, and some simple transactions such as sale of money orders, and loan payments—but *not* passbook savings deposits or withdrawals. It took awhile for customers to get used to this, but it was a successful system for this bank which had a number of passbook accounts with a high number of deposits and withdrawals per account. The point is, that depending on the situations in a particular bank, variations can be developed in the type of teller services provided by certain tellers.

6. *Statement Savings versus Passbook Savings.* The last two factors described above introduced a problem that most bankers are familiar with the teller time consuming aspects of passbook savings accounts. One need only consider the types of transactions to passbook accounts that create activity for tellers and sometimes out of balance conditions which in turn creates research necessary to balance passbooks. The advent of Certificates of Deposit and the interest credited to passbook savings, and the direct deposit of Social Security and other payments credited to passbook savings have aggravated the already existing problems of interest postings and teller posting errors that traditionally create both teller transaction activity and out of balance passbook conditions. The answer to this problem is the statement savings account. All transactions are recorded on a statement which is mailed to the customer on a quarterly basis. Under this system there is no passbook and therefore, tellers do not have to take the time to post transactions or interest into a passbook or to research and correct out of balance passbooks.

Some banks have solved this problem by not offering passbook savings to customers. Other banks offer both types of accounts but encourage statement savings by offering a higher rate of interest on statement savings (will pay a lower than maximum rate on passbook savings), will service charge passbook savings at a higher rate than a statement savings, and/or will only allow direct deposit and ATM transactions to be used with statement savings accounts. With all this the passbook still remains a favorite service for many customers. It is a service that most bankers still feel they have to offer because these passbook accounts are a major source of deposits, and in this day and age they are an inexpensive source. Each bank has to consider how far it is willing to go to discourage passbook savings—but some customer discouragement is certainly indicated. Conversely, it seems prudent that bankers should continually seek new ways to promote statement savings.

7. *Automated Teller Machines.* Be careful of this one! When ATMs were first introduced they were publicized as being a bank's answer to decreasing teller salary expense. We all read of the success stories that some banks had (mostly giant metropolitan banks) with these machines. And even today, they are being used in some banks to directly replace tellers in branch offices. ATMs are a good idea if your customers use them. Getting a large base of your customers to use them for a variety of transactions is the problem. Recent surveys indicate that these machines are only being used by about a third of the customer base in most banks and the customers who are using them, use them primarily just to obtain cash. One could argue that more cash type transactions are generated because of the machines rather than the machines being a major influence in reducing lobby transactions. In any event, if you already have these machines they should be constantly marketed to your customer base. If you don't have them and you are thinking about it, you should know that they are expensive to buy, to house, to market, and to maintain. But if for competitive purposes you feel the need to purchase them, consider locating them in your branch drive-up facilities and particularly in those drive-ups that are located near your younger customer base (especially college students). Studies show that customers perceive drive-up ATMs to be safer and more convenient than walk up or stand alone units.

SUMMARY

The first part of this chapter described a simple approach to determine optimum teller staffing requirements. Although this approach uses some basic statistics which must be collected by any bank using this system, it is an approach that is much less confusing and laborious than other statistical approaches used in banks today. This approach involves only four steps:

1. Tabulating the current number of teller work days per week being used, by location for a sufficient meaningful number of weeks preferably a nine-week period.
2. Tabulating transactions volumes, per day, by location for a normal volume week and for a heavy volume week.

3. Determining optimum teller staffing levels by relating teller work days used to transaction counts and comparing each branch office's results with the other branches.

4. Implementing optimum staffing requirements as developed in the first three steps. In this step actual salary expense is reduced.

Throughout this chapter several important factors are described that are effective in reducing teller salary expense:

1. The ongoing tabulating of teller time used by each location and the consistent publishing of this information for all managers of tellers to review is in itself an automatic motivating force for all concerned, which will continually control the quantity of teller time used.

2. Determining optimum goals for each location gives added impetus to controlling and reducing the teller staff.

3. Even after attaining optimums, managers can possibly reduce staffing further by eliminating the highs in the teller days worked per week that produced the averages upon which the optimums were based. Instructing managers in how to staff for each day of the week will help eliminate these highs.

4. Tabulating transactions will dispel any incorrect assumptions that certain days of the week or weeks in the month are busier than others.

5. Consider using part-time tellers in a one-to-one ratio with full time tellers in order to obtain maximum flexibility in staffing each location during low and peak volume periods.

6. Beware of a manager's tendency to overstaff during moderate volume periods as a result of the staffing requirements needed during extremely heavy volume periods.

7. Remember, when determining staffing requirements in relation to the volume of transactions, that if a location is open longer on one or two days during the week than on the other days, the volume of transactions has to be adjusted because the teller day is also longer (but there is little or no increase in salary expense).

8. Employing a sufficient number of well-qualified teller supervisors is a key factor in controlling and reducing a teller staff.

9. Establishing workable teller approval limits for transactions and limits for signature verification will help reduce the time required to process a transaction, which in turn will lead to staff reductions.

10. Consider establishing separate higher limits for senior experienced tellers. These tellers can help the more junior tellers by approving

some of their transactions. This eliminates any possible time wasted in waiting to obtain an approval from a teller supervisor.

11. Make sure that the teller area has sufficient equipment for signature and balance lookups and for obtaining other necessary account information to reduce teller walking and/or waiting time.

12. Route time consuming teller transactions to specialized tellers or to desk personnel.

13. Consider using a mix of both universal-type tellers and tellers specializing in either the demand or the savings function.

14. Market statement savings accounts to reduce the teller activity caused by passbook savings accounts.

15. ATM machines will reduce lobby teller transactions but only if customers use them extensively.

Chapter 3

Reduce Personnel Related Expenses

This chapter shows many practical ways a bank can reduce personnel type expenses. These ways are divided into eight major interrelated areas, most are within the area of personnel administration. Personnel administration in banks today has become a highly specialized function that requires expertise in a number of areas: wage and salary administration, fringe benefit programs, and development of personnel policies. This book is not a manual for personnel administrators. What is presented in this chapter is an identification of those critical areas within the scope of the personnel function that should be investigated by managers who are responsible for reducing expenses. The material shown in each section of this chapter is presented in a non-technical way so that any member of management regardless of his or her expertise in the field of personnel administration can easily supervise a campaign to reduce these expenses.

REDUCE STAFF

The best way to reduce salary expense is to reduce staff! *Every* bank is overstaffed. It doesn't matter how large or small the bank is, overstaffing exists to some degree in all banks. Unless your bank has seriously investigated and reduced staff recently it would be safe to say that it is overstaffed by at least 5% and probably by 10%. So if you have a total of 100 employees, you have five to ten employees you really don't need. Overstaffing is really like a bacteria that always exists in an institution and unless it is controlled frequently with heavy doses of antibiotics it will quickly spread and grow into a very expensive "disease." But how does one detect and treat this problem? In this section we will explore some concepts that will be helpful in controlling overstaffing. There is no quick cure. Remember it is always present; but the major concern is how rampant it is.

Chapter 2 described in detail how to control teller salary expense. Even if you only address this area of the bank, you will be going a long way toward controlling expenses. But in addition to the principles described there are other concepts for staffing all departments which should not be overlooked.

1. It all starts at the top. If the president is adamant about reducing staff, the staff will be reduced one way or another. One way senior management can start is to put a bankwide freeze on the hiring of additional staff (not replacement staff) for at least a six-month period. It is amazing how managers will get the work done without the addition of the extra help they thought they needed. This will make them staffing conscious and it will bring them to the realization that the well is not bottomless. But even after this freeze is lifted it will be important to continue with a strict policy of requiring managers to substantiate to senior management the need for additional help. This substantiation should include volume statistics concerning their operation which support their request for additional staff.
2. The subject of substantiation with volume statistics, which relates to number 1 and number 3, brings up a major consideration in the proper staffing of a department. Do the managers know the quantity of clerical type duties their employees perform per hour, per day, per week, per month, per quarter, or on a per year basis, whichever time frames are pertinent to their specific departments? This whole book is filled with ways statistics can help you make more profitable decisions. The formats shown in the various chapters can be adapted to formulate overall departmental and specific per employee volumes.

3. The best time to assess staffing in a department is when one of the employees is leaving the department. This is a golden opportunity to ask if you really need to replace that person. Can this person's job duties be assigned to someone else or spread among many doing similar work? Is the function that person performs even needed at all? If the function is needed, is it also being done in another department and can that department take over this function without replacing this person? If a replacement is necessary and the person leaving is a full-time employee, can that employee be replaced with a part-timer? It is important for a manager to answer these questions before automatically assuming that the person "has" to be replaced.
4. The previous chapter discussed the use of part-time employees for teller staffing. This concept is equally important in other departments in a bank—bookkeeping, proof, loan department—or any other departments that use clerks. Part-time help is cost effective because of the reduced fringe benefit costs, reduced salary expense, ease in laying off the employee if the need is reduced, and they can more easily be transferred to other departments as the need arises. Part-time help is often easier to recruit. Some banks, for instance, cooperate extensively with local high school and community college coop programs which provide students for part-time work.
5. Finally, one should focus on how profitable it really is to save just one employee. In this labor market the annual base salary expense saved probably averages $10,000 per year for clerical employees. But what about all those other direct and indirect employee expenses that most personnel experts advise cost an additional 40% of base salary! The list as shown below is imresively expensive:

   Medical plans (hospial, surgical, major medical)
   Dental plan
   Retirement plan
   Profit sharing
   Social Security
   Insurance plans (life, long-term disability)
   Unemployment insurance
   Worker's compensation

Blanket bond insurance

Vacation time

Sick pay

Training time and supplies

Education subsidies (AIB, college courses, seminars)

Free bank services (checking accounts, safe deposit boxes, travelers checks, credit cards, reduced interest rates on loans)

Lunch and/or other food subsidies, including employee parties

Travel time and expenses

Furniture (desk, chair, filing cabinet, etc.)

Equipment (typewriter, adding machine, calculator, telephone, CRT, etc.)

Supplies (pens, pecils, paper, etc.)

Space (work space, closet space, eating space, rest room space, parking space)

Utilities (light, heat, cooling, water, telephone lines)

Management time

Employees are certainly a bank's most important asset, but they are also its most expensive asset.

WAGE AND SALARY ADMINISTRATION

No presentation about ways to reduce expenses related to personnel would be complete without a commentary about wage and salary administration. This personnel function has become, particularly in recent years, increasingly important in controlling salary expense. Unfortunately, to develop and establish a meaningful wage and salary administration program in a bank requires a high degree of expertise. This expertise can be developed, however, through private study and attending a course or two, or a two- or three-day seminar on this subject. Establishing this program requires a written description of every specific job within a bank, a ranking of these jobs into grade levels, and assigning starting salaries, midpoint salaries, and maximum salaries for each grade level. This all sounds relatively simple but the ranking of jobs into grades can become a complex project. It requires the development of some sort of a system to determine which jobs in a bank are more important than others, are harder to perform, or require specialized education. After this is done, the development of salary scales for the different grades, once some basic assumptions are determined, is merely an exercise in mathematics. Superimposed on this whole project, however, is the need to know what other banks, and to some extent what other industries in your area are paying for employees doing similar work. Another important aspect of this project is to simultaneously develop an organized system for rating employees' performances so that salary increases can be based on merit rather than seniority.

Most banks start this project on a simple basis, by making a lot of assumptions without the aid of adequate job descriptions or outside salary market research, but as each year goes by, they continually refine their approach and eventually end up with a fairly sophisticated program.

A meaningful wage and salary administration program is an important part of a bank's efforts to control salary expense, because without it many employees could be overpaid, either when beginning employment with the bank; through too many unnecessary or generous salary increases granted through the years; or merely because their job duties are not commensurate with the high salaries they are being paid. A salary program will identify these areas of excessive salary expense, and will provide a means to stop these excesses and to prevent them from happening in the future.

MAJOR FRINGE BENEFITS

In recent years direct fringe benefits have become very sizeable expense items for banks. With some of these benefits, such as Social Security and unemployment insurance there is very little a bank can do to reduce these expenses, except to reduce the staff. What follows are a series of ways to reduce expenses in those more direct type of benefits.

Profit sharing plans. Bankwide profit sharing plans are a waste of money! Now there is a startling statement. How many companies and banks in the country have profit sharing plans and claim they are worthwhile? If one could question each chief executive officer of these institutions about the value of their plan with regard to increasing profits, and obtain an unbiased answer, I wonder what they really would say. The concept of profit sharing is based on the motivational premise that the more employees work toward increasing income or decreasing expenses in their own job environment, the more money in the form of profit sharing they will earn. There are several problems with this theory. First of all, senior management, who decides whether or not to establish a profit sharing plan in an institution, views profit sharing differently than does the rank and file employee. By the nature of their responsibilities senior management is more naturally motivated toward increased profits. Increasing profits is an integral part of their overall job duties. If profits are not good, they may lose their jobs. In addition, each senior manager gets a larger slice of the profit sharing pie than a rank and file employee, because most plans are designed around the pie being divided according to the employees' base salary. The typical employee however, has difficulty seeing how he or she can really increase profits in his or her own job assignment, and even if it was possible for an employee to increase profits a few hundred dollars, only a small percentage of that would go into the profit sharing fund, and then that percentage is divided among many. In the employee's mind, therefore, personal efforts involved to increase profits do not translate to any appreciable dollar amount ending up in the employee's pocket. The whole program then is at first viewed by employees as an extra benefit and perhaps even as a reward. But as time goes on it is more often viewed as a basic fringe benefit that is rightfully owed to them. Also, any book on management will point out that money does not rank very high as an employee motivational factor. And so the whole theory of a profit sharing plan starts out on a marginally motivating premise. But it certainly would be logical to assume, considering all the comments made above, that regardless of how basically motivating profit sharing really is to any employee, there is probably some direct relationship between the degree of motivation toward increasing profits and the degree of employee job responsibilities. In other words, the greater the job responsibilities an employee has, the more disposed he or she is toward increasing profits.

If the reader basically agrees with the comments made so far about bankwide profit sharing plans, the natural conclusions to be drawn about these plans are that if you don't have a profit sharing program, think twice about offering one; and if you already have a plan think twice about ever increasing it, and better yet try to reduce it or eliminate it. If you want cash incentives consider those that are more meaningful such as a cash bonus plan based on profits, but only paid to higher level employees. Of course there is not as much of a personal tax advantage for these employees, but then the cost to the bank is not as great.

Retirement plans. This is another costly fringe benefit, and anything that can be done to reduce its negative effect on profits is worth the effort. Retirement plans are complicated, and therefore, when establishing or revising a retirement plan, it is worth the money to hire a consultant from a larger public accounting firm.

There are basic points about retirement plans that should always be considered in the effort to reduce or control expense in this area. For example, retirement plan benefit formulas should always include a tie to Social Security benefits. Banks, like all institutions, pay half the Social Security taxes necessary to support their employees' Social Security benefits, and so whatever benefit formula a bank devises should at least include half the Social Security benefit. For example, if a benefit formula will pay an employee $1,000 per month, upon retirement, then this amount should be reduced by half the Social Security benefit that the employee will receive at retirement. Another advantage to this approach is that as basic Social Security benefits increase the amount of the bank's liability and resultant funding requirements decreases.

Other factors that should be considered when reviewing the expense of a retirement plan are (1) the lower the age limit of employees eligible to join the plan the more employees whose benefits have to be funded; (2) the more employees who contribute to their own retirement, the less the bank has to contribute and (3) actuaries base funding requirements on a number of factors including the bank's employee turnover rates, rate of return on assets in the fund, duplication of benefits, and rate of inflation. Some of these factors are known and others are assumed. The assumed ones such as rates of turnover, return on fund assets, and inflation, should be questioned. Too conservative an approach in these assumptions can cause very high funding requirements, thus funneling unnecessary assets into a retirement plan rather than having them available to invest in loans or other higher yielding investments.

These factors should point out the importance of reviewing a retirement plan for profit improvement purposes, and the prudence of enlisting the aid of a consultant.

It should be noted here that there has been a recent active interest among banks to offer the tax advantaged 401(k) plan to employees as supplement to retirement benefits. The 401(k) can be offered with or without a matching contribution from the employer. In either event the 401(k) is an excellent way for employees to add to their retirement income themselves. This in turn reduces the need for the bank to increase its benefits under its formal retirement plan.

Medical and dental plans. The following ways can be used by any bank officer, regardless of his or her expertise in this area, to reduce and control costs.

1. If your costs are rising rapidly in this area, obtain quotations from several other reputable insurance carriers. There will always be one or two that will charge you less than your present carrier and at least you can reduce this expense for a year or two, and then, if necessary, repeat the process. Don't be surprised to find that some of these quotes could be as low as half the rate you are paying now.
2. If you don't have a dental plan, avoid establishing one, if at all possible. The current dental plans being offered are used extensively by employees and use determines rates. Initial rate quotations often underestimate use and after a year's experience the rate may increase substantially.
3. If you are a large bank, consider funding your own medical plans using an insurance policy as a stop loss for large claims. This stop loss limit can be set at any individual or combined claim amount you wish.
4. Investigate your local health maintenance organizations (HMOs). Their rates may be lower than those offered by your insurance carrier and/or may be rising at a slower pace. It would be more profitable therefore, to increase your internal marketing efforts to encourage employees to take advantage of the more comprehensive service usually offered by HMOs in contrast to those plans offered by other organizations.
5. If at all possible try to get your employees to pay some of the cost of your medical and/or dental plan. If you have to, reduce the negative effect on morale by offering another benefit at the same time, (not related to medical or dental plans) such as a more liberal vacation or personal day off policy. This would have two positive effects on controlling these expenses. If an employee contributes toward payment of the plan, the bank's premium outlay would be reduced; but in addition it makes the employee a partner in absorbing costs and rising costs. This in turn could make the employee think twice before using the plan unnecessarily, thus controlling use.

EMPLOYEE TURNOVER

The rate of employee turnover, particularly as related to the clerical work force in a bank, is considered to be a factor in controlling expenses.

High turnover rates indicate excessive training and recruiting costs. Low turnover rates indicate low costs in these areas. Therefore high turnover rates should be avoided to reduce training and recruiting costs. There are however, other factors to consider when investigating turnover in relation to controlling expenses. In some instances turnover can in fact reduce expenses. For example, the turnover of employees who have been working a number of years in basically the same type of work, such as teller work, can reduce expenses. These employees are almost always being paid a salary at the high end of the scale because of the raises they have received through the years. Often they have even been promoted to higher teller grades with little change in duties, so that they would not reach a maximum salary for their job. The difference between the salary that a beginning teller would be paid and a teller with years of seniority is often substantial. For example, if a starting teller's salary is $9,000 per year, it would not be unusual in some banks for a teller with ten years on the job to make $15,000 or more per year and still get raises. No matter how you compute it, it doesn't cost the difference to recruit and train a teller, particularly when you consider that once this type of turnover takes place the reduction in salary expense is not just for the first year but also for a number of future years as well.

Turnover of unproductive employees is another way to reduce expenses. Most banks hesitate to dismiss this type of employee; but if they do leave of their own accord, for the profit-minded banker the occasion should be privately viewed as a time of jubilation!

All turnover is not categorically an expense to the bank and in some instances it can substantially reduce expenses. It is important, therefore, in analyzing turnover to consider not only how many employees left the bank, but also the salary they made, and how productive they were.

This whole discussion about employee turnover presupposes that a bank records turnover. Some banks, I'm sure, merely estimate turnover rates rather than calculate them. To really know your own turnover rates you should make the calculation at least once a year. You could be surprised to find that the rate is higher than you think. The following points should be considered when determining turnover rates.

1. Keep a record during the year of each employee that leaves the bank, the reason why the employee left, the employee's department, the date hired, the date of termination, and whether the employee was full-time or part-time at the time he or she left the bank. This record will provide you with the information you will

need if you ever want to do an in-depth analysis of turnover in your bank.

2. Turnover rates are computed by dividing the number of employees who left the bank by the average number of employees in the bank during a specific period of time. Turnover rates should be calculated with the average number of employees for one quarter or annually and not by the number of employees as of one point in time (such as the end of a year). However, to compute this average it is sufficient to record the number of employees in the bank as of a certain time in each month rather than each day or each week which would be too cumbersome.
3. If turnover rates are high, a more complete analysis is desirable, turnover rates by department and/or by quarter can be calculated using the same method described in number 2. When determining turnover rates for a department only the employee statistics for that department are used. Also, if a quarterly turnover rate is desired, only statistics related to the specific quarter are used.
4. Banks with high turnover should take the time to keep good records regarding turnover, and compute rates quarterly by departments or areas within the bank. For comparison purposes these rates should be reported by quarter for several quarters. In addition, an analysis should be made of the reasons that employees left the bank and their length of employment. With these records you will be able to find out at what times during the year the turnover is the highest and in what areas of the bank; why people are leaving; and whether or not the turnover in these areas is with employees who have been with the bank for a short period of time. High turnover rates with newer employees does create excessive recruiting and training expenses. An administrator cannot correct high turnover without facts. There are almost always patterns that can be found when high turnover rates exist. Without knowing the facts, however, it is impossible to determine these patterns.

OVERTIME

When was the last time you looked at the overtime expense? When examining overtime, you should adopt the philosophy that most overtime is a waste of time! This is particularly true if the overtime is paid for

Figure 3–1 Summary Overtime Report of Dollars Spent 19xx (Previous Year) versus 19xx (Present Year)

(1) Month	(2) Proof Department		(3) Loan Department		(4) Maintenance Department		(5) North Branch		(6) West Branch		(7) Miscellaneous		(8) Bank Totals	
	19YY	19XX	19YY	19XX	19YY	19XX	19YY	19XX	19YY	19XX	19YY	19XX	19YY	19XX
January														
February														
March														
Qtr. total														
April														
May														
June														
Qtr. total														
July														
August														
September														
Qtr. total														
October														
November														
December														
Qtr. total														
Year total														

employees working past an eight hour day or a forty-hour week, which is usually the case. The reason why most overtime is a waste is that in most situations a bank is paying time and a half for hours worked beyond a normal day when employees are tired and inefficient. So if their efficiency is reduced during overtime hours, the bank is paying premium prices for less production.

In examining overtime, the first step is to develop a historical record of overtime dollars spent by month, by location, for all the months of the previous year as compared to the months of the current year. Figure 3–1 illustrates a format that could be used to display this information. Only those departments or branch offices that have significant overtime should be identified. Departments or branch offices with insignificant amounts should be lumped together in the miscellaneous column. This will make the report easier to read. Actually, Figure 3–1 is a summary report. To arrive at this summary information a worksheet in the same format may have to be used showing every department and branch office that had overtime in order to determine in which locations the overtime was significant for the previous year.

The format used in Figure 3–1, when completed with dollar amounts, will show you at a glance which departments, in which months, quarters, and for the year, are the big overtime spenders. Once you know where the overtime is being spent, the next step is to determine who is being paid the overtime in each department. This can easily be tabulated using the same format shown in Figure 3–1. But in place of the department names, the names of the employees that received significant overtime should be shown. Again use the miscellaneous column for insignificant amounts. The "Bank Total" column becomes the "Department Total" column. You will find it helpful to also note the number of hours on overtime worked in small print next to the dollars paid.

Upon examining the report that identifies who worked the overtime, don't be surprised to see that most of the overtime is worked by only a few of the employees in the department, rather than being spread evenly among all the employees in the department. This is particularly true in a department with many employees. This phenomenon exists for several reasons. These, as well as other reasons that cause overtime, and suggested corrective measures, are shown below.

1. Some employees like to work overtime because of the extra money, and will always volunteer to work when the work is available. Some may just spend a little extra time after the

department closes doing their normal work, or they may punch in early in the morning or early from lunch. A series of extra quarter, half or full hours worked each day or every other day adds up over a period of a year. The punching-in time that often goes undetected by the department manager is the early punching-in time in the morning. Some employees are early risers and like to get in early in the morning (usually between 15 to 60 minutes early) and start their work whether or not they are directly interested in building up overtime hours. The way to counsel these employees is to mention to them that they are welcome to come in early, but that they are not required to start work before the normal starting time, and so are not to punch in on the time clock before the normal starting time.

With regard to those who volunteer to work overtime when there is a need, the manager should be careful to choose only those who are the most productive. Allowing slow workers to work overtime only compounds the expense.

2. Another reason why only certain employees may work most of the overtime in a department is because managers will often choose the same employees to work each time overtime has to be worked. This may be because the manager, who often works later along with the employee(s), likes to work or works well with some employees rather than others; or certain jobs require specialized expertise and only those employees with that expertise can perform the overtime work. There is nothing wrong with these reasons. In fact matching an employee's expertise with the work to be performed should be encouraged.
3. Sometimes an excess number of employees are scheduled to work overtime on a special project that has a short deadline. This "overkill" is often done because a manager has an uneasy feeling about completing a project on time. The result, however, particularly if the project requires input from another area in the bank, may be that the scheduled employees are sitting around waiting for the input, or when the input arrives there isn't enough of it to keep all the employees busy. Some planning and forethought about the nature of the project in relation to the number of employees required would eliminate this overkill. Also, there is no reason why some of them could not be sent home early if too many employees are scheduled to work. Too many employees

scheduled for any job only slows down all the employees on the job.

4. Some banks have a general policy of paying overtime for any employee who works on a scheduled day off, regardless of whether the employee will exceed 40 hours during that week. Obviously this policy should be reexamined or at least invoked only when there is dire need.

In any event, regardless of the reasons for overtime, any consistent overtime expense in a department should be investigated. And if it is found to be needed, alternate ways of getting the work done should be instituted such as hiring part-time employees, rescheduling present employees to begin later and work later, or splitting employees into two or more shifts, or a combination of all of these practices. If the need for this overtime appears marginal, sometimes the only sure fast way to eliminate it is for higher management to refuse to grant a manager any authority to allow overtime in his or her department unless it is approved in advance by the manager's manager. This usually eliminates the "need" in any marginal situation.

WORKING HOURS

If you are paying for 40 hours of work per week, are all your employees working a full 40 hours? Surprisingly, it is fairly common in banks to have shorter work hours in some of its departments or branches. These practices creep into a bank over a period of years. One department starts letting the employees go home early one or two days a week and then after a time the "standard" hours become the early hours. Even among branches within the same bank, starting times and/or the length of the lunch hours could vary. The best way to check to see if any of these variances exist within your bank is to survey starting and ending times and the length of the lunch hours in every branch and department in the bank. Standardizing these times will inevitably increase the number of actual working hours, which should decrease the need for additional employees as volume increases.

VOLUME CHANGES

Most bankers are aware of volume increases, if for no other reason than that department and branch managers are always first in line to complain about the need for more help and they use the reason that volume has increased. The continual growth in the banking industry and the population growth, as reported by the media has programmed us to increases in volume. We live in a relatively new country and we have a history of growth. Growth is expected. But when managers request additional help, and cite volume increases as the reason, make them prove it statistically. This will force them to keep better statistical records in their departments and branches.

Even though we are programmed toward growth and volume increases, there are times when volume *decreases*—during an economic recession, either locally or nationwide, and when the need for a function or a service either decreases or is replaced with a new need. The point is that there are decreases as well as increases in volume and therefore, there will be times when the need for personnel will decrease. Loan volumes and teller and proof transactions, for example, can and do decrease and it is prudent to be watchful, primarily through statistical review, for these decreases.

THE SIX-DAY WORK WEEK

Probably the worst impact on salary expense in any bank is the effect that a six-day work week has on the number of employees required to staff for the extra work day. Even if that extra day is only a half-day—such as a Saturday morning—banks will often give employees who work on Saturdays a full day off during the week to compensate them for the loss of a full two-day weekend. The result of this is an approximate 20% increase in the staffing levels for those branches and support departments affected. That is a big increase because the number of employees that work the sixth day often approaches 80% to 90% of the bank's total work force. For example, if a bank employs 100 people 80 to 90 of them may work on the sixth day and take a compensating day off. To supply a staff to work for those 80 or 90 employees when they are on their day off, requires the hiring of 16 or 18 more employees. This 20% factor comes from the simple logic that a six-day work week is 20% longer than a five-day work week! One could present an argument against using this same percentage when relating it to an increase in staff, by proposing that just because the number of days increases, doesn't mean that the volume has increased, it is just spread over a longer period of time. Unfortunately staffing is not solely dependent on volume. A certain staff base is required just to open the doors each day even if a minimum number of customers are serviced. In any event, if a bank is only open five days per week and is considering opening a sixth day or is now open six days and is considering returning to five days the respective increase or decrease in salary expense is just as major a consideration as the effect on customer service. To reduce the effect, in either situation, the following alternatives should be considered.

1. Rather than keeping the bank's lobbies open on the sixth day, keep only the drive-ins and walk-up teller stations. This not only substantially reduces the number of tellers required but also eliminates the need for lobby desk personnel and support department staffs.
2. If the lobbies are to remain open do not open support or other departments, or at least keep them open with only a skeleton staff. The most logical area to investigate first is the bookkeeping/proof function. Depending on processing time procedures and deadlines it may make no difference whether or not the normal day's work performed on Saturday in these departments is done on Saturday or Monday, because all of Saturday's work may be considered by computer processors as Monday's work anyway.
3. Consider keeping some of the branch lobbies open with the remaining branch lobbies closed with only their drive-ins open, or with the remaining branches closed entirely. Depending on the geographic locations of a branch banking network, these combinations could be very practical from a customer service point of view as well as for cost effective reasons. If two branches are located within a block or two of each other, it might be just as effective to keep only one of these offices open on the sixth day. Or if some of the branches are miles apart from one another and serve distinct communities, the need for the sixth day opening could depend on the need of the community being served.
4. Up to this point the sixth day has been presumed to be a Saturday. If Saturdays are busy traditionally, some other day could be considered as the "sixth" day and the above mentioned alternatives could be applied to this day.

In conclusion it should be mentioned that all the considerations and alternatives so far mentioned with regard to a six-day work week would also apply to a seven-day work week, or even to extended banking hours on any day of the week.

SUMMARY

This chapter described thirty-five ways to reduce personnel related expenses. Shown below for easy reference is a brief description of each of these ways, shown in the same sequence as presented in the chapter.

1. Believe that your bank is always overstaffed. You must determine the degree of overstaffing.
2. Put a bankwide freeze on hiring any additional staff for at least a six-month period.
3. Institute a strict policy of requiring managers to fully substantiate requests for additional staff through the use of departmental volume statistics.
4. Assess staffing in departments when an employee is leaving. Is it really necessary to replace that employee?
5. Use part-time clerical help whenever possible.
6. Focus in on how profitable it really is to vigorously control staffing levels.
7. Institute a meaningful wage salary administration program to control starting salaries and merit raises, and to determine the correct salary ranges for each job function, thereby eliminating the possibility of overpaying employees.
8. Consider the premise that a bankwide profit sharing program is virtually a useless attempt to improve profits and therefore an unnecessary expense.
9. Tie retirement benefit formulas to Social Security benefits.
10. Review the age required for your employees to join your retirement plan.
11. Consider instituting or increasing the employees' contribution rate with regard to your retirement plan.
12. Question the assumptions made by actuaries to determine your retirement plan's funding requirements (i.e., turnover rates, rate of return on fund assets, inflation rates).
13. Consider instituting a 401(k) plan for employees to decrease the need to improve your formal retirement plan.
14. Obtain quotations from competing carriers, particularly when your medical or dental plan costs are increasing at an alarming rate.
15. Avoid instituting an employee dental plan, if at all possible.
16. Investigate funding your medical plan yourself.
17. Investigate your local HMOs medical plan rates.

18. Consider requiring employees to pay a share of their medical and/or dental plan coverages.

19. Reduce turnover among newer employees.

20. Accept turnover of clerical employees with several years of seniority.

21. Encourage turnover of unproductive employees.

22. Keep accurate turnover records.

23. Consider the premise that most overtime is a waste of time.

24. Keep detailed overtime pay records.

25. Identify those employees who consistently work overtime. This may help identify the cause and eliminate the problem.

26. Watch out for the early starter.

27. Do not permit unproductive workers to work overtime.

28. Carefully match the expertise of the employees who are to work overtime to the work to be performed.

29. Watch out for the "overkill" scheduling of employees to work overtime on a special project that has an early deadline.

30. Use alternate methods of getting the work done when overtime is being scheduled consistently in a department.

31. Reconsider any personnel policy that pays overtime as a reward for working on a normal day off.

32. Require department managers to obtain approval in advance for anticipated overtime.

33. Eliminate inconsistent working hours between departments and/or branch offices.

34. Become aware of department or branch office volume decreases.

35. Consider the devastating effect that the six-day work week has on salary expense, and reduce this effect by using skeleton staffing techniques.

PART THREE

INCREASE FEE INCOME

Chapter 4

Checking Account Service Charges

INTRODUCTION

In the past few years there has been a lot written in banking periodicals about checking account service charges. All of these articles warn bankers that if they don't start charging fees more closely related to the true costs of providing this service, they will lose the war against declining profit margins—and they might.

What many bankers don't realize is how to price this service and therefore they are often reluctant to charge as much as they think they should. This reluctance to increase their fees stems from a clouded view of the true costs of providing this service.

This chapter provides guidelines to determine reliable costs for maintaining the various types of checking accounts offered by banks today—personal checking, the regular and Super NOW accounts, and business checking accounts. The subject of checking account costs involves the development of transaction costs, volumes of transactions within a bank and the formation of this information into reports. Then the profitability of these accounts can be accurately determined, and finally the profitable (but competitive) pricing of these accounts can be established. Samples of these reports with representative statistics are shown throughout the chapter. But the keystone of all the reports shown is the "Profitability Analysis Worksheet" (Figures 4–11 and 4–12). All other reports shown lead up to this final statistical report, which displays all information about accounts in a bank from which to make correct profitable decisions about pricing.

This chapter shows you how to develop these statistics for your own bank by using a combination of your bank's own records and reliable outside statistical data. This approach, therefore, will not involve the development of an in-bank cost accounting system. Also, these statistics can be developed with or without the aid of a computer, as will be shown. The end result of this approach that I have tested and used will be the ability to price checking account services both profitably and competitively.

It should be noted here that this chapter describes in detail the methodology of pricing checking accounts. This methodology was developed and tested several years ago and is as appropriate today as it was then. In developing this methodology several examples of costs, volumes, and interest rates were used to develop pricing structures. Many of these examples, since they were written several years ago, do not necessarily reflect current costs, volume, and rates. To update these factors for a book format would require yearly supplements because of the fast changing nature of these factors. What is important in this chapter is to understand the methodology used and then apply it with the most current information available. This chapter tells you where and how to find this current information.

DETERMINE BASIC CHECKING ACCOUNT COST STATISTICS

How much does it cost a bank to provide a checking account service for its customers? At first, the answer to this question may seem awesome, because as any banker knows there are many departments involved in providing this service—new accounts, teller, proof, bookkeeping data processing, and marketing. And since some of these departments also help provide other bank services, how does a bank isolate just the checking account related expenses of these departments and the other departments of the bank that help provide this service, to determine the true cost of maintaining a checking account for a customer? The answer that immediately comes to mind is that a bank should develop a cost accounting system that could be used to develop its costs. This sounds good but many bankers are not inclined, for whatever reasons, to hire an outside accounting firm to come in and develop such a system and then to spend more money to maintain this system on an ongoing basis.

Fortunately there is such a cost accounting system available that was developed for commercial banks by bankers that has been in existence and continually refined since 1957. It is called the Functional Cost Analysis (FCA) and the program is administered by the Federal Reserve System. To my knowledge the FED's FCA is the only cost accounting system for banks that is in wide use in banking today. Some of the larger banks have, of course, developed their own systems. The unique advantages of the FCA is its wide use throughout the country, its scope, and its refinements through the years. But there's another advantage to this system, which for most banks could be the most important: the results of the participating banks' cost analysis are published during the third quarter of each year for the preceding calendar year. And these results are averaged and broken down into three bank size groups. Any bank therefore, whether a participant or not, can substantially benefit from reviewing these results. Before describing how any bank can benefit from these published reports, it would be appropriate and informative to include a general description of the FCA system as written by the Federal Reserve in their introduction to the published results. The following is a direct quote of their entire introductory page as it is printed in the beginning of each of their published reports.

INTRODUCTION

> The Functional Cost Analysis (FCA) program is a cooperative venture between the Federal Reserve Banks and the participating banks. With uniform reporting procedures, it is designed to serve as a tool for bank management in evaluating performance. FCA develops individual bank income and cost data along functional lines and provides comparisons of these data within each bank from year to year and with groups of other banks on an annual basis. It is specifically designed to assist a participating bank in increasing overall bank earnings as well as improving the operational efficiency of each bank function. The current format is the product of ongoing review since the inception of the program in 1957,

and reflects many suggestions offered throughout the years by participating banks.

Bank cost accounting is not an exact science. Because of differences in concepts and in degree of sophistication as well as heavy reliance on human judgment, it has been virtually impossible in the past to compare with confidence one bank's costs with those of another bank and at times impractical even to compare year-to-year results within an individual bank.

Prior to the development of the Functional Cost Analysis program, the banking industry lacked a simplified uniform system of cost accounting that would require only modest data collection and would eliminate as many difficult judgments as possible. The Federal Reserve's Functional Cost Analysis program is intended to fill this void. In cases where differences in methods of accounting could not be eliminated by definitions or standard data collection procedures, adjustment techniques were developed and applied uniformly to all participating banks.

Functional Cost Analysis is by most cost study standards, a very simple system. Information on bank assets, income, expense, and item counts is collected by banks with the guidance of uniform instructions.

Bankers must use judgment in making certain expense distributions particularly in the allocation of wages and salaries. Expenses not functionally distributed by the bankers are allocated by the computer on the basis of "experience factors" developed from expense data of participating banks. This technique has helped to minimize inconsistencies of interbank comparisons.

If bank management can obtain: (1) reasonable approximations of functional costs, (2) year-to-year cost comparisons within the bank, and (3) reliable interbank comparisons with group averages for similar banks, then decision-making can be greatly assisted. The Functional Cost Analysis program helps to achieve this purpose.

The Functional Cost Analysis data of participating banks is summarized in this booklet. The reporting banks are separated into three groups by deposit size:

Columns (1) and (2) Average figures for member banks with deposits up to $50 million

Columns (3) and (4) Average figures for banks with deposits from $50 million to $200 million

Columns (5) and (6) Average figures for banks with deposits over $200 million

This booklet provides a great deal of information concerning bank costs and earnings. Before using this report, one should become familiar with the general objectives of the Functional Cost Analysis program as well as with the accounting and technical procedures used to obtain the figures on the following pages. If you have any questions about this data, contact the Federal Reserve Bank in your district.

This report is published annually and is available to any bank, member or not, from any Federal Reserve Bank or branch bank.

In this chapter as well as other chapters in this book, sample published results from the FCA are used. But when they are used, a complete explanation is given of the information presented along with a description of where to find this information. No matter what year in the future you wish to use this report, therefore, you will be able to find and understand the data described. It is important to note, however, that these sample FCA statistics, although reflecting current costs and volumes are shown primarily for methodology purposes for a bank to use in developing its own checking account fee program. You should therefore obtain from a local Federal Reserve Bank the most current FCA statistics available before using this methodology.

As mentioned before, participating banks who submit their own statistics can determine their own costs for providing checking accounts but even nonparticipating banks can substantially benefit from reviewing this report. It provides a basis for banks to compare costs with banks of the same size. This gives a bank a strong base on which to build an equitable fee structure for a service for your customers and your bank.

FCA per Item Costs

To determine the cost of maintaining customer checking accounts, participating banks in the FCA include an exhaustive list of expenses that relate to the costs involved in every department that provides any part of this service. The list of expenses involved are as follow:

Officer salaries	Occupancy
Employee salaries	External examinations and audits
Fringe benefits	Directors fees
Off-premise computer expense	FDIC insurance
Furniture and equipment	Other insurance, except realty or life
Printing, stationery, and supplies	Travel
	Dues and memberships
Postage, freight and delivery	Books, periodicals, information services
Publicity and advertising	Telephone and Telegraph
Fees, legal & other (including holding company mgmt. fees)	All other expenses

From the list of expenses actual dollars spent for the demand deposit function are determined through the use of detailed worksheets provided by the FED to participating banks. Next, yearly volumes of items relating to the demand deposit function are tabulated by category (for example the number of checks posted to accounts, the number of deposits posted to accounts, the number of items deposited). Finally standard weights are used which define the time required to perform all tasks related to the processing of each type of item as it is handled in various departments of the bank. The standard weight for each type of item is the same for all banks regardless of their size.

With the knowledge of the total dollars spent for the demand deposit function, the volume of the different items processed and the application of the weighting system, a cost per item can be determined.

The information concerning FED's method of determining and calculating the cost per item was presented to show you that considerable work is involved in arriving at these costs, and to show the logic used, which add to the validity and credibility of the resulting figures. These figures are ones that any bank can rely on when developing a fee structure for checking accounts. Because if it costs these banks these amounts to perform a checking account service to their customers, it probably costs your bank approximately the same amount. Unless you are a participating bank in the FCA or you have your own highly structured cost accounting system, you don't know your exact costs. It will be appropriate, therefore, throughout the rest of this chapter to use what is known—the FCA cost figures.

As mentioned earlier FED FCA reports show cost and other data for banks in three different deposit size categories up to $50 million, $50 to $200 million and over $200 million. Of course when developing the fee structure for your bank you should use the category closest to your deposit size or, if you are near a deposit size borderline, you may wish to use an average of the figures shown in the two of the three nearest categories. Let us assume that for banks of your size the costs for providing checking accounts according to the current FCA reports for the banks in your bank's deposit size category are as follows:

15.325 cents for each on us check or deposit processed and posted to a DDA account
31.494 cents for each deposit processed and posted to a DDA account
8.479 cents for each transit check deposited to an account
$4.24 per month to maintain each account

For future reference note that the above cost figures can be found in the FCA report "Demand Deposits—Weights-Units and Item Costs" under the subtitle "Cost Per Item in Cents." An example of this report is shown in Figure 4–1, and the costs shown above have been boxed in for easy reference.

The above cost per item figures are not related to the type of checking account. If it costs 15.325 cents for each on us check processed and posted to a checking account, this figure is the same regardless of whether the check is posted to a personal checking account, a NOW account or a business checking account. And the same is true for the other cost per item figures shown. What does make a difference, however, when further developing costs, is the average number of the different types or items processed for a particular type of account—the average number of on us items, deposits and transit items processed per personal checking account, per NOW account, and per business account. So far we know the cost of processing each on us item, each deposit, and each transit item regardless of the type of account. Next we have to determine how many on us items, deposits, and transit items are processed on average for each type of account in order to complete our determinations regarding the cost of providing this service. There are two ways to determine these average volumes per account. Analyze your own volumes or use FCA average figures. We will first present the FED's FCA figures.

Figure 4–1 Demand Deposits—Weight-Units and Item Costs

	Weight	200 Banks Deposits up to $50M Number	200 Banks Deposits up to $50M Weight-units	286 Banks Deposits $50M–$200M Number	286 Banks Deposits $50M–$200M Weight-units	75 Banks Deposits over $200M Number	75 Banks Deposits over $200M Weight-units
Weight-Unit Calculation							
1 On-Us Debits		999,619	1,813,952	2,724,364	4,924,068	14,776,901	26,746,191
2 Deposits		195,901	729,456	510,868	1,897,607	2,646,507	9,845,006
3 Transit Checks Deposited		692,814	692,814	2,593,487	2,593,487	15,799,455	15,799,455
4 Account Maintenance		4,507	2,694,617	11,344	6,807,945	58,062	34,691,777
5 Checking Accounts, Subtotal			5,930,840		16,223,108		87,082,430
6 On-Us Checks Cashed		101,135	284,189	266,105	747,756	1,560,016	4,383,647
7 Transit Checks Cashed		107,068	407,930	231,185	880,818	1,323,237	5,041,533
8 Official Checks Issued		17,858	97,505	53,711	293,265	295,776	1,614,939
9 TT&L Deposits		1,880	6,185	9,097	29,930	24,457	80,463
10 Total Weight-Units			6,726,651		18,174,879		98,203,014
11 Total Operating Exp		$	495,946	$	1,541,013	$	9,220,868
12 Cost per Weight-Unit (in cents)			7.373		8.479		9.390

Figure 4–1 Demand Deposits—Weight-Units and Item Cost (continued)

		Cost per Item in Cents				
Item Costs						
13 On-Us Debit		13.379		15.325		16.995
14 Deposit		27.453		31.494		34.929
15 Transit Check Deposited		7.373		8.479		9.390
16 Account Maintenance per Month		$ 3.67		$ 4.24		$ 4.67
17 Check Cashing		24.509		27.767		30.694
18 Official Check Issued		40.256		46.294		51.267
19 TT&L Deposit		24.257		27.895		30.892
Analysis of Expense by Activity						
20 On-Us Debits	$133,740	26.96%	$ 417,502	27.09%	$ 2,511,359	27.23%
21 Deposits	53,781	10.84	160,894	10.44	924,406	10.02
22 Transit Checks Deposited	51,080	10.30	219,896	14.27	1,483,505	16.08
23 Account Maintenance	198,670	40.05	577,232	37.45	3,257,418	35.32
24 Checking Account Exp., Subtotal	$437,272	88.16%	1,375,526	89.26%	$ 8,176,689	88.67%
25 Check Cashing	$ 51,029	10.28%	$ 138,083	8.96%	$ 884,986	9.59%
26 Official Checks Issued	7,188	1.45	24,865	1.61	151,636	1.64
27 TT&L Deposits	456	.09	2,537	.16	7,555	.08
28 Non-Checking Expense, Subtotal	$ 58,673	11.83%	$ 165,486	10.73%	$ 1,044,178	11.32%
29 Total Operating Expense	$495,496	100.00%	1,541,013	100.00%	$ 9,220,868	100.00%

FCA Average Volumes per Account

In order to determine costs it is important to know, on an average, how much activity there is in each type of account. The average activity per account per month is presented by the FCA in five separate reports. Each report covers a specific type of checking account or a mixture of accounts. The activity per account per month is shown on the last three lines on each report. These five reports are:

Demand Deposits–Commercial Checking Account Analysis
Demand Deposits–Personal Checking Account Analysis
Demand Deposits–Special Checking Account Analysis
Demand Deposits–Interest Bearing Checking Account Analysis
Demand Deposits–Regular Checking Account Analysis

Figure 4–2 is a sample composite of the activity per account per month to be found on the last three lines of these five reports for banks in the $50 to $200 million deposit category. Also shown in Figure 4–2 is a description of the types of accounts included in each of the five reports and the number of banks that reported information in each category. All of the information shown in Figure 4–2 should be considered when reviewing these FCA activity reports. For example, as bankers we have all heard the statistic that on average a checking account customer writes approximately 22 checks per month. That statistic is quoted most often from the FCA Demand Deposits – Regular Checking Account Analysis. What we don't hear is that the FCA report from which this statistic is taken is an analysis of a combination of business accounts and personal type accounts (see Figure 4–2 regular checking account analysis, column 2, which shows the type of accounts included in the analysis). Accordingly, of all the volume figures shown on Figure 4–2, I would be inclined to rely more on those shown for special checking accounts and interest bearing checking accounts, since there were a sufficient number of banks in this size category (73 and 290, respectively) that reported their volumes in these two types of account categories. In the commercial checking account and personal checking account categories there were not a sufficient number of banks that reported their volumes and so the volumes shown are suspect. What is consistent among all personal type account categories is the number of deposits – three per account per month (as shown in Figure 4–2, column 5). For transit checks deposited the averages shown per account per month for special checking accounts (2.14 transit checks) and NOW accounts (9.10 transit checks) would be the most reliable for the reasons stated above. Note that the NOW account figure for transit checks deposited is high. This is because nonprofit organizations are also permitted to have these accounts and the number of items deposited as reported include these accounts as well as personal accounts.

Note also that the FED only separates out the number of transit checks deposited and only shows separate cost figures for these items. The cost for on us checks deposited and for deposited cash are included in the cost per on us debit and per deposit respectively.

In summary, the average volume figures that we could obtain from the FED's FCA reports, as shown in Figure 4–2, that would be of use in determining average costs for maintaining a checking account would be as follows. These figures have been rounded to the closest whole number. The average special checking account customer wrote 13 checks, made 3 deposits, and deposited 2 transit checks per month. The average NOW account customer wrote 17 checks, made 3 deposits, and deposited 9 transit checks per month. The average personal checking account customer made 3 deposits per month. What still hasn't been determined are the volume figures for business accounts and the number of on us debits and transit checks deposited for personal accounts (excluding NOW accounts and special checking accounts). This leads us into the next section which will show a much more accurate way to accumulate volume statistics by type of account.

Determine Your Own Volumes

Any bank that processes checking accounts with a computer can determine, from monthly summary reports, the number of checks posted and the number of deposits posted in total to all accounts in a particular category (i.e., personal accounts and NOW accounts). Also available from these reports are the number of accounts in each of these categories. By dividing the number of checks posted by the number of accounts it is easy to arrive at the average number of checks posted to each account. This same simple formula can be used, of course, to arrive at the number of deposits posted on average to each account for a given month. Since most banks analyze business account volume on a per account basis, we will confine our present discussion about determining your own volumes to personal checking and NOW account categories.

Figure 4–2 Composite of FRB's Functional Cost Analysis Volume Statistics

Name of FCA demand deposit report	*Types of accounts included*	*Number of reporting banks $50–200 million deposits*	*Average activity per account per month*		
			On us debits	*Deposits*	*Transit checks*
Commercial Checking Account Analysis	Business Accounts	26	54.23	9.72	99.22
Personal Checking Account Analysis	Individual and Household Accounts, Special Checking Accounts, NOW Accounts	25	14.76	2.72	15.45
Special Checking Accounts Analysis	Fee per Check Written Type of Accounts	73	12.61	2.62	2.14
Interest Bearing Checking Account Analysis	NOW Accounts	290	17.13	3.33	9.10
Regular Checking Account Analysis	Business Accounts, Individual and Household Accounts, NOW Accounts (Not Special Checking Accounts)	286	21.16	3.92	22.17

Even if your bank does not process checking accounts with a computer-system you may still have these monthly volume figures available to you from other manual reports you currently prepare. But if you don't, you should count these items for a month by type of account. Your proof department machines, which automatically count the items sorted into each pocket, could be used to partially automate this counting task as the items are processed in your proof department.

Whether or not your DDA function is processed by a computer, determining the number of transit items deposited to personal and NOW accounts could be difficult and it is recommended, as will be shown later, that the FED's FCA volume statistics for transit items be used.

Figure 4–3 introduces another important element in developing and presenting volume statistics. It is the FCA checking account size analysis, which shows the percent of total volume (dollar amount of balances) and the percent of total number of accounts for different balance categories for those reporting banks in the three deposit size categories. The reporting banks, when they compile these statistics, slot each account by the balance in the account as of a point in time. They are not slotted by the average balance in the account. All types of checking accounts are included in these statistics business accounts, personal accounts and special checking accounts. NOW accounts, however, are excluded. What this analysis shows is that, on line one for the 156 reporting banks in the $5–$200 million deposit size category, when each account with a balance of less than $200.00 was slotted, the total dollar amount of balances of all these accounts amounted to less than 1% (.91%) of the total balances of all the DDA accounts. And the number of accounts in the

Figure 4–3 Checking Account Size Analysis

	97 Banks Deposits up to $50M		*156 Banks Deposits $50M–$200M*		*42 Banks Deposits over $200M*	
	Volume	*Accounts*	*Volume*	*Accounts*	*Volume*	*Accounts*
1 Under $200	1.37%	34.99%	.91%	34.37%	.63%	32.19%
2 $ 200 to $ 500	3.31	20.37	2.73	20.51	2.46	22.29
3 $ 500 to $ 1,000	5.52	16.49	4.58	16.42	4.40	17.98
4 $ 1,000 to $ 5,000	20.46	20.39	18.15	20.89	15.02	20.62
5 $ 5,000 to $ 10,000	12.40	3.94	9.91	3.82	7.31	3.29
6 $ 10,000 to $ 25,000	17.31	2.60	13.69	2.40	9.80	2.02
7 $ 25,000 to $100,000	20.18	1.00	21.00	1.27	16.22	1.19
8 $100,000 and Over	19.40	.18	28.98	.28	44.11	.38
9 Totals	100.00%	100.00%	100.00%	100.00%	100.00%	100.00%

less than \$200.00 category amounted to 34.37% of the total number of all the DDA accounts. If, therefore, the average number of checking accounts for each of the 156 reporting banks was 10,000 accounts with total balances of \$20,000,000, then 3437 accounts (.3437 × 10,000) had an aggregate of only \$182,000 in balances (\$20,000,000 × .0091). To go a step further, if you add the first three lines of "volume" and "accounts" percentages for these 156 banks, 71.3% of the number of accounts accounted for only 8.22% of the balances in the whole DDA portfolio—or in our example of 10,000 accounts with \$20,000,000 in balances 7130 accounts would have only \$1,644,000 in total balances!

The information presented above in conjunction with the statistics reported by the FED's FCA as shown in Figure 4–1 was presented only to point out the importance of knowing the balance makeup of your own DDA accounts and to combine this information when you develop your own volume statistics.

Formulate Your Own Volume Statistics

It is important in any analysis of DDA volume to report this volume in conjunction with the number of accounts by balance categories. Figures 4–1 and 4–5 are examples of a basic analysis of a bank's personal DDA account (NOW accounts and special checking accounts were excluded). The figures shown are based on an actual bank's records as extrapolated from the bank's main computer files. Although the information shown was obtained from computerized DDA files by using a special computer program, these statistics can be obtained manually. Both Figures 4–4 and 4–5 show an analysis of the same DDA personal accounts during the same one month period, but these accounts were analyzed two different ways by the average balance in each account for the month (Figure 4–4) and by the lowest balance in each account for the month (Figure 4–5). Both of these reports or profiles show three types of information—the number of accounts, the balances in these accounts and the activity in these accounts.

Figure 4–4 shows an analysis of a total of 8,657 personal checking accounts with a total positive average balance of \$5,831,944, total number of debits (including checks and internal debits) posted to these accounts of 111,584, and total number of credits (including deposit slips and internal credits) posted to these accounts of 23,240 (see line 13). In Figure 4–4 each of this bank's 8,657 accounts was analyzed according to the account's 31-day average balance and then depending on the amount of

Figure 4–4 Statistical Profile of Personal Checking Accounts Based on Average Balances for June, 19xx

(1) Balance Categories	(2) Number of Accounts	(3) Average Balances	(4) Number of Debits	(5) Number of Credits
1 O.D. Accounts	152	($ 7,843)	308	135
2 $.01 to $99	1,566	73,838	8,348	2,782
3 $100 to $199	1,248	184,356	14,404	3,854
4 $200 to $299	1,027	254,801	15,508	3,326
5 $300 to $399	775	270,359	12,222	2,481
6 $400 to $499	658	294,087	10,253	1,988
7 $500 to $999	1,830	1,297,144	28,092	5,030
8 $1,000 to $1,999	912	1,237,679	14,743	2,420
9 $2,000 to $2,999	238	576,715	3,576	544
10 $3,000 to $4,999	141	540,173	2,299	392
11 $5,000 to $9,999	75	507,828	1,180	173
12 $10,000 and Over	35	602,807	651	115
13 Totals	8,657	5,831,944	111,584	23,240

that average balance, was slotted into one of the balance categories shown in column one. If, for example, the average balance for a particular account was $512 then that account was slotted into the $500 to $999 category. Once these accounts were properly categorized by their average balance, the number of accounts in each category together with the total

Figure 4–5 Statistical Profile of Personal Checking Accounts Based on Lowest Balances for June, 19xx

(1) Balance Categories	(2) Number of Accounts	(3) Average Balances	(4) Number of Debits	(5) Number of Credits
1 O.D. Accounts	913	$ 155,749	11,053	2,617
2 $.01 to $99	3,753	891,759	48,140	10,805
3 $100 to $199	860	372,358	12,222	2,430
4 $200 to $299	522	351,695	7,722	1,440
5 $300 to $399	554	379,424	7,049	1,392
6 $400 to $499	452	370,406	5,877	1,141
7 $500 to $999	943	1,030,811	11,716	2,117
8 $1,000 to $1,999	403	789,252	4,847	782
9 $2,000 to $2,999	117	374,359	1,319	233
10 $3,000 to $4,999	79	383,653	922	160
11 $5,000 to $9,999	43	366,495	499	79
12 $10,000 and Over	18	365,983	218	44
13 Totals	8,657	$5,831,944	111,584	23,240

of these accounts' average balances, and number of debits and credits posted, were tabulated. As shown on line 6, there were 658 accounts with average balances of between $400 and $499 and the average balances for these 658 accounts totaled $294,087. And there were a total of 10,253 debits and 1,988 credits posted to these accounts during the month.

Figure 4–5 shows an analysis of the same 8,657 accounts done in the same manner as in Figure 4–4. But instead of categorizing each account by its average balance for the month, each account was categorized by its lowest balance during the month.

In this section of this chapter my aim is to show ways a bank can determine its own volume statistics rather than use FCA averages. The statistical information displayed in Figures 4–4 and 4–5 shows basic information about a bank's personal DDA accounts. All of this information will be used in this section or in succeeding sections of this chapter to develop a knowledgeable and profitable service charge structure for DDA accounts.

Some of you by now may be thinking that it would be nice to have all this information about your own bank's checking accounts but for one reason or another you don't have access to a computer from which to obtain this information. The computer was used to slot the accounts into balance categories and to tabulate the balances and volume statistics for these slotted accounts. For those banks whose DDA accounts are processed by a computer system programs are available that will tabulate these statistics. These programs may be available at your computer center or can be purchased from an outside firm. Your own CPA firm may even have them. If, however, you either cannot obtain these programs or your DDA accounts are not processed by a computer system, slotting accounts into balance categories can be done manually by using a multi-pocket proof machine or any accounting machine that has multiple totals. It is almost impossible to tabulate manually the number of debits and credits posted for accounts by balance category. The method described in the section of this chapter entitled "Determine Your Own Volumes," that uses the average number of debits and credits posted per account should be used. These average volume statistics per account will be sufficiently accurate to develop costs and establish a pricing structure for checking accounts. The following paragraphs will show how to manually tabulate the statistics shown in Figures 4–4 and 4–5. There are three ways to slot accounts manually by balance category. These accounts can be slotted by lowest balance, by current balance, or by average balance. The way you want to service charge these accounts will determine the way to slot these balances. Figures 4–4 and 4–5 showed the slotting of these accounts by average balances and lowest balances respectively because most banks service charge accounts if either the minimum or the average balance falls below a certain level. Service charges for personal checking accounts should be triggered on the minimum (lowest) balance during the month and fortunately slotting accounts by their lowest balance, manually, is a relatively easy process. The only way to slot accounts by balance categories manually would be to use the customer's monthly statement. A clerk could scan down the balance column of each statement and easily spot the lowest balance shown during the month. But the average balance of the month is usually not shown on the statement and, therefore, a clerk would manually have to compute the average balance for each statement before the account was slotted. Since the time involved would be almost prohibitive, an alternative method would be to extract a balance from each statement at a particular point in time (current balance)—for example, the balance at the end of the month. The current balance would be a reasonable substitute for the average balance since the tabulation of a succession of current balances within a certain balance category would statistically result in the approximate average balances of all accounts in that category. To be statistically accurate, however, once the point in time is selected use the same date for each account.

To manually slot accounts by balance categories with a proof machine first select the balance categories into which you wish your accounts slotted (OD accounts, $.01 to $99, $100 to $199, etc.). When selecting balance categories, always remember to include the balance category that represents your present service structure for the type of account being analyzed. If, for example your cutoff for triggering a service charge on personal accounts is $350 then choose a category that ends with $350 (i.e., $300 to $350). Also, you should choose a category that represents a future trigger point ($450 for example). The reason for this forethought in choosing balance categories will become evident when we discuss costs and pricing. But to continue, once the balance categories have been selected assign a proof machine pocket for each category selected. Use a proof operator to scan each monthly account statement for the type of balance upon which you choose to analyze the account (lowest balance for an analysis of your accounts based on their lowest or minimum balance, *or* current balance as a substitute for analyzing your accounts based on their average balance). The proof operator now knows into which pocket to put the balance but it is important to know what balance. Since the statistics we are trying to obtain are the same as those obtained in Figures 4–4 and 4–5, we wish to know how any accounts fall into the various balance categories. But we also wish to know the cumulative average balances of these accounts in these categories. We have also decided that it would be best to substitute current balance for an average balance because of the amount of time it would take to calculate the average balance. And so the balance the proof operator puts into the selected pocket is the *current* balance. Of course if you already know the average balance for each account, this average balance is put into the selected pocket. Therefore, if you wish to analyze your accounts based on their lowest balance, select the pocket based on the lowest balance in the account but put the *current* balance in that pocket. If you wish to analyze your accounts based on their average balance, select the pocket based on a balance as of one point in time (current balance to be used as a substitute for the average balance) and place that current balance in the selected pocket. Let us assume that you wish to analyze your accounts according to their lowest (minimum) balance during the month. The proof operator scans a statement and finds the lowest balance to be $20.00 overdrawn and the balance at the end of the month (current balance) to be $55.00 (positive balance). Pocket 1 has been designated as the pocket into which those accounts that have an overdrawn balance as their lowest balance should be put. The proof operator then puts $55.00 into pocket 1. After all the statements have been visually scanned and the accounts have been categorized and all the balances have been registered in the proof machine, total all the pockets. The total dollar amount in each pocket will give you the total of all the current balances for accounts categorized by their lowest balance by the various balance categories. Most proof machines' pocket totals will also give you a count of the number of balances put into each pocket. This figure tells you the number of accounts in each category. If your machine does not give you this count, merely hand count the number of balance entries listed on the pocket tape. The debit and credit volume statistics are calculated by multiplying the average number of debits posted and credits posted per account by the number in each balance category. For example, if you had determined earlier that on average, for all your personal checking accounts, 12 debits are posted to each account per month, (and this was determined earlier by dividing the grand

Figure 4–6 Statistical Profile of NOW Accounts Based on Average Balances for June, 19xx

	(1) Balance Categories	(2) Number of Accounts	(3) Average Balances	(4) Number of Debits	(5) Number of Credits
1	OD Accounts	20	($264)	22	5
2	$.01 to $99	60	2,000	155	55
3	$100 to $199	68	10,291	574	150
4	$200 to $299	76	19,105	950	194
5	$300 to $399	91	31,798	1,066	216
6	$400 to $499	79	35,820	972	225
7	$500 to $999	295	213,749	3,551	656
8	$1,000 to $1,999	343	503,625	4,046	771
9	$2,000 to $2,999	179	443,184	2,025	383
10	$3,000 to $4,999	187	729,044	2,409	407
11	$5,000 to $9,999	113	783,752	1,322	248
12	$10,000 and over	66	1,207,717	825	179
13	Totals	1,577	$3,979,821	17,917	3,489

total of all debits posted to all accounts during the month analyzed by the total number of accounts) and your "proof machine survey" showed you that 585 accounts were slotted into the balance category of lowest balances of between $.01 to $99, then 7,020 (585 × 12) debits were posted to those 585 accounts during the month.

Figure 4–7 Statistical Profile of NOW Account Based on Lowest Balances for June, 19xx

	(1) Balance Categories	(2) Number of Accounts	(3) Average Balances	(4) Number of Debits	(5) Number of Credits
1	OD Accounts	46	$ 12,461	449	99
2	$.01 to $99	239	96,069	3,189	661
3	$100 to $199	116	73,371	1,438	310
4	$200 to $299	98	66,166	1,089	209
5	$300 to $399	83	69,250	991	179
6	$400 to $499	74	66,996	756	150
7	$500 to $999	215	269,613	2,243	417
8	$1,000 to $1,999	299	583,390	3,323	631
9	$2,000 to $2,999	148	484,731	1,715	303
10	$3,000 to $4,999	129	609,678	1,283	234
11	$5,000 to $9,999	88	740,210	956	194
12	$10,000 and over	42	907,886	485	102
13	Totals	1.577	$3,979,821	17,917	3,489

Although I have never timed it, I would judge that a good proof operator could survey and tabulate between 300 and 500 accounts per hour. And so if you had 3000 personal accounts it would take one proof operator 6 to 10 hours to complete the survey. If you don't have a multi-total machine, you should be statistically accurate if you survey only every fifth statement and manually slot and record the balances using a separate sheet of paper for each balance category, and then at the end add all the figures up on an adding machine, and finally multiply each total figure by 5.

And so either the computer or a manual system can be used to determine volume and balance information about any type of checking account. If you're using the computer method and you offer personal, special checking, and NOW accounts to your customers you should analyze all of these types of accounts at the same time and produce separate reports for each type of account using the same format as shown in Figures 4–4 and 4–5. If you are using a manual system you may wish to analyze each type of account in succession rather than all at the same time. It would make the project less confusing. If you are deciding which type of accounts to analyze first and are tempted to skip one of the files, I suggest that you analyze the larger of the two personal type of account files (personal accounts or special checking accounts) first. It is always worth the effort to analyze the NOW account files because of its mix of personal and nonprofit type of accounts and its peculiar cost ramifications (the interest paid on the balances). Figures 4–6 and 4–7 show an example of an analysis of a bank's NOW accounts which varies substantially from this same bank's personal accounts as shown in Figures 4–4 and 4–5.

With regard to business accounts most banks currently already analyze, either by hand or electronically, volume and balance statistics on a per account basis and so it is not necessary to analyze these accounts and develop the type of statistics shown in Figures 4–4, 4–5, 4–6, and 4–7.

DETERMINE COSTS BY TYPE OF ACCOUNT

Now, armed with sufficient and reliable per item cost figures and statistical data, you can develop a complete cost picture for different types of checking accounts. As shown earlier in this chapter the FCA told us that the average cost per type of item processed for participating banks in your bank's deposit category is:

Costs	
Per on Us Debit	15.325 cents
Per Deposit	31.494 cents
Per Transit Check Deposited	8.479 cents
Account Maintenance per Month	$4.24

These cost figures are the same for all types of checking accounts. Volume and average balance figures for the various types of accounts are not necessarily the same for all types of accounts. I will therefore present the complete cost figures for the three major types of checking accounts—personal accounts, NOW accounts, and business accounts. In developing these costs I will use the FCA cost figures shown above, and of course, the volume and balance statistical information developed in Figures 4–4, 4–5, 4–6 and 4–7.

Personal Checking Accounts Costs

Figures 4–4 and 4–5 analyzed the same personal accounts for the same period in two different ways: by average balance in each account for the month (Figure 4–4) and by the lowest balance in each account for the month (Figure 4–5). Upon scanning either group of statistics, it is obvious that the major volume in these accounts is in the lowest balance categories.

Since most banks service charge personal accounts on a fee per check basis, a flat monthly fee basis, or a combination of these, it is important to know what the volume is in relation to the balance in the account in order to determine the net cost to the bank to maintain these accounts. Also, many banks offer free checking to customers who maintain a certain balance in their accounts. That certain balance could be on a lowest (or minimum) basis (service charge free if the balance does not fall below a certain amount during the month), free checking if an average balance of a certain amount is maintained during the month, or a combination of these. Assuming that a bank does not offer free checking account service to all its personal account customers regardless of the balance in the account, it will make a difference in service charge income depending on whether service charges are levied based on lowest (or a minimum) balance maintained or the average balance maintained during the month. Figure 4–8 shows a simple comparison of cumulative volume type statistics, that would relate to a service charge structure,

Figure 4–8 A Comparison of Volume Statistics for Personal Checking Accounts Lowest Profile versus Average Balance Profile

(1)	(2)		(3)		(4)		(5)	
	Based on Lowest Balance				Based on Average Balance			
Balance Categories	Cumulative Number of Accounts	Cum. %	Cumulative Number of Debits	Cum. %	Cumulative Number of Accounts	Cum. %	Cumulative Number of Debits	Cum. %
1 OD Accounts	913	10.5	11,053	9.91	152	1.76	308	.28
2 $.01 to $99	4,666	53.9	59,193	53.1	1,718	19.8	8,656	7.8
3 $100 to $199	5,526	63.8	71,415	64.0	2,966	34.3	23,060	20.7
4 $200 to $299	6,048	69.9	79,137	70.9	3,993	46.1	38,568	34.6
5 $300 to $399	6,602	76.3	86,186	77.2	4,768	55.1	50,790	45.5
6 $400 to $499	7,054	81.5	92,063	82.5	5,426	62.7	61,043	54.7
7 $500 to $999	7,997	92.4	103,779	93.0	7,256	83.8	89,135	79.9
8 $1,000 to $1,999	8,400	97.0	108,626	97.3	8,168	94.4	103,878	93.1
9 $2,000 to $2,999	8,517	98.4	109,945	98.5	8,406	97.1	107,454	96.3
10 $3,000 to $4,999	8,596	99.3	110,867	99.4	8,547	98.7	109,753	98.4
11 $5,000 to $9,999	8,639	99.8	111,366	99.8	8,622	99.6	110,933	99.4
12 $10,000 and over	8,657	100	111,584	100	8,657	100	111,584	100

between accounts slotted by their lowest balance during the month and the same accounts slotted by their average balance during the month. All statistics shown were extracted from those in Figures 4–4 and 4–5. From reviewing the comparisons shown in Figure 4–8, it is obvious that more service charge income would be collected if a service charge structure is based on a lowest balance rather than on an average balance. For example, if a bank decided to charge a service charge when a balance in an account fell below $300, then that bank would collect more service charges if it based its fee (regardless of whether the fee was charged as a flat amount per month and/or on a per check posted basis) on the lowest balance in the month. This is because at the $300 and below category almost 70% of the number of accounts and 70% of the number of debits posted would be affected. Whereas only 46.1% of the number of accounts and 34.6% of the number of posted debits would be affected if the fee was charged on an average balance during the month. To illustrate this more graphically let us assume that this bank had a fee structure of a $2.00 flat maintenance charge plus $.15 per check posted when the balance fell below $300. Then using the statistics shown on line 4 of Figure 4–8 the bank would collect $12,096 ($6,048 × $2.00) from the flat maintenance charge and $11,870.55 (79,137 × $.15) from the per check fee or a total of $23,966.55 if it used lowest balance statistics. In contrast, by using average balance statistics the bank would collect only $13,771.20 for the month (3,993 × $2.00 + 38,568 × .15¢). The annualized difference is a potential $122,344.20 ($23,966.55 – $13,771.20 = $10,195.35 × 12).

Figure 4–9 shows the cost involved in maintaining the personal checking accounts profiled in Figure 4–5. The number of accounts, debits, and credits used are the same as those shown in Figure 4–5. The FCA costs per item used of 15.3 cents per debit, 31.5 cents per credit, 8.5 cents per transit item, and $4.24 per account for maintenance are the same as those shown earlier in this chapter. The number of transit items deposited was conservatively estimated at two items per month per account (see Figure 4–2, line for Special Checking Account Analysis). The number of transit items deposited per account for Special Checking Accounts rather than for Personal Checking Accounts was used because the number of banks reporting personal checking account statistics as per Figure 4–2 was low and the number of transit checks reported for this category seemed too high compared to the number of deposits per month reported. The costs per account per month for debits and for credits were computed by multiplying the cost per item times the num-

Figure 4–9 Costs of Personal Checking Accounts Based on Lowest Balance Statistical Profile

(1)	(2)	(3)	(4)	(5)	(6)	(7)	(8)	(9)	(10)
				Costs per Account per Month					
Balance Categories	Number of Accounts	Number of Debits	Number of Credits	Debits @ 15.3 Cents	Credits @ 31.5 Cents	Transit Items @ 8.5 Cents	Mainten-ance @ $4.24	Total Cost per Account per Month	Total Cost per Month
1 O.D. Accounts	913	11,053	2,617	$1.85	$.90	$.17	$4.24	$7.16	$ 6,537
2 $.01 to $99	3,753	48,140	10,805	1.96	.91	.17	4.24	7.28	27,322
3 $100 to $199	860	12,222	2,430	2.17	.89	.17	4.24	7.47	6,424
4 $200 to $299	522	7,722	1,440	2.26	.87	.17	4.24	7.54	3,936
5 $300 to $399	554	7,049	1,392	1.95	.79	.17	4.24	7.15	3,961
6 $400 to $499	452	5,877	1,141	1.99	.80	.17	4.24	7.20	3,254
7 $500 to $999	943	11,716	2,117	1.90	.71	.17	4.24	7.02	6,620
8 $1,000 to $1,999	403	4,847	782	1.84	.61	.17	4.24	6.86	2,765
9 $2,000 to $2,999	117	1,319	233	1.72	.63	.17	4.24	6.76	791
10 $3,000 to $4,999	79	922	160	1.79	.64	.17	4.24	6.84	540
11 $5,000 to $9,999	43	499	79	1.78	.58	.17	4.24	6.77	291
12 $10,000 and over	18	218	44	1.85	.77	.17	4.24	7.03	127
Totals	8,657	111,584	23,240						$62,568

ber of items in that category and then dividing by the number of accounts in that category. For example, in Figure 4–9 line 2 the \$1.96 amount in column 5 represents the average monthly cost of processing all debits for each account that had an average balance of between \$.01 and \$99 for the month of June; and this was determined by multiplying the number of debits in that category (48,140) times the cost per debit (15.3¢) and then dividing the total (\$7,365.42) by the number of accounts in that category (3,753).

Column 9 of Figure 4–9, total cost per account per month, was computed by adding the various costs per account per month shown in columns 5, 6, 7, and 8. The total cost per month shown in column 10 was computed by multiplying the amount shown in column 9 by the number of accounts shown in column 2.

We now know the costs for providing personal checking accounts to customers and we have shown this information by cost per account per month and total cost. Before developing statistics to determine the profit or loss for providing this service we will briefly explore methods of obtaining cost figures for NOW accounts and business checking accounts.

NOW Account Costs

You can develop cost figures for NOW accounts (and "Super NOW" accounts) by using the same method that was used in developing cost figures for personal accounts. Figure 4–10 shows the costs for maintaining this bank's NOW accounts. The basic statistical information was taken from the statistical profile of NOW accounts based on lowest balances (Figure 4–7). The same per item costs for debits and credits and for maintaining accounts were used in Figure 4–10 and in Figure 4–9 (costs for processing personal checking accounts). There are two differences in computing the costs of NOW accounts in contrast to personal checking accounts. An interest expense column (column 10) was added to Figure 4–10. This interest expense was calculated by first computing average balance per account (the average balances for each category as shown in column 5 of Figure 4–10 divided by the number of accounts in each category as shown in column 2 of Figure 4–10). Then this average balance for each balance category was multiplied by .0525 and divided by 12 to arrive at a monthly interest expense. The second difference is in the number used for transit items deposited. Rather than using two items per account per month as for personal checking accounts, 9 items

Figure 4–10 Costs of Processing NOW Accounts Based on Lowest Balance Statistical Profile

(1)	(2)	(3)	(4)	(5)	(6)	(7)	(8)	(9)	(10)	(11)	(12)
					Costs per Account per Month						
Balance Categories	Number of Accounts	Number of Debits	Number of Credits	Average Balances	Debits @ 15.3 Cents	Credits @ 31.5 Cents	Transit Items @ 8.5 Cents	Maintenance @ \$4.24	Interest Exp. @ 5¼%	Total Cost per Account per Month	Total Cost per Month
1 OD Accounts	46	449	99	\$ 12,461	\$1.49	\$.68	\$.77	\$4.24	\$ 1.19	\$ 8.37	\$ 385
2 \$.01 to \$99	239	3,189	661	96,069	2.04	.87	.77	4.24	1.76	9.68	2,314
3 \$100 to \$199	116	1,438	310	73,371	1.90	.84	.77	4.24	2.77	10.52	1,220
4 \$200 to \$299	98	1,089	209	66,166	1.70	.67	.77	4.24	2.95	10.33	1,012
5 \$300 to \$399	83	991	179	69,250	1.83	.68	.77	4.24	3.65	11.17	927
6 \$400 to \$499	74	756	150	66,996	1.56	.64	.77	4.24	3.96	11.17	827
7 \$500 to \$999	215	2,243	417	269,613	1.60	.61	.77	4.24	5.49	12.71	2,733
8 \$1,000 to \$1,999	299	3,323	631	583,390	1.70	.66	.77	4.24	8.54	15.91	4,757
9 \$2,000 to \$2,999	148	1,715	303	484,731	1.77	.64	.77	4.24	14.33	21.75	3,219
10 \$3,000 to \$4,999	129	1,283	234	609,678	1.52	.57	.77	4.24	20.68	27.78	3,584
11 \$5,000 to \$9,999	88	956	194	740,210	1.66	.69	.77	4.24	36.80	44.16	3,886
12 \$10,000 and over	42	485	102	907,886	1.77	.77	.77	4.24	94.57	102.12	4,289
Totals	1,577	17,917	3,489	3,979,821							\$29,153

were used as per the FCA (Figure 4–2). The reason why more transit items are deposited to NOW accounts than to personal accounts is because NOW account statistics include not only personal NOWs but also nonprofit organization NOW accounts.

Business Account Costs

Fortunately most banks already analyze their monthly business account activity by each account and therefore can easily determine costs on a by account basis (rather than by a balance category basis as was done for personal and NOW accounts) by multiplying the known debit, credit, and transit item activity in each account by the FCA costs per item and then adding the flat maintenance cost also shown by the FCA. These cost per item and maintenance costs are the same as those used for both personal and NOW accounts, and are found in the FCA report "Demand Deposits—Weights-Units and Item Costs."

DETERMINE CHECKING ACCOUNT PROFITABILITY AND THE PRICING OF CHECKING ACCOUNTS

Now, having developed a procedure to determine the costs of providing the various types of checking accounts to customers, we can proceed to the final stage—determining profitability and pricing for profitability. Determining profitability involves two elements—income from account balances and service charges, and the competitive pricing of this service. Since the three basic types of checking account services—personal accounts, NOW accounts and business accounts—have their individual characteristics with regard to income and pricing, it is appropriate to determine the profitability of these accounts separately.

Personal Checking Account Profitability

Figure 4–11 shows a profitability worksheet that can be used to determine profitability by balance category for personal checking accounts. As we saw in Figure 4–8, it is more profitable to use minimum balances rather than average balances to determine the balance level at which service charges are to be imposed, the volume statistics used in Figure 4–11 are based on the lowest balance profile for personal checking accounts (Figure 4–5). In addition, to complete the worksheet a hypothetical service charge schedule is used. This schedule consists of a $.15 per

Figure 4–11 Profitability Analysis Worksheet Personal Checking Accounts

(Based on lowest balance profile and a $300 minimum balance requirement to avoid service charges)

	(1) Balance Categories	(2) Number of Accounts	% of Total	(3) Cumulative Number of Accounts	% of Total	(4) Average Balances	% of Total	(5) Cumulative Average Balances	% of Total	(6) Number of Debits	% of Total	(7) Cumulative Number of Debits	% of Total
1	OD Accounts	913	10.5	913	10.5	$ 155,749	2.7	155,749	2.7	11,053	9.9	11,053	9.9
2	$.01 to $99	3,753	43.4	4,666	53.9	891,759	15.3	1,047,508	18.0	48,140	43.1	59,193	53.0
3	$100 to $199	860	9.9	5,526	63.8	372,358	6.4	1,419,866	24.3	12,222	11.0	71,415	64.0
4	$200 to $299	522	6.0	6,048	69.9	351,695	6.0	1,771,561	30.4	7,722	6.9	79,137	70.9
5	$300 to $399	554	6.4	6,602	76.3	379,424	6.5	2,150,985	36.9	7,049	6.3	86,186	77.2
6	$400 to $499	452	5.2	7,054	81.5	370,406	6.4	2,521,391	43.2	5,877	5.3	92,063	82.5
7	$500 to $999	943	10.9	7,997	92.4	1,030,811	17.7	3,552,202	60.9	11,716	10.5	103,779	93.0
8	$1,000 to $1,999	403	4.7	8,400	97.0	789,252	13.5	4,341,454	74.4	4,847	4.3	108,626	97.3
9	$2,000 to $2,999	117	1.4	8,517	98.4	374,359	6.4	4,715,813	80.9	1,319	1.2	109,945	98.5
10	$3,000 to $4,999	79	.9	8,596	99.3	383,653	6.6	5,099,466	87.4	922	.8	110,867	99.4
11	$5,000 to $9,999	43	.5	8,639	99.8	366,495	6.3	5,465,961	93.7	499	.4	111,366	99.8
12	$10,000 and over	18	.2	8,657	100	365,983	6.3	5,831,944	100	218	.2	111,584	100
13	Totals	8,657				$5,831,944				111,584			

Figure 4–11 Profitability Analysis Worksheet Personal Checking Accounts (continued)

(8) Average Balance per Account	(9) Income per Account per Month @ 10%	(10) Number of Debits per Account	(11) Debit Charges @ $.15	(12) Mainte-nance Charge @ $2.00	(13) Total Service Charge Income	(14) Total Balance and Service Charge Income	(15) Cost per Account per Month	(16) Net Profit or (Loss) per Account	(17) Net Profit or (Loss) per Month
$ 171	$ 1.43	12.11	$1.82	$2.00	$3.82	$ 5.25	$7.16	($1.91)	($1,744)
238	1.98	12.83	1.92	2.00	3.92	5.90	7.28	(1.38)	(5,179)
433	3.61	14.21	2.13	2.00	4.13	7.74	7.47	.27	232
674	5.62	14.79	2.22	2.00	4.22	9.84	7.54	2.30	1,201
685	5.71	12.72	–0–	–0–	–0–	5.71	7.15	(1.44)	(798)
819	6.83	13.00	–0–	–0–	–0–	6.83	7.20	(.37)	(167)
1,093	9.11	12.42	–0–	–0–	–0–	9.11	7.02	2.09	1,971
1,958	16.32	12.03	–0–	–0–	–0–	16.32	6.86	9.46	3,812
3,200	26.67	11.27	–0–	–0–	–0–	26.67	6.76	19.91	2,329
4,856	40.47	11.67	–0–	–0–	–0–	40.47	6.84	33.63	2,657
8,523	71.03	11.60	–0–	–0–	–0–	71.03	6.77	64.26	2,763
20,332	169.43	12.11	–0–	–0–	–0–	169.43	7.03	162.40	2,923
									$10,000

check or debit charge, and a flat $2.00 per month maintenance fee both of which are to be charged if the minimum balance in the account falls below $300 at any time during the month. An explanation of the information shown in each column is as follows:

Columns 1, 2, 4, and 6 are basic statistics that were copied from Figure 4–5. Columns 3, 5, and 7 are cumulative amounts that were calculated by hand and included as an aid in analyzing the basic volume and balance data. Note the percentage of total amounts next to each figure in columns 2 through 7. These were also computed by hand and included as a further aid in the analysis.

Column 8—Average balance per account is computed by dividing the average balances in column 4 by the number of accounts in column 2.

Column 9—Income per account per month @ 10% is computed by multiplying the average balance per account shown in column 8 by 10% and dividing the product by 12 to arrive at a monthly income amount. Note that the 10% income figure used here and in other parts of this chapter is of course used as an example. An actual income percentage should be used when developing your own bank's statistics.

Column 10—Number of debits per account is computed by dividing the number of debits in column 6 by the number of accounts in column 2.

Column 11—Check and debit charges @ 15¢ is computed by multiplying the number of debits posted in each account as shown in column 10 by 15¢. Note that debits include checks and other customer generated debits such as those created by the customer's use of an ATM machine.

Column 12—Maintenance charge @ $2.00 is a flat charge per account per month regardless of activity; the charge is the same for each category of accounts that were charged.

Column 13—Total service charge income is computed by adding the debit charge in column 11 to the maintenance charge in column 12.

Column 14—Total balance and service charge income is computed by adding the income per account per month in column 9 to the total service charge income in column 13.

Column 15—Cost per account per month are figures that were copied from column 9 in Figure 4–9 which detailed the costs of processing personal checking accounts.

Column 16—Net profit or loss per account is computed by subtracting the cost per account per month in column 15 from the total balance and service charge income in column 14.

Column 17—Net profit or loss per month is computed by multiplying the net profit or loss per account in column 16 by the number of accounts in column 2.

This profitability analysis worksheet (Figure 4–11) is a composite of all the statistics that have been developed for personal checking accounts that effect profits—volume data, balance information, income from balances and service charges, costs for maintaining accounts and finally net profit or loss computations; and all of these statistics are presented by balance category. At first glance, since so many statistics are presented on one worksheet, it might appear to be a complicated report to prepare at your bank. In reality, once the basic volume and balance statistics have been determined and recorded in the format shown in Figure 4–5, developing the processing costs (Figure 4–9) and finally the worksheet (Figure 4–11) would not take one clerk with a pocket calculator more than three hours to complete!

As will be shown, this worksheet (Figure 4–11) is invaluable in determining the pricing of personal checking accounts. But before discussing the pricing of these accounts it is appropriate to note a few things about personal checking which can be applied to many banks.

The majority of personal checking accounts are not profitable to the bank because of the low balances maintained in these accounts. Lines 1 and 2 of the worksheet show this dramatically. On a cumulative basis 53.9% of the total number of accounts maintain only 18% of the total balances of all personal checking accounts (column 5) and the net loss per month to the bank for these accounts is \$6,923 (column 17: \$1,744 + \$5,179) or \$83,076 on an annualized basis (\$6,923 × 12).

The whole portfolio of personal checking accounts is profitable because the balances maintained by a minority of customers generate sufficient income to pay for the costs of maintaining the majority and to produce an overall profit. On the worksheet the total of column 17 shows overall profit of \$10,000 per month.

It should be emphasized that this analysis is of personal checking accounts only. This bank with \$5,831,944 in personal checking account balances has total DDA balances of \$30 million which consists of \$4 million in NOW balances and \$20 million in business and nonprofit account balances. This bank had a total number of 12,500 DDA accounts. So when analyzing the personal checking account statistics on the worksheet maintain a perspective. For example, upon examining line 2 of the worksheet (Figure 4–11) we find that on a cumulative basis 53.9%

(4,666 accounts) of the total number of personal checking accounts keep 18% ($1,047,508) of the total personal checking average balances. If we combine these statistics with the NOW account statistics of this bank we find that the 4,666 personal accounts represent 45.6% of the total number of personal and NOW accounts combined, and the average balances of $1,047,508 represent only 10.7% of the total balances in these two types of accounts. Finally, if we compare the 4,666 accounts with $1,047,508 in average balances with the total DDA portfolio of 12,500 accounts with total balances of $30 million, 37.3% of the accounts keep only 3.5% of the total average balances in the bank!

Pricing Personal Checking Accounts

Although the pricing of any product including checking account services can be complex, there are two basic factors that should be kept in mind profit and competition. The statistics on the worksheet (Figure 4–11) give us enough information to reasonably determine the profitability of an account at whatever price we wish to charge for checking accounts. It is also important to determine what your competition is charging for this service. A survey of charges, therefore, should be compiled. This survey should be large enough to give you a complete picture. Accordingly it should include other commercial banks and savings and loan associations in your area. If your bank is located in a small community this survey should include financial institutions in several surrounding communities. When taking this survey find out what the other institutions are charging for NOW accounts, business accounts, and special checking accounts. Since overdraft, personalized checkbook and stop-payment charges directly relate to checking accounts, these charges should also be included in the results of the survey.

Once you know what the institutions in your area are charging for checking account services you can begin the process of weighing this information with the profitability aspects as developed on the worksheet. When weighing all this information and developing a profitable but competitive pricing structure, consider the following:

1. If you are giving good service and are a recognized leading bank in the community, your customer base, your balances, and your share of market will probably not diminish if your prices are slightly higher than your competition's prices, and your profits will be higher!

2. I'm thoroughly convinced that pricing low to obtain volume only attracts more accounts into the unprofitable balance categories. It is much better to improve service levels by continually hiring personable employees at all levels who will treat customers efficiently and in a helpful way, and to train these employees in all the aspects of the services your bank offers. Good service, not low service charges, builds customer base.
3. Consider pricing accounts so that those who use the service pay for it. When you compile your own profitability worksheet (Figure 4–11) you will find that a vast number of accounts keep low balances in their accounts; these accounts should be priced so that your bank at least makes a small profit on them, never loses money.
4. The worksheet (Figure 4–11) shows both income and expense statistics on a per account basis. The expenses (cost per account per month in column 15) usually never go down, and often go up. The balance income per account (income per account per month in column 9) however, can fluctuate dramatically. Always use a conservative percentage figure in this column when computing the income to allow for fluctuations.
5. There are various ways to structure service charges for personal accounts. The most common way is to charge on a per check paid basis combined with a flat maintenance fee per month, both of which are charged if the balance in the account falls below a certain amount. When deciding which of these two fees to increase and by how much, remember that $.05 increase in the check fee will produce more income than a $.50 increase in the maintenance fee. To prove this, refer to the cumulative number of accounts and number of debits at the highest balance category within which service charges are imposed. In Figure 4–11, for example, line 4 is the balance cut-off level for imposing service charges in this bank. The cumulative number of accounts at this level is 6,048. And the cumulative number of debits posted at this level is 79,137. A $.05 increase in the check posted fee would produce additional monthly income of $3,956.85 (79,137 × $.05). Whereas, by comparison, a $.50 increase in the maintenance fee would produce additional monthly income of $3,024.00 (6,048 × $.50). Of course, if you can increase both fees, that is even more

profitable. But if you feel you must make a choice on increasing one fee or the other, increase the check fee. It is not only more profitable, but also the charges relate more to activity, which is easier to explain to customers.

6. Examine the level at which service charges are imposed. In Figure 4–11, the minimum balance level of $300 is too low, because those accounts in which the minimum balance falls into the $300 to $399 and into the $400 to $499 balance category produce on average a $ 1.44 and a $.37 loss per account per month (see lines 5 and 6, columns 14, 15, and 16). In this example the minimum balance cutoff level should be $500. Also, when considering an increase in fees, review the substantial impact of just increasing the minimum balance level at which service charges are imposed. This impact is easily computed from the information shown on the profitability analysis worksheet.
7. Some banks incorporate an average balance feature into their personal checking account service charge structure in order to protect those customers who usually keep high balances in their checking account, but on occasion the lowest balance in the account during a month is low enough to trigger a service charge. The average balance feature is combined with the low balance requirement so that customers can avoid service charges by maintaining a minimum balance of x or an average balance of y. When deciding upon the average balance level be sure it is high enough. The statistics shown in columns 8, 9, and 15 will indicate what average balance to quote to produce a profit. Column 9 figure assumes a 10% earnings rate and produces $9.11 on an average balance of $1,093 which is enough to make a profit against a cost per account per month of $7.02 (see line 7). A drop to an 8% earnings rate, however, would require an average balance of $1,053 ($7.02 ÷ $.08 × 12) just to break even.
8. Often banks will add another feature to their personal checking account pricing structure, which takes into account the balances in affiliated savings accounts or CDs. Accordingly, the customer has the option of maintaining the required balance levels in her or his checking account or maintaining a required level in a savings account to avoid a service charge in his or her checking account. This feature is advantageous to the customer, who might maintain a low balance in a checking but keeps a good balance

in a savings account. It is also advantageous to the bank because it encourages customers to use more than one of the bank's services. And as marketing experts tell us, the more bank services a customer uses in one bank, the more likely that customer will remain a customer of that bank. But here again when using balance levels to waive service charges, make sure the level used is high enough to offset costs and to produce a profit.

Pricing Checking Accounts in Relation to Savings Accounts

The main consideration when relating savings account balances to waiving checking account service charges is the required balance level in the savings account. Banks who do not know their costs for maintaining checking or savings accounts will have a tendency to require too low and therefore unprofitable balance levels. First of all, it is best to require a minimum balance rather than an average balance. This will promote higher average balances. The profit consideration, however, between a minimum balance versus an average balance requirement is not as great in a savings account as it is in a checking account because the balance in a savings account does not fluctuate to the extremes that it would in a checking account. Also, there is little or no difference between a minimum and an average balance in a certificate of deposit because the balance in a CD usually does not fluctuate at all. And, since many banks use average balances in savings accounts to waive checking account charges, our study will confine this subject to average balances.

In order to decide the profitable average balance level requirement in a savings account in order to waive a checking account service charge, the profitability balance levels of savings accounts should be known. Again, we can turn to the FED's functional cost analysis (FCA) reports to arrive at a reasonable cost. The FED's FCA report "Time Deposits—Cost per Weight-Unit and Item Costs Calculations" will show the cost for handling each deposit, withdrawal, and interest posting, and the annual account maintenance cost for savings accounts. The FCA report "Analysis of Regular Savings Accounts" shows on average the number of deposits, withdrawals, and interest postings made to each account each year. Note that the FCA does not give us separate costs or volumes for passbook accounts and statement savings accounts. These statistics represent both types of savings accounts. From these FCA reports we can determine the average cost per month for maintaining a savings account as follows:

Volume		*Cost per Item*		*Total Annual Cost*
5.78 Deposits per Year	×	@ $ .78	=	$ 4.51
4.33 Withdrawals per Year	×	@ 1.51	=	6.54
4 Interest Postings per Year	×	@ 2.95	=	11.80
Annual Maintenance Cost				19.99
Total				$42.84
Total monthly cost per account ($42.84 ÷ 12) =				*$ 3.57*

Note that the above cost figures do not include interest expense. Now that we know that it costs $3.57 per month to maintain a savings account, we can determine balance profitability levels for savings accounts as follows:

Average Balance in Savings Account	*Cost per Account per Month*	*Interest Expense per Month @ 5¼%*	*Total Cost per Month*	*Income per Month on Balance @ 10%*	*Profit or Loss per Account per Month*
$300	$3.57	$1.31	$4.88	$2.50	($2.38)
400	3.57	1.75	5.32	3.33	(1.99)
500	3.57	2.19	5.76	4.17	(1.59)
600	3.57	2.63	6.20	5.00	(1.20)
700	3.57	3.06	6.63	5.83	(.80)
800	3.57	3.50	7.07	6.67	(.40)
900	3.57	3.94	7.51	7.50	(.01)
1,000	3.57	4.38	7.95	8.33	.38
2,000	3.57	8.75	12.32	16.67	4.35

Obviously the low average balance savings accounts are not profitable. So trying to attract customers by offering free checking account service to customers who keep low average savings account balances is not profitable. Also, it should be kept in mind that even if free checking is offered to those savings account customers who maintain average balances of $2,000, the effect is a trade between a profit of $4.35 per month income on the savings account balance against reduced profits of about $4.00 per month in checking account charges (Figure 4–11, column 13—Total service charge income). If you decide to offer free checking for savings account customers who maintain a certain balance level in their account, then make the savings balance level as high as possible and *don't make it automatic*. Require the customer to sign up for the service. This will reduce the number of customers who will take advantage of the service.

Free checking for customers who have certificates of deposit is even worse for the profit picture than it was for savings account customers. Assuming a 2% profit spread between the income earned and the interest paid on a certificate of deposit and using, for example, an FCA account maintenance figure of $4.69 per month (which can be found in the FCA report "Time Deposit—Cost per Weight-Unit and Item Costs Calculations" in the section labeled Certificates of Deposit under $100,000) the profitability of selected balance levels could be displayed as follows:

Amount of Certificate	*Cost per month*	*Income per Month with a 2% Spread*	*Profit or Loss per CD*
$ 500	$4.69	$ .83	($3.86)
1,000	4.69	1.67	(3.02)
1,500	4.69	2.50	(2.19)
2,000	4.69	3.33	(1.36)
3,000	4.69	5.00	.31
4,000	4.69	6.67	1.98
5,000	4.69	8.33	3.64

Here again, by offering free checking, even to customers who have a $5,000 CD, we are trading $3.64 per month profit in the CD for a $4.00 per month reduction in checking account service income.

Bankers are becoming more and more aware of the unprofitable nature of low balance savings accounts, whether these accounts are in passbook, statement savings, or CD form. And what makes matters worse is not the one account that may result in a monthly loss of a dollar or two, but that over half of the accounts in a bank's portfolio may be losing money. And this same approximate loss percentage of accounts is also true of checking accounts. If a bank has 10,000 savings accounts and 1,000 checking accounts and half of each type of account is losing $1.50 per month, the total loss annually is $180,000!

Figure 4–12 Profitability Analysis Worksheet NOW Accounts

(Based on lowest balance profile and a $1000 minimum balance requirement to avoid service charges)

	(1) Balance Categories	(2) Number of Accounts	% of Total	(3) Cumulative Number of Accounts	% of Total	(4) Average Balances	% of Total	(5) Cumulative Average Balances	% of Total	(6) Number of Debits	% of Total	(7) Cumulative Number of Debits	% of Total
1	OD Accounts	46	2.9	46	2.9	$ 12,461	.3	$ 12,461	.3	449	2.5	449	2.5
2	$.01 to $99	239	15.2	285	18.1	96,069	2.4	108,530	2.7	3,189	17.8	3,638	20.3
3	$100 to $199	116	7.4	401	25.4	73,371	1.8	181,901	4.6	1,438	8.0	5,076	28.3
4	$200 to $299	98	6.2	499	31.6	66,166	1.7	248,067	6.2	1,089	6.1	6,165	34.4
5	$300 to $399	83	5.3	582	36.9	69,250	1.7	317,317	8.0	991	5.6	7,156	39.9
6	$400 to $499	74	4.7	656	41.6	66,996	1.7	384,313	9.7	756	4.2	7,912	44.2
7	$500 to $999	215	13.6	871	55.2	269,613	6.8	653,926	16.4	2,243	12.5	10,155	56.7
8	$1,000 to $1,999	299	19.0	1,170	74.2	583,390	14.7	1,237,316	31.1	3,323	18.5	13,478	75.2
9	$2,000 to $2,999	148	9.4	1,318	83.6	484,731	12.2	1,722,047	43.3	1,715	9.6	15,193	84.8
10	$3,000 to $4,999	129	8.2	1,447	91.8	609,678	15.3	2,331,725	58.6	1,283	7.2	16,476	92.0
11	$5,000 to $9,999	88	5.6	1,535	97.3	740,210	18.6	3,071,935	77.2	956	5.3	17,432	97.3
12	$10,000 and over	42	2.7	1,577	100	907,886	22.8	3,979,821	100	485	2.7	17,917	100
13	Totals	1,577				$3,979,821				17,917			

Figure 4–12 Profitability Analysis Worksheet NOW Accounts (continued)

(8) Average Balance per Account	(9) Income per Account per Month @ 10%	(10) Number of Debits per Account	(11) Debit Charges @ $.25	(12) Mainte-nance Charge @ $5.00	(13) Total Service Charge Income	(14) Total Balance and Service Charge Income	(15) Cost per Account per Month	(16) Net Profit or (Loss) per Account	(17) Net Profit or (Loss) per Month
$ 271	$ 2.26	9.76	$2.44	$5.00	$7.44	$ 9.70	$ 8.37	$ 1.33	$ 61
402	3.35	13.34	3.34	5.00	8.34	11.69	9.68	2.01	480
633	5.28	12.40	3.10	5.00	8.10	13.38	10.52	2.86	332
675	5.63	11.11	2.78	5.00	7.78	13.41	10.33	3.08	302
834	6.95	11.94	2.99	5.00	7.99	14.94	11.17	3.77	313
905	7.54	10.22	2.56	5.00	7.56	15.10	11.17	3.93	2.91
1,254	10.45	10.43	2.61	5.00	7.61	18.06	12.71	5.35	1,150
1,951	16.26	11.11	-0-	-0-	-0-	16.26	15.91	.35	105
3,275	27.29	11.59	-0-	-0-	-0-	27.29	21.75	5.54	820
4,726	39.38	9.95	-0-	-0-	-0-	39.38	27.78	11.60	1,496
8,411	70.09	10.86	-0-	-0-	-0-	70.09	44.16	25.93	2,282
21,616	180.13	11.55	-0-	-0-	-0-	180.13	102.12	78.01	3,276
$ 2,524									

Determining NOW Account Profitability

Figure 4–12 is a profitability analysis worksheet for NOW accounts that follows the same format that was developed for the personal checking account profitability worksheet (Figure 4–11). The basic volume and balance information was taken from the statistical profile of NOW accounts (Figure 4–7) and the cost per account per month amounts shown in column 15 of this NOW account worksheet were taken from the costs developed for NOW accounts as shown in Figure 4–10. Note that the interest expense is included in the costs shown in Figure 4–10.

Upon examining the NOW account profitability worksheet we can see that the service charge structure of $.25 per check and a $5.00 maintenance fee when the minimum balance falls below $1,000, is profitable in every balance category. It is curious that even with a high minimum balance requirement and the substantial service charge imposed if the balance in the account falls below this minimum, 55.2% of the number of accounts fall below the minimum (see column 3, line 7) and that, cumulatively, these accounts only account for 16.4% of the total average balances in the NOW account portfolio (column 5, line 7).

Pricing NOW Accounts

The service charge structure of $.25 per check and a $5.00 maintenance fee if the minimum balance falls below $1,000 was used in the NOW account profitability analysis worksheet because it is a common structure used by many banks, and it is a profitable structure. Fortunately when banks were first pricing NOW accounts, they were able to draw upon the New England experience and accordingly priced these accounts high enough to make them profitable from the beginning, rather than offer them as loss leaders. Also, this type of structure discourages low balance customers from being attracted to NOW accounts. Too low a service charge, either in the amount of fees or in the amount of minimum balance requirement, would drive too many regular DDA account customers into the NOWs and banks would only incur the additional interest expense on a large number of low balance accounts.

By using the format shown in the NOW worksheet (Figure 4–12) any bank can easily calculate the effect its own service charge structure has on profits. If you are anticipating changing fees, you would need only to complete columns 11 through 17 and overlay it on the worksheet, probably a twenty-minute job.

From reviewing the sample worksheet, it is easy to see why many banks have chosen the $1,000 level for a minimum balance requirement. Because it is only at that level, without service charge income, that the NOW account is barely profitable—$.35 per account per month (see column 16, line 8 of Figure 4–12). A lower minimum balance would only make the affected accounts unprofitable to maintain. All of this is based on the supposition that a bank could invest these balances at a minimum 10% per year return.

Some banks may wish to offer its customers the option of either keeping a minimum balance in the account during the month to avoid a service charge, or of keeping an average balance in the account during the month to avoid a service charge. If you wish to offer this option be sure the average balance requirement is high enough. From examining line 8, columns 8, 9, 15, and 16, we see that an average balance of $1,951.00 at a 10% income rate produces $16.26 per month of income against a cost of $15.91 per month. To produce a small profit of $.35 per month, an approximate $2,000 average balance requirement would be necessary. The effect of a $1,500 average balance requirement per month could be calculated as follows. The only unknowns would be the exact number of debits and credits posted to accounts at this level. It would be sufficient to use the costs as developed for the $1,000 to $1,999 minimum balance level as shown in columns 6 and 7 in line 8 of Figure 4–10 and calculate a new interest expense amount at the 5¼% rate for a $1,500 average balance. The result would be $1.70 + $.66 + $.77 + $4.24 + $6.56 = $13.93. Then upon comparing the income earned on the $1,500 of $12.50 ($1,500.00 × 10% ÷ 12) per month against the cost of $13.93, the loss per month per account affected would be $1.43. Determining the exact number of accounts affected would not be possible with any of the statistics developed since the surveys taken did not include this particular balance cutoff. However from the average balance survey taken of NOW accounts (Figure 4–6) we know that 343 accounts have average balances between $1,000 and $1,999 (see column 1, line 8), and if we assume that half of these would have average balances of less than $1,500, then 171 accounts would have average balances between $1,000 and $1,500. Adding the 171 accounts in this catagory to the other seven lower balance catagories (OD to $999) we arrive at a total of 860 accounts that would be charged because they had an average balance below $1,500. From reviewing the profitability analysis worksheet (Figure 4–12) we know that 871 accounts are subject to charge because their minimum balance is below $1,000 (column 3, line 7). What we don't know is how many of the 860 accounts are the same as the 871 accounts. In any event, it would appear that the additional accounts that would not be service charged if the average balance required was dropped to $1,500 would be insignificant. This whole explanation only points out the fact that before taking any account surveys it is best first to determine the possible balance cutoffs that might be used in pricing NOW accounts, so that they can be included in the survey. This statement, of course, also would be true in relation to pricing personal checking accounts.

The Profitability and Pricing of "Super NOW" Accounts

The only difference between a NOW account and a Super NOW account (also known as a money market checking account) is that Super NOWs usually pay higher interest rates. It should not be absolutely necessary, therefore, to develop seperate volume statistics for these accounts in order to determine profitability levels. Merely compute the interest expense (based on the interest rate you are currently paying) and overlay these amounts in column 10 of Figure 4–10. Then recompute the total cost per account per month shown in column 11 of Figure 4–10 and overlay these amounts in columns 11 through 17 on the NOW account profitability worksheet (Figure 4–12) using your current service charge structure in columns 11 and 12 and the recomputed total cost per account per month amounts from column 11 of Figure 4–10, which will be used in column 15 of Figure 4–12.

Most banks in pricing their Super NOW accounts learned from their NOW account pricing experiences and are pricing their maintenance charges on these accounts at two or three times their NOW maintenance charge, and are requiring large minimum balances to waive the service charge. Also, some banks are paying a bonus interest amount if a customer keeps a large balance ($25,000 to $50,000 minimum or average) in their account at all times during a statement cycle period. As a result of this pricing, in many banks the Super NOW account is only attractive to those customers who traditionally keep large balances in their checking accounts.

As a final comment in the pricing of both NOW and Super NOW accounts, many banks are paying interest on only the average *collected* balances in these accounts rather than the average ledger balances. Collected balances introduces the subject of determining float on funds deposited which is covered in the next section. The comments made regarding float could also be applied to NOW type accounts.

The Profitability and Pricing of Business Accounts

Most banks analyze the activity in their business accounts on an individual account basis and so the profitability of *each account* can be determined. The grouping of accounts by balance category, therefore, is unnecessary. The per check, per credit, per transit item and the maintenance costs as per the FCA are the same as they are for personal checking and NOW accounts. The factors needed to determine the profitability of a business account would be as follows:

The number of checks posted	@ 15.3¢
The number of deposits and credits posted	@ 31.5¢
The number of transit items deposited	@ 8.5¢
Maintenance cost per month	@ $4.24

In addition, most banks give the customer an earnings allowance to be credited toward the calculated service charge. This earnings allowance is usually computed on the average available balance during the month. Available balance is defined as that which can be invested by the bank. The available balance should take into condideration float time for the checks the customer deposits into the account and reserve requirements for your bank.

With regard to the float factor in determining available balance, banks can either compute float exactly for each customer's account or use a factor. Many banks do not have the sophisticated equipment necessary to compute float on an exact basis and use a factor of between one and two business days for the amount of each transit item deposited (float is not computed on "on us checks" and cash deposited). Modern proof machines in combination with computer processing of DDA accounts will seperate out cash and on us checks deposited from transit items deposited. In the absence of these, however, an even more arbitrary float factor has to be developed or a hand analysis of each business account deposit slip has to be made.

The amount of the earnings allowance is, of course, the bank's choice, but it should be competitive with those of other financial institutions and tied to an investment index, thereby making it easier to explain to a commercial customer. The profit margin for maintaining the account can be built into the service charge structure, the earnings allowance, or both. There will always be a profit margin in the earnings allowance if the investment index used is lower than the overall yield in the bank's investment and loan portfolio. When selecting an allowance based on an investment index it is advisable to adjust the earnings allowance rate as often as practical (at least quarterly, but monthly is better) so as not to be locked into a high rate in a falling market or to be noncompetitive in a rising market.

A typical commercial DDA account service charge formula, therefore, that takes into account all the factors previously mentioned could be described as follows.

Debits and checks posted	@ $ .20
Credits and deposits	@ .35
Transit item deposited	@ .10
Monthly maintenance	@ 6.00

The balances in the account earn a credit toward the service charges calculated at a rate based on the 13 week U.S. Treasury Bill rate and are computed on the average collected balances for the month less reserve requirements.

Note that in the above example, profit was built into each part of the service charge structure (and could be built into the earnings rate because of the words "at a rate based").

In conclusion, it should be emphasized that when pricing any banking service banks must price their services for profit or eventually face declining profits and risk going out of business altogether.

SUMMARY

A review of this chapter shows fourteen ways a bank can substantially improve profits through the skillful pricing of checking accounts.

1. Analyze the profitability of your own bank's personal checking accounts and NOW-type of accounts by preparing a profitability analysis worksheet for these accounts (examples shown in Figures 4–11 and 4–12). This worksheet, when completed, will provide at a glance a myriad of information related to your own accounts, and it will profile this information by balance catagory. This balance category profile format will be extremely useful in making profitable decisions about the pricing of these accounts.

2. Conduct a market survey, at least on a yearly basis, of what other financial institutions in your *whole* geographical area are charging for checking accounts.

3. Always program a service charge fee to be triggered when a balance in a personal or NOW account reaches a *minimum* balance level, not an average balance level.

4. If you are giving good customer service, consider pricing your checking accounts slightly higher than your competition's prices.

5. Do not price low to obtain volume. Good service builds customer base – not low service charges.

6. Price accounts so that those who use the service pay their share of the cost. Do not let high balance customers pay for the cost of maintaining low balance accounts.

7. If your fee structure for personal-type checking accounts is a combination of a flat maintenance charge and a fee for each check posted, and you're considering increasing these fees, remember that a small increase in the fee for each check posted will produce more income than a large increase in the maintenance fee.

8. When increasing your checking account fees, always consider the substantial impact (determined from your profitability analysis worksheet) of even a small increase in the balance level at which fees are imposed.

9. When you are considering waiving checking account charges for customers who maintain a certain balance in a savings account or CD, make sure you know the average costs of maintaining the savings instrument so that you do not fall into the trap of requiring a savings balance that is too low and therefore unprofitable. If this balance requirement is too low, your bank can end up with a multiplicity of low balance, unprofitable savings *and* checking accounts and no service charge income for maintaining the related checking accounts, all of which result in a triple negative effect on overall bank profitability.

10. When relating savings and checking accounts for the waiving of service charges, require that customers sign up for this relationship. Do not automatically sign up all customers who would qualify.

11. Price NOW accounts high enough so that it is not attractive to the mass of low balance regular-type checking accounts in your bank.

12. Price Super NOW accounts high enough so as not to attract the mass of low balance NOW accounts in your bank.

13. If you wish to price either type of NOW account according to an average balance formula rather than minimum balance, be sure you review your profitability analysis worksheet for NOW-type of accounts to be certain that the average balance level is high enough to produce a reasonable profit.

14. When tying an earnings allowance on a business checking account to an index, change the rate as often as possible so it responds more accurately to changes in general money market rates.

Chapter 5

N.S.F. Charges

Recent litigation by consumer groups against large banks on the west coast has drawn considerable attention to the fee for checks on an overdrawn account. This litigation seems to center around the amount of the fee and whether the same fee should be charged for each check causing the overdraft on the account. This chapter will not explore this issue but rather will discuss administrative ways to increase the income in this area regardless of the amount of the fee.

REVIEW THE FEE

When was the last time you reviewed this fee? Does it cover your current costs? Some things to consider when you are calculating expenses are the costs of an officer's or manager's time in reviewing overdrafts and making a decision whether to pay or return the checks; clerical costs of processing the checks involved and in mailing out customer notices; computer costs in preparing customer notices and management reports; other employee time costs in consulting with customers on the telephone or in person about the cause of the overdraft; and the bank's income loss on the overdrawn balance.

CHARGE ON A PER CHECK BASIS

Charge this fee on a per check basis, not on a per overdraft basis (i.e., for each day the account is overdrawn), and charge a fee whether you *pay or return the check(s)*. By charging only on a per overdraft basis, you could be losing 30% of your income in this area. Frequently more than one check has contributed to the overdraft; this is particularly true for business accounts. You may want to put a limit on the dollars charged per day for any one account for this service or charge a reduced fee per check if a number of checks are causing the overdraft on a particular day.

FORCE CHARGE YOUR OVERDRAFT FEE

If you are on an automated DDA system, instruct the computer center to charge the fee on every account for each check. If you're not on a computer, instruct your bookkeepers to automatically charge the fee during the check posting process. This forces those managers who feel they must reverse the fee, to do it manually. More often managers will take the easier way out on borderline decisions and will not reverse the fee.

ESTABLISH A STRONG MANAGEMENT POLICY AGAINST REVERSING FEES

If you don't have a strong policy against reversing overdraft fees considerable income will be lost. This policy should come from the top of the organization. Clerks should not be given authority to reverse the fee if the fee is forced charged or to waive the fee if the fee is not forced charged. Only managers or officers should be given the authority to reverse or to waive an overdraft fee.

There are, of course, occasions when it is prudent to consider giving a customer a break in these fees, particularly when there are other high balance accounts related to the overdrawn account or when a customer has never been overdrawn before. But even in these cases consider only reversing one half the fee, and only for this time.

RECORD AND REVIEW OVERDRAFT FEE STATISTICS

Review the total fees charged and waived per branch office on a monthly basis. This is particularly important when a new fee structure

Figure 5–1 Sample Monthly Historical Report of N.S.F. and Overdraft Fees

		January	*February*	*March*	*Year's total*
Main office	Fees Charged	$2,225	$1,912	$2,575	
	Fees Reversed	212	175	275	
	Net Fees Collected	2,013	1,737	2,300	
	% of Fees Reversed	9.5	9.1	10.7	
North branch	Fees Charged	1,515	1,400	1,858	
	Fees Reversed	50	65	0	
	Net Fees Collected	1,465	1,335	1,858	
	% of Fees Reversed	3.3	4.6	0.0	
South branch	Fees Charged	1,600	1,545	1,635	
	Fees Reversed	215	125	195	
	Net Fees Collected	1,385	1,420	1,440	
	% of Fees Reversed	13.4	8.0	11.9	
East branch	Fees Charged	850	600	925	
	Fees Reversed	30	0	65	
	Net Fees Collected	820	600	860	
	% of Fees Reversed	3.5	0.0	7.0	
West branch	Fees Charged	1,000	950	1,275	
	Fees Reversed	20	57	0	
	Net Fees Collected	980	893	1,275	
	% of Fees Reversed	2.0	6.0	0.0	
Total bank	Fees Charged	7,190	6,407	8,268	
	Fees Reversed	527	422	535	
	Net Fees Collected	6,663	5,985	7,733	
	% of Fees Reversed	7.3	6.6	6.5	

has been introduced. This review will help ensure continued profit increase in this area. Figure 5–1 shows a simple report format for reviewing N.S.F. and overdraft fees. This format assumes that fees are force charged and manually reversed. By showing the months across the top of the page, a historical review is automatically produced as the months

Figure 5-2 Estimate of Potential Annual Income from N.S.F. and Overdraft Fees per the Number of Accounts and the Fees Schedules Shown

Total number of checking accounts in bank	*$3.00 Fee per check paid or returned*	*$4.00 Fee per check paid or returned*	*$5.00 Fee per check paid or returned*	*$6.00 Fee per check paid or returned*	*$7.00 Fee per check paid or returned*	*$8.00 Fee per check paid or returned*	*$10.00 Fee per check paid or returned*
5,000	$ 46,500	$ 61,980	$ 77,460	$ 93,000	$108,000	$123,960	$154,920
8,000	74,400	99,168	123,936	148,800	173,760	198,336	$247,872
10,000	93,000	123,960	154,920	186,000	217,200	247,920	$309,840
15,000	139,500	185,940	232,380	273,000	325,800	371,880	$464,760
20,000	186,000	247,920	309,840	372,000	434,400	495,840	$619,680

progress. Unit banks and banks with two or three branches may wish to separate the fees charged and reversed by type of account (such as by personal accounts and business accounts). To do this in a bank with several branches, however, produces a report that is too cumbersome to read and review. It is more important for interbranch comparison purposes that just the basics are presented for each branch so that fee statistics for several branches can appear on one page. Then if it appears that a particular branch is reversing too much fee income, a more detailed analysis of that branch can and should be made. The most important statistic for reviewing purposes is the percentage of fees reversed. This represents a measure of fees reversed as related to fees charged and is computed by dividing the fees reversed amount by the fees charged amount. These statistics represent a force charge system where all fees are indiscriminately and automatically charged when the overdraft occurs, and any fees to be reversed are done manually upon review.

The fees charged figure represents potential income, and the percentage figure represents an easy-to-review measure of the potential income that was lost to the bank. Also, these percentage figures can be used to set future standards for each branch. For example, the percentages shown in Figure 5–1 would indicate that the Main Office and the South Branch are reversing too many fees in relation to the other branches and the bank as a whole. Whereas an average standard of 5% to 7% of fees reversed would be more acceptable.

Finally, any report of the fees generated by management should be sent to all those officers and managers who are involved in charging and reversing these fees. It serves as a report of progress made, but more importantly it shows managers how well they are doing in relation to each other. This will help motivate those who are not doing as well as they should.

Figure 5–2 is an educated estimate of the annual income that could be earned by banks that institute the administrative approaches described in this chapter. This estimate was derived from actual earnings achieved by banks in this area. These figures are only presented to show graphically how important this fee income can become in your bank in relation to the actual income you are receiving. For a quick review compare your current actual annual income in this area to that shown in the column that is closest to your present fee. To determine more accurately your own bank's potential income, count the number of checks presented against insufficient funds for all checking accounts for a two week period, apply your selected fee schedule, divide the result by 2 to obtain a weekly average, and multiply by 52 to arrive at an estimated annual income. Now compare this estimate to your present actual annual income.

SUMMARY

The following is a summary of the suggested techniques that should be used to achieve optimum income from N.S.F. and O.D. fees.

1. Review the fee itself.
2. Charge the fee on a per check paid or returned basis.
3. Force charge the fee.
4. Institute a strong management policy against reversing the fee.
5. Review the fees that are charged, waived, and collected by branch on a monthly basis.

Chapter 6

Important Fee Incomes That Are Often Overlooked

This chapter describes those fee incomes that either could be or are overlooked by many bankers because they are unaware of volumes of items that are associated with these transactions or of the amount of time required to perform the service. Some of these types of fees are obvious but they are shown in order to draw attention to them, so that they are not overlooked in the banker's quest to increase income. All of the fees described are common to every bank, are easy to increase, and will provide a substantial increase in income for most banks.

SAVINGS ACCOUNT LOW BALANCE FEE

Today, bankers are taking a hard look at those thousands of passbook and statement savings accounts that maintain a low balance. According to the Federal Reserve Bank's *current* functional cost analysis (FCA), it costs a bank an average of $4.24 per month to maintain a savings account. In addition, for a regular savings account, most banks pay 3.50% interest on the balance. The $4.24 per month cost includes the Fed's FCA per item cost and average per account volume figures for deposits, withdrawals, transit checks deposited, interest payments, and account maintenance (for banks in the $50 million to $200 million range). For a savings account with a balance of $100, the cost of maintaining this account would be $4.24 + .24 for interest ($100 × 3.5% ÷ 12) or $4.53 per month or $54.36 per year. Assuming the bank could invest this $100 at a 9% per year rate, the loss per year for maintaining this account would be $45.36. According to these cost and income figures, a balance in a savings account of $604 would be required just to break even.

Another factor involved in discussing the expense of maintaining savings accounts is the number of these accounts that exist in banks. According to a recent FCA regular savings account size analysis report, approximately 64% of all savings accounts have balances of less than $500. So if a bank had 10,000 savings accounts, 6,400 of them would be unprofitable.

All of the above would indicate the importance of imposing a service charge on low balance savings accounts. Banks are using two ways to improve profits on low balance savings. Either they are not paying interest on an account if the balance falls below a certain dollar amount, or they are service charging the account on a monthly or quarterly basis. Given the choice of the two methods, I prefer paying interest. It seems more palatable from the customer's point of view to pay the interest and to charge a maintenance fee for a low balance, rather than not pay the interest and not charge a fee. Also, if you charge a fee you can increase it in the future.

Some other points to remember when charging a fee:

1. More income is derived from a fee if the charge is based on a minimum balance amount rather than on an average balance.
2. More income is usually collected if the fee is charged on a monthly basis rather than on a quarterly basis. A fee of $2.00 per month is almost as palatable to a customer as $4.00 per quarter, but the amount collected is 50% greater.
3. Notify your customers by mail so they are fully informed.
4. You may wish to exempt minor accounts, but if you do, make the exemption on a customer request basis—do not automatically exempt every minor account.
5. Expect a substantial number of savings accounts to close out. A lot of these closeouts, however, will not represent customers leaving the bank but rather customers consolidating accounts.

6. Make the balance limit as high as possible—no less than $150.
7. Service charges are a substantial source of income. For example, 3,000 accounts with balances of less than $150 × $2.00 per month would equal $72,000 per year in income.

DORMANT ACCOUNT CHARGES

State escheat laws vary with regard to dormant accounts. Also your state may have restrictions on how much you may charge an account that has not had activity. These laws and restrictions have to be investigated. Every bank has many dormant accounts in both checking and savings and most of these accounts have balances below $100. These accounts should be serviced charged on a monthly basis to cover your cost of maintaining them. These dormant account charges could be in addition to your low balance fee as described in the previous section, but again, check your state's regulations.

The object of service charging these accounts, of course, is to increase your income. But in addition, the sooner you get these accounts off your books the sooner you will reduce your overall expense of maintaining them.

Also, remember to review all your accounts for a possible dormant charge—regular checking, special checking, NOW accounts, regular savings, time savings, Xmas clubs, and vacation clubs.

MONEY ORDER AND CASHIER'S CHECK FEES

If you don't know how many money orders your bank sells each year, you should find out right away. Many medium-size banks literally sell thousands of these money orders each year and the fees generated from these sales can be substantial.

What was said about money orders is also true for cashier's checks sold. I'll wager that if you don't know how many money orders and cashier's checks are sold, you will be amazed when you find out. The volume of these services are almost always underestimated. Whatever your charges are now, a $.25 increase is easy to institute for both money orders and cashier's checks and the profit increase will be immediate and substantial.

SAFE DEPOSIT BOX FEES

This is an obvious fee schedule to review but because it is so obvious it could be overlooked. For example, if you have 3,000 safe deposit boxes in your whole bank, a simple decision to raise each box fee only $1.50 would *increase* your annual income in this area by $4,500. Annual safe deposit box fees in most banks are extremely reasonable considering the protection and security a safe deposit box offers. Also, in many communities, there is a scarcity of boxes, so this fee structure should be one of the first to be reviewed by any bank that is serious about increasing annual income.

CHECKBOOK CHARGES

Many banks mark up their personalized checkbook costs a percentage of the amount it costs them. For example, if the check printing company charges the bank $9.00 for a reorder of 200 personalized checks, a bank will add 5% to 25% of this cost to the charge quoted to the customer. A $9.00 cost to the bank would increase the price to $10.80 for a 20% markup. If the average personal checking customer writes 14 checks per month, these customers will on average order new checks every 14 months (200 ÷ 14). If a bank had 5,000 of these accounts, 357 customers (5,000 ÷ 14) would be ordering checks each month. If the profit markup was 20% or $1.80 per order, the income derived would be $7,711.20 ($1.80 × 357 × 12). Also, since banks open and close a number of checking accounts each year, the number of checkbook orders actually ordered each year is considerably higher than the 357 per month shown in the example. Business account customers, of course, write a lot more than 14 checks per month and so they order in larger quantities which adds to the profit for the bank. Consequently, if you don't mark up these prices or you haven't reviewed your current markup on this item, it should be considered, because it is an effortless way to increase income.

RETURNED DEPOSITED CHECK CHARGE

The income derived from this type of fee will vary depending on the bank. But here again, if you do not know how many returned deposited checks you have on average each day, it could be worth the effort to find out. I know of one bank in a suburban area that had 10,000 checking accounts, 2,000 of which were business accounts, and after a simple survey found out that on average they were processing a total of 35 returned deposited checks per day. It took considerable effort and expense to track down the account into which these checks were originally deposited so that these returned checks could be charged back to the proper accounts and then mailed back to the customers. The bank decided to start charging $1.00 per check and to add this amount to the debit ticket used to charge back the item. Business account customers were also charged this fee the same way—on a direct rather than an analysis basis. The net result of this decision was an immediate $35.00 per day increase in fee income or $9,100 per year. After a year of charging for this service, the fee could easily be increased to $2.00 per check.

STOP PAYMENT, COLLECTION, AND WIRE TRANSFER CHARGES

The volume of each of these three services will vary from bank to bank. But for many banks the volume in one or two of these services will be substantial. And an increase in the fee will increase income.

Stop payment fees have been on the rise in recent years and a fee of $15.00 or more per stopped check is common in many urban areas. Considering the liability of the bank for a stopped check written for any sizeable amount, this fee is certainly reasonable.

There are some banks, depending on the trade area in which they service customers, that do a brisk business collecting negotiable instruments that cannot be collected through normal bank check clearing channels. The amount of paperwork involved in accounting for these items is considerable and so are the problems if these items are lost. The fees, therefore, for this type of service should be a direct charge and should reflect the true cost of providing this service. To estimate this cost, multiply the number of full-time employees (or the full-time equivalent) who provide this service by their average salary + 50% for fringe benefits and general overhead. Then divide this amount by the total number of items handled per year and you will obtain a good indication of the costs involved in providing this service on a per item basis. This amount added to any charges a correspondent bank may levy, plus a small percentage for a profit will give you a reasonable fee that should be charged for this service.

The volume of wire transfers may fool you if you don't already know the volume. But whether the volume is great or small, always pass on to your customer any charge your correspondent bank may charge you for this service, and add on your own fee which should at least cover your costs. These costs can be approximated in the manner used for determining collection item costs.

SUMMARY

For the banker, who up to this point has not recently reviewed the fees for the services described in this chapter, there are thousands of dollars per year in additional fees that could and should be collected. A suggested priority of services for reviewing fee structure according to volume, and potential dollar increase in income is as follows:

1. Savings account low balance
2. Money order
3. Cashier's check
4. Dormant account
5. Safe deposit box
6. Checkbook
7. Returned deposited check
8. Stop payment
9. Collection service
10. Wire transfer

Chapter 7

A Catalogue of All Bank Fees

The following pages list all types of fees charged by commercial banks. These fees are divided into three main categories: fees for deposit services (checking accounts, savings accounts, supplies for deposit customers, ATM service, and cash services for deposit customers); fees for loan services (commercial loans, installment loans, and mortgage loans); and fees for other bank services (official and special type check issuance, safe deposit boxes, security transactions, credit cards, collections, utility and tax payments, and miscellaneous services).

This comprehensive list of fees was developed from listings obtained from several banks. All the fees shown are for services performed by most banks. Fees for trust services, however, were omitted because only 25% of the banks in the country offer this service and not all of these banks offer all possible trust type services. Also, the variety of trust services offered by large metropolitan banks is almost endless. The complete trust fee schedule for one multi-billion dollar metropolitan bank, for example, is printed on thirty-five pages. To improve profits, those banks who offer trust services should review their schedule of fees for the trust services they offer. This review should include a comparison of fees with those charged by correspondent banks.

The list of fees shown in this chapter includes all those that were covered in other chapters in this section of the book. The profit improvement minded reader should review each fee shown to be sure that his or her bank is charging for each service in accordance with bank policy. Also, the amount of the fee should be examined to be certain that it is sufficient to cover the cost of the service plus profit.

FEES FOR DEPOSIT SERVICES

Checking and NOW Account Charges

A. Per item fees for:

1. Checks and debits
2. Deposits and credits posted
3. Transit items deposited
4. Large quantities of rolled coin deposited (per roll)
5. Large quantities of currency deposited (per strap)
6. Large quantities of food stamps deposited (per strap)
7. Stop payments
8. Returned deposited checks
9. Returned checks
    a. Insufficient funds
    b. Uncollected funds
    c. Stale dates
    d. Post dates
10. Checks paid that cause an overdraft (overdraft charges)
11. Faxing commercial statement daily
12. Mailing ACH receipt
13. ACH transaction
14. Fee to mailing checks with statements
15. Undeliverable statement
16. Lost checkbook

B. Monthly account maintenance

C. Miscellaneous charged for:

1. Customer balance inquiries
2. Duplicate statements
3. Special cutoff statements
4. More than one statement per month
5. Month-end sorting of paid checks by account number

6. Account reconciliation service
7. Photostatic copies of checks and deposit tickets
8. Checkbook orders
9. Reconciling checkbooks for customer (per hour fee)
10. Transfer of funds to or from another account
11. Dormant or inactive accounts
12. Held statements not picked up by customer
13. Night deposit service
14. Lost night deposit bag keys
15. Certifying a check
16. Endorsement stamp

Savings Account Charges

1. Monthly or quarterly low balance
2. Excessive withdrawals
3. Overdrafts
4. Duplicate passbooks
5. Dormant or inactive account
6. Paying interest by check
7. Reconciling customer's passbook (per hour fee)
8. To close account
9. Transfer of funds to or from another account
10. Money market savings monthly maintenance and per debit transaction fees

ATM Fees

1. Transaction fees (in-house and network)
    a. Withdrawals from checking accounts
    b. Withdrawals from savings accounts
    c. Balance inquiries
    d. Deposits (network transactions)
2. New card
3. Card replacement
4. Pin reissue
5. Monthly or annual cardholder fee

Supplies for Deposit Customers

1. Currency straps
2. Coin wrappers
3. Deposit bags
4. Lead seals

5. Pay envelopes
6. Payroll envelopes
7. Endorsement stamps

Cash Services for Deposit Customers

1. Coin orders (per roll)
2. Coin wrapping (per roll)
3. Currency orders (per strap)
4. Fast cash orders (per package)
5. Foreign currency orders (per order)
6. Foreign currency tip packs

FEES FOR LOAN SERVICES

Commercial Loan Fees

1. Loan commitment
2. Unused portion of a line of credit
3. Construction loans to cover on-site inspections before loan draws are made (inspection fee)
4. Loan participation sold
5. Defaulted loans
6. Appraisal of property
7. Setup fee for small commercial loans
8. Letters of credit
9. Loan history printout fee
10. Credit report fee
11. Line of credit annual fee
12. Collateral protection insurance fee
13. Loan renewal fee
14. Loan rewrite fee
15. Loan extension fee
16. NSF loan payment fee

Installment Loan Fees

1. New loan (setup fee or loan processing fee)
2. Extension of payment
3. Late payment
4. Investigation (direct FHA property improvement loan)
5. Repossession

6. Storage for repossession
7. Credit report fee

Mortgage Loan Fees

1. Appraisal of property
2. Inspection during construction
3. Mortgage assumption
4. Closing a new mortgage (settlement fee)
5. Prepayment of mortgage
6. Points to seller of property (FHA and VA mortgage)
7. Late payment
8. Foreclosure
9. Interim escrow analysis

FEES FOR OTHER BANK SERVICES

Official and Special Type Checks Issuance Fees

1. Cashier checks
2. Money orders
3. Domestic drafts
4. Foreign drafts
5. Gift checks
6. Traveler's checks

Safe Deposit Box Fees

1. Box rental (amount determined by size of box)
2. Drilling
3. Lock change
4. Lost key
5. Safe deposit box lifetime rent
6. Bulk storage service
7. Late payment
8. Box inventory

Security Transaction Fees

1. Purchase or sale of stocks, bonds, commercial paper, bankers acceptances, government issues
2. Safekeeping of securities
3. Stock and bond transfer
4. Coupon clipping

Credit Card Fees and Charges

1. Cardholder's annual fee
2. Cardholder's interest charges
   a. Outstanding balance over 30 days
   b. Immediate on cash advances
3. Merchant's monthly imprinter/supplies fee
4. Merchant's monthly dial terminal fee
5. Merchant's monthly discount on sale charge
6. Cash advance fee
7. Overlimit fee

Collection Service Fees for Processing

1. Drafts with attached documents (bills of lading, warehouse receipts, securities, mortgages, deeds, savings passbooks)
2. Foreign checks
3. Promissory notes
4. Trade acceptances
5. Maturing bonds
6. Maturing bond coupons (per envelope)
7. Previously dishonored checks
8. Checks and drafts with specific instructions or requiring special handling

Note: Fees could be on a flat charge basis or based on the dollar amount of the item handled. All fees should be in addition to bank's out-of-pocket expense, i.e., correspondent bank charges, postage and insurance expenses, wire, or telephone costs.

Utility and Tax Payment Fees

1. City taxes
2. County taxes
3. Water bills
4. Telephone bills
5. Electric bills
6. Gas bills

Miscellaneous Fees

1. Notary fees
2. Document photocopies
3. Lottery sales
4. Issuing state license plates
5. Signature guarantee

6. Check cashing (for noncustomers)
7. Lock box service
   a. Per check deposited
   b. Per check photocopied
8. Payroll service
9. Wire transfers
   a. Domestic
   b. Foreign
10. Microfilm/fiche research (per hour)
11. Garnishments
12. Levies
13. Immigration letters
14. Issuing and redeeming U.S. savings bonds in quantity
15. Precious metal transactions
    a. Purchase or sale of gold and silver (coins or bullion)
    b. Safekeeping
    c. Delivery
    d. Appraisals
16. Brokerage service
17. Sweeping funds
18. Land contract processing
    a. Set up
    b. Each payment
       1. Cedited to customer's account
       2. Remitted to the customer by check
19. Direct cash management service
    a. Setup fee
    b. Monthly fee
20. Home banking service
21. IRA fees
    a. Annual fee
    b. Transfer fee
    c. Closeout fee
    d. Low-balance annual fee
    e. Partial withdrawal fee
22. Fax service fee

This chapter concludes this section that covered in detail the substantial income that can be gained from service charges and fees. But to maximize profits from this source of income, it cannot be overemphasized that a review of all your various fees should be done, at the very least, on a yearly basis. And those fees that were covered in detail in this chapter and in chapters 4, 5, and 6 should be reviewed every six months.

PART FOUR

CASH AND CASH ITEMS

Chapter 8

How Much Cash Do You Really Need?

VAULT CASH AND RESERVE REQUIREMENTS

For those banks that cannot use a large percentage of their teller cash as part of their reserve requirement, controlling teller cash is an area that can really boost income. If, for example, you are earning 10% on your investments for every $10,000 reduction in teller cash your bank can earn an additional $1,000 per year. Even if you rate low on peer bank statistical comparisons for cash on hand, don't be lulled into a sense of complacency. These surveys are often too general and don't take into consideration the number of each bank's branch offices, tellers, business accounts, and cashed checks, all of which affect cash requirements. There is a very practical and simple way that I have used to determine how much teller cash is required, which will produce dramatic results. Actually, it is so simple you might question its merit. But it works.

Use your past historical records to review the history of cash kept on hand. Compute, from daily teller cash recap sheets the *average* cash kept on hand *per week per location* for the past twelve weeks. Use the format shown in Figure 8–1. Note in Figure 8–1 that the branches are identified in the first column and are always shown vertically—the

Figure 8–1 Historical Record of Average Cash on Hand for *Past 12 Weeks* Ending:

Branch	*# DDA Accts.*	*% of Total DDA Accts.*	*5/15*	*5/22*	*5/29*	*6/5*	*6/12*	*6/19*	*6/26*	*7/3*	*7/10*	*7/17*	*7/24*	*7/31*	*12 Week Average*
Main Office															
North Branch															
South Branch															
East Branch															
West Branch															
Bank Total															

weekly periods are shown horizontally. This format was designed to compare each branch's weekly variances and cash levels; and then to compare these cash levels and variances to the other branches' cash levels and variances. The format used in Figure 8–1 has a column for showing the number of DDA accounts for each branch as well as a percentage of total DDA accounts. These statistics are added to give the officer who reviews this report additional comparisons. Cash on hand is affected considerably by the number of checking accounts serviced by a branch and to a lesser degree by the number of savings accounts. It is easier to compare the percentage of total number of DDA accounts statistics than the number of accounts themselves. At the end of the row of cash on hand boxes for the twelve-week period is a box to average all the figures shown in that row.

Figure 8–2 shows a completed twelve-week historical record of cash on hand for a hypothetical bank with five branches and a total of 10,009 checking accounts. The figures are representative of a bank that has not effectively controlled its teller cash. Upon reviewing Figure 8–2, the variances from week to week for some branches seem almost ridiculous. But I've seen them worse than this. And you will never know how your bank looks until you spread your weekly cash totals in this format.

Now comes the task of determining the proper cash levels for each branch. It is a problem that is solved logically. The first step is to forget the high cash figures and concentrate on the lowest three or four cash figures. No matter how often some branch managers overstock their branches with cash, they will slip up on occasion and fall down to what is usually an optimum cash level. Figure 8–3 outlines the three *consistantly* lowest cash amounts for each branch. If you find in your survey one amount considerably lower than the next three lowest amounts, you may wish to disregard the lowest one since it is not a consistent figure. From the outlined amounts in Figure 8–3 prepare a chart of these amounts as shown in Figure 8–4. Figure 8–4 also shows an average amount column. From this average amount a target or suggested cash level figure for each branch and the whole bank can be estimated by rounding the average to the nearest $5,000 figure. Then compute the percent of total figure that the target figure for every branch represents in relation to the total bank target amount. For example, the target figure of $320,000 for the main office represents 35.5% of the bank total target amount of $900,000 (320,000 ÷ 900,000 = 35.5%). To double check the target figures, compare the percent of total figures to the percent of total

Figure 8–2 Historical Record of Average Cash on Hand for *Past 12 Weeks* Ending:

Branch	*# DDA Accts.*	*% of Total DDA Accts.*	*5/15*	*5/22*	*5/29*	*6/5*	*6/12*	*6/19*	*6/26*	*7/3*	*7/10*	*7/17*	*7/24*	*7/31*	*12 Week Average*
Main Office	3,514	35.1%	415,271	445,703	387,007	315,200	480,650	318,958	404,714	350,111	470,150	455,957	475,215	330,177	404,093
North Branch	2,488	24.9%	265,750	252,157	275,110	210,778	247,975	195,550	273,950	210,998	242,412	290,510	192,115	204,315	238,302
South Branch	1,519	15.2%	173,912	142,518	160,782	157,592	181,687	149,515	161,958	150,570	145,057	140,997	169,720	159,315	157,802
East Branch	1,464	14.6%	151,215	167,212	140,315	142,111	161,919	137,812	150,500	140,888	142,728	135,593	155,123	130,917	146,361
West Branch	1,024	10.2%	98,153	115,721	110,444	107,125	111,877	95,253	117,613	113,192	119,212	113,717	113,527	104,391	110,019
Bank Total	10,009	100.0%	1,104,301	1,123,311	1,073,658	932,806	1,184,108	897,088	1,108,735	965,759	1,119,559	1,136,774	1,103,700	929,115	1,056,577

Figure 8–3 Historical Record of Average Cash on Hand for *Past 12 Weeks* Ending:

Branch	# DDA Accts.	% of Total DDA Accts.	5/15	5/22	5/29	6/5	6/12	6/19	6/26	7/3	7/10	7/17	7/24	7/31	12 Week Average
Main Office	3,514	35.1%	415,271	445,703	387,007	315,200	480,650	318,958	404,714	350,111	470,150	455,957	475,215	330,177	404,093
North Branch	2,488	24.9%	265,750	252,157	275,110	210,778	247,975	195,550	273,950	210,998	242,412	290,510	192,115	204,315	238,302
South Branch	1,519	15.2%	173,912	142,518	160,782	157,592	181,687	149,515	161,958	150,570	145,057	140,997	169,720	159,315	157,802
East Branch	1,464	14.6%	151,215	167,212	140,315	142,111	161,919	137,812	150,500	140,888	142,728	135,593	155,123	130,917	146,361
West Branch	1,024	10.2%	98,153	115,721	110,444	107,125	111,877	95,253	117,613	113,192	119,212	113,717	113,527	104,391	110,019
Bank Total	10,009	100.0%	1,104,301	1,123,311	1,073,658	932,806	1,184,108	897,088	1,108,735	965,759	1,119,559	1,136,774	1,103,700	929,115	1,056,577

Figure 8–4 Average Cash on Hand for the Three Lowest Weeks

Branch	*Week One*	*Week Two*	*Week Three*	*Average*	*Target Figure*	*% of Total Cash*	*% of Total # of DDA Accts*
Main Office	315,200	318,958	330,177	321,445	320,000	35.5%	35.1%
North Branch	210,778	195,550	192,115	199,481	200,000	22.2%	24.9%
South Branch	142,518	145,057	140,997	142,857	145,000	16.1%	15.2%
East Branch	137,812	135,593	130,917	134,774	135,000	15.0%	14.6%
West Branch	98,153	95,253	104,391	99,265	100,000	11.1%	10.2%
Bank Total	904,461	890,411	896,597	897,822	900,000	99.9%	100.0%

figures for the number of DDA accounts. They should be reasonably close.

The logic applied to determining acceptable cash levels is that if a branch can operate on the lesser cash figure for three weeks out of twelve, why not every week.

Note that the total target figure for the bank as shown in Figure 8–4 is $900,000 compared to $1,056,577 which is the total average cash on hand figure for the bank for a twelve-week period (Figure 8–2 and Figure 8–3). In this example, the potential average reduction in cash is $156,577. And this is not uncommon for banks that have not examined their cash on hand figures recently. Actually, don't be surprised if the percentage decrease in cash required is higher in your bank than the 10% shown in the example. I have seen it as high as 20%.

Now the important part of this cash reduction campaign begins—implementation. Schedule a branch managers' meeting and at the meeting explain that for profit improvement and security purposes, you wish to control cash requirements better. Then produce the reports of your completed study (as shown in Figures 8–2, 8–3, and 8–4) and explain how you arrived at the suggested target figure for each branch. Mention the basic logic you used to determine the target. Ask the managers to review these reports and ask if they wish to discuss the suggested target figures. Change any agreed upon target figures. Once the target figures are finalized, produce a report each week of the average cash on hand for the previous week. Use the format shown in Figure 8–5. Note that the twelve week's historical record is shown on top for reference. After the first twelve weeks of publishing this report you can eliminate the original twelve week's history section. Publish this report on Monday of each week and include last week's cash figures. This makes the report current, and the cash can be very easily adjusted this week if last week's figures were too high. The format shown in Figure 8-5 will display the progress that has been made. By developing this report and sending it to the branch managers week after week, you will find the psychology of this system will automate to some extent the review of the cash on hand. The branch managers will see how they are doing in relation to their goal and in relation to the other branches. They will be motivated to look good on the report not only to higher management, but also to their peers.

If a particular branch is not meeting its target figure for some reason or you suspect that too much cash is still being kept on hand in a

Figure 8–5 Historical Record of Average Cash on Hand for *Past 12 Weeks* Ending:

Branch	*# DDA Accts.*	*% of Total DDA Accts.*	*5/15*	*5/22*	*5/29*	*6/5*	*6/12*	*6/19*	*6/26*	*7/3*	*7/10*	*7/17*	*7/24*	*7/31*	*12 Week Average*
Main Office	3,514	35.1%	415,271	445,703	387,007	315,200	480,650	318,958	404,714	350,111	470,150	455,957	475,215	330,177	404,093
North Branch	2,488	24.9%	265,750	252,157	275,110	210,778	247,975	195,550	273,950	210,998	242,412	290,510	192,115	204,315	238,302
South Branch	1,519	15.2%	173,912	142,518	160,782	157,592	181,687	149,515	161,958	150,570	145,057	140,997	169,720	159,315	157,802
East Branch	1,464	14.6%	151,215	167,212	140,315	142,111	161,919	137,812	150,500	140,888	142,728	135,593	155,123	130,917	146,361
West Branch	1,024	10.2%	98,153	115,721	110,444	107,125	111,877	95,253	117,613	113,192	119,212	113,717	113,527	104,391	110,019
Bank Total	10,009	100.0%	1,104,301	1,123,311	1,073,658	932,806	1,184,108	897,088	1,108,735	965,759	1,119,559	1,136,774	1,103,700	929,115	1,056,577

Figure 8-5 (continued) Average Cash on Hand for Weeks Ending:

Branch	*Target Figure*															
Main Office	320,000															
North Branch	200,000															
South Branch	145,000															
East Branch	135,000															
West Branch	100,000															
Bank Total	900,000															

Figure 8–6 North Branch Teller Ending Cash Report

Teller	*Monday 9–12–XX*	*Tuesday 9–13–XX*	*Wednesday 9–14–XX*	*Thursday 9–15–XX*	*Friday 9–16–XX*	*Monday 9–19–XX*	*Tuesday 9–20–XX*	*Wednesday 9–21–XX*	*Thursday 9–22–XX*	*Friday 9–23–XX*	*First Week's Average*	*Second Week's Average*
H. Hart												
F. Cooke												
T. Carani												
A. Raz												
C. Palonis												
Total												

branch, develop a two-week record of ending cash by *teller* by day for that branch. Use the same basic format that was used in developing the twelve-week branch historical record. Figure 8–6 is a sample of this format. From this report it will be easy to isolate those tellers who are consistently ending up the day with too much cash on hand. Branch managers will find this type of report helpful when determining which tellers are consistently keeping too much cash, and if those reports are maintained for a two-month period or more, it will help them determine their future cash ordering requirements.

Review Your Cash on Hand Records Again

After you have established the control system and it has been operating for about three months, review these three month's records to determine if the original target figures were too high for one or more of the branches. Again, identify the lowest three week's cash amounts. If their average is substantially below the original target amount a new lower target figure can be established. By repeating this procedure, you may find that you can reduce your cash by an additional 5% to 10%.

In conclusion, the historical records approach to cash management, as described up to this point in this chapter, is a control tool. It is a way to establish, maintain, and review goals easily. This simple control tool will go a long way toward permanently and almost automatically controlling any bank's cash requirements. Although the examples given show the development of cash control for banks in a branch system, the theory will work for unit banks as well. It would be impossible to compare branches but this is not a vital part of this historical records approach. The important part of this whole approach is to determine the goal based on the logic that if a bank or a branch can operate for at least three weeks out of twelve with a consistently lower average amount, it can operate every week with that amount. They can and should—now that that amount (goal) has been determined.

Review Cash Order Timing

When interest rates are high it pays to review the timing of cash orders. Ordering too far in advance, even one day in advance of need, can be expensive. At a 10% investment rate, for example, $100,000 in cash ordered too early costs your bank $27.40 per day and if this is done each week the annual loss in interest income is $1,424.80. It pays, therefore to examine each branch's cash delivery schedule. If a branch needs the cash for a Friday afternoon's anticipated heavy check cashing activity, order the cash for Friday morning delivery not for delivery on Thursday.

If a particular correspondent bank can't have your cash order ready early in the morning so that it can be delivered to the branch early for use that day, shop around for a correspondent that will—and don't forget to investigate the cash services of your nearest Federal Reserve bank. Their services are very competitive and even if you don't clear checks with them you can still order cash from them.

To facilitate the movement of a cash shipment to the tellers, particularly when the cash is needed in the branch immediately upon delivery, I don't think it is necessary to verify each bill in each package. Verify only the number of packages and quickly fan each package to be certain it was labeled correctly by denomination. You will probably find that cash shipped from your correspondent rarely is missing a bill. For the one or two times a year that a small error occurs it isn't worth the time it takes to count each bill.

There are, of course, auxiliary benefits to be obtained from eliminating excess cash in a branch. The most obvious benefit is security. Robberies and mysterious disappearances of cash are an increasing problem for banks. Also, less cash in a branch translates to less cash per teller, less cash for tellers to count, to balance and therefore, fewer teller cash differences.

Reduce Correspondent Bank Balances

The subject of excess cash also applies to correspondent bank balances. If you haven't reviewed this recently it is well worth the effort. Banks often keep $5,000 and $10,000 balances in correspondent banks more from habit or a long forgotten reason than because of a need. Just because a correspondent banking officer treats for lunch once a year is no reason to keep a balance in that bank. It is a very expensive lunch—$1,000 ($10,000 balance at a 10% rate).

If you must keep balances in a correspondent bank for specific services try to consolidate these balances into one or two banks that offer all the services you need. At least you reduce the risk of keeping too much in balances to pay for services.

SUMMARY

There are good reasons for controlling cash: more funds are available for investment, less cash is exposed to the possibility of theft or mysterious disappearance, and teller productivity is increased by reducing the volume of cash to be counted, balanced, and stored.

This chapter has described several ways to reduce the volume of cash maintained in a bank. The most dramatic way is to determine required cash levels. The historical records approach will control cash requirements by setting realistic goals and automatically will show the progress toward realizing these goals. Other ways of reducing cash include analyzing cash order schedules and reducing correspondent bank balances. This chapter introduced the more obvious ways of reducing correspondent bank balances. The next chapter will explore the more technical ways of reducing these balances.

Chapter 9

Reduce Float, Correspondent Bank Check Clearing and Other Costs

REDUCE FLOAT

The subject of float cannot be separated easily from its companion subject—correspondent bank check clearing costs. All banks use other banks to clear checks. This includes the Federal Reserve system. How fast these checks clear introduces the subject of float, and how much a correspondent bank charges to clear these checks introduces the subject of correspondent bank pricing. This chapter will explore these subjects in combination because of their close interrelation. At the end of the chapter comments about other correspondent bank costs are presented.

In very large banks, analyzing float has become a highly skilled profession within the operations division of a bank. Senior bankers will spend days trying to devise ways to transport checks to end points in a day or even hours sooner. Checks in float cannot be invested and they are a large nonearning asset. In these days of high interest rates and the FED's role in check clearing, all banks regardless of size, should monitor this function carefully. Once a way is discovered to collect a certain group of check one day sooner, the funds represented by the amounts of these checks can be invested one day earlier each day this group of checks is processed by your bank. So, if this group of checks totals on average $100,000 per day, then the increase income is the earnings on the $100,000 for each day of the year. If for example, this $100,000 can be invested at a 10% rate, then the increased earning is $10,000 per year.

The following is a list of ways to reduce the clearing time for checks received by your bank.

Relate Proof Operation to Limited Customer Banking Facilities

Many banks in the country close their lobbies on a particular weekday and leave only their drive-in and/or walk-up facilities open. If this is the situation in your bank and your proof department is closed during this day, consider running at least a skeleton crew in the proof department to process and send out for clearing the checks received by these drive-ins and walk-up tellers. You may be holding over millions of dollars worth of checks for that day each week. At an earning rate of 10%, the loss of income per million dollars worth of checks is $\$1{,}000{,}000 \times 10\% \div 365 \times 52 = \$14{,}246.57$ per year. Of course the cost of operating a minimum proof operation on these days would have to be subtracted from this increase in earnings. Also, if your facility tellers are not processing mail deposits, have them process and clear these checks too. For some banks, the total dollar amount of a day's mail deposits is considerable.

Relate Posting of "On Us" Checks to Limited Customer Banking Facilities

On the day your lobby is closed it is important to post your own checks that were received the day before via the tellers and those received from your correspondent bank (inclearings). If you delay the posting of these items one day, you're giving credit to your customers (or in the case of inclearings, your correspondent bank is charging your account) a day before you are being paid for these items. This can be as expensive in lost earnings as not clearing your outgoing items on the day they are received (relating the proof operation to limited customer banking facilities).

Relate Proof Operation to Late Walk-up and Drive-in Banking Hours

Many banks keep their drive-in and walk-up teller windows open later than their lobby tellers. But they hold over all items received by these late tellers after the main lobby closes. These cutoff times should be examined to determine if the proof department's schedule could be rearranged to accept work up to a later hour and still make cash letter delivery deadlines. If you have a sorter reader in your bank, you may be able to at least sort out and send the larger dollar amount items.

Relate Proof Operation to Saturday Customer Banking Hours

If your bank is open on Saturdays, are you sending your checks out to your correspondent bank on Saturdays for clearing? Check your correspondent's receiving deadlines for Saturday in order to determine if you could receive credit on Monday instead of Tuesday for one day items, and Tuesday instead of Wednesday for two day items.

CORRESPONDENT BANK CHECK CLEARING SERVICES

Up to now we have identified ways to increase income by getting checks out of your bank faster for clearing. Next we shall examine ways to clear these checks faster in the vast national check clearing system. This, of course, introduces the subject of pricing of correspondent bank check clearing services.

There are many services a correspondent bank provides to other banks. The most important of these from a cost and pricing point of view, however, is the check clearing service. Traditionally, correspondent banks relate the cost of their services to collected balances required, because they usually prefer that you keep balances in their banks rather than to pay them a direct charge for their services. Since the volume of items involved in clearing checks is large, they obtain more balances for clearing checks than for all other services combined. Because of the cost in lost earnings for balances required and the pricing complexity of the correspondent bank's check clearing service, it is important that you thoroughly review your bank's present balance costs for this service and compare them to what other correspondent banks offer.

The pricing of a check clearing service basically involves only three factors the per item processed cost, the availability of the dollars deposited, and the earnings credit given for the collected (available) balance. All three of these factors have to be considered as one package because each factor directly relates to the other two. One bank may charge more for each item processed than another but may provide earlier availability for certain items.

The best way to start this review is to determine the mix of checks in your present cash letters—both in volume and in dollars. This can be obtained from your correspondent bank's billing, from an end point analysis, which many correspondents will provide upon request, and/or from your own proof department's records. The information obtained should include the number and dollar amount per month and availability of the following types of items.

1. Checks drawn on the correspondent bank itself.
2. Government checks.
3. Postal money orders.
4. Checks (if any) for which same day availability is given.
5. Checks for which one (next day) availability is given.
6. Checks for which two day availability is given.
7. Checks (if any) for which more than two day availability is given.

Same day availability means you can use the cash letter amount the same day it is received by the correspondent bank. Often the amount can be anticipated and used before the checks will arrive at the bank before their evening deadline. One day and next day availability are often synonymous and mean that if the checks arrive at the correspondent bank by their evening deadline on Monday, you can invest the money on Tuesday. Two day availability means that if the checks arrive on Monday evening, you can invest the money on Wednesday. Be certain to ask each correspondent bank with which you are comparing prices to define what they mean by immediate, same day, one day, and two day availability;

if the days are business days or calendar days; and what their deposit time deadlines are for receiving this availability. Also, find out how availability is affected for deposits made during the weekend and on holidays.

The availability factor is the most important of the three factors mentioned in the pricing of this service. One earlier day's availability for a group of checks totalling $100,000 could mean an additional $10,000 per year in income at a 10% rate of return. Therefore it is important that you know your mix of checks deposited to correspondent banks and their availability schedules.

Figure 9–1 shows a basic format that you can use in compiling the statistics necessary to analyze a cash letter going to a particular correspondent bank or to FED. Use this format for each correspondent bank. Your correspondent bank should be able to give you the statistics and information indicated.

The sample analysis form (Figure 9–1) has been completed with statistics that could represent a bank with $200 million in assets and 12,000 checking accounts that sends 80% of its transit items to correspondent bank A.

The following is a detailed explanation of the information shown in Figure 9–1 which will lead to a description of a number of ways in which you will be able to either increase availability or decrease costs.

No Fee for Correspondent Bank Items

The first column, "Type of Item," shows a group of representative categories of items. Some correspondent banks will not charge a fee for their own items if sorted, particularly if you are using that bank to clear the majority of your transit items. When picking a major correspondent bank to clear your items, therefore, it is important to choose the one that offers this free service and the one for which your bank receives a large dollar volume of checks.

Dollar Sorting

A good end point analysis from a major correspondent bank will show the number and dollar amount of items deposited for the month broken down by drawee banks, and/or drawee banks within certain areas of the

Figure 9–1 Cash Letter Analysis of Checks Being Sent to Correspondent Bank—August, 19xx

Type of Item	*Average Daily Deposit*	*Number of Items for Month*	*Cost Per Item*	*Total Price for Month*	*Collected Balance Required*	*Availability*	*Sort Required*
Checks drawn on correspondent bank A	$ 502,294	26,981	$ .00	$ .00	$ .00	1 Day	Sorted
Checks drawn on bank X	50,554	3,967	.02	79.34	27,202.91	1 Day	None
Checks drawn on bank Y	175,095	10,064	.02	201.28	69,011.86	1 Day	None
Checks drawn on bank Z	68,621	4,186	.02	83.72	28,704.66	1 Day	None
Government checks	105,620	5,010	.02	100.20	34,355.07	1 Day	None
Postal money orders	30,200	1,998	.02	39.96	13,700.88	1 Day	None
RCPC items	853,338	46,100	.02	922.00	316,121.51	1 Day	None
All other items	586,536	27,155	.04	1,086.20	372,419.94	1 & 2 Day	None
Total	2,372,258	125,461	–	2,512.70	861,516.83	–	–
Return items	–	1,078	.75	808.50	277,206.33	–	–
Grand Total	$2,372,258	–	–	$3,321.20	1,138,723.16	–	–
Quoted earnings rate=3.5%							

Note: Deposit deadline for delivery to correspondent bank for all items is 10:30 p.m. If government checks and postal money orders are sorted and delivered by 3:00 p.m., same day (immediate) availability is given by FED.

country, and a break out of these items by dollar amounts. For example, it will show the number and dollar amount of items drawn on the State Bank of Chicago, Illinois, under $250.00, under $500.00, and under $1,000,000. In most cash letters containing any volume at all the majority of items are each for a small dollar amount (under $250.00), but these items represent only a small percentage of the total dollar amount of items being deposited. The principle of dollar sorting can also be used to break out larger dollar amount items faster to meet earlier clearing deadlines or to send separate cash letters direct to specific banks for faster clearing.

Dollar sorting, however, in some proof departments may not be practical. A sufficient number of proof machine pockets may not be available and it could be difficult to train proof operators to sort by drawee bank and by dollar amount at the same time. Proof departments that use electronic sorter reading machines for processing checks, however, can easily adapt their operation to this type of sorting.

The next three items shown in Figure 9–1 (checks drawn on banks X, Y, and Z) will show from which drawee banks your bank is receiving quantities of checks totaling substantial dollar amounts. Statistics for only three banks are shown for illustrative purposes. From this analysis you should select the names of those drawee banks from which you could possibly receive earlier credit, or be able to reduce your clearing costs, by using the following methods.

Exchanging Local Checks

If the drawee banks identified are local, consider exchanging checks with these banks directly each day through your local clearinghouse or in the absence of one, by organizing one. The purpose of exchanging checks through a clearinghouse arrangement is usually not to obtain earlier availability, but rather to save the per item or balance requirement cost charged by a correspondent bank to process these items.

Direct Deposit of Local Checks

If the drawee banks identified are local but are much larger than your bank and direct exchange of checks is not feasible, consider trying to obtain same day availability from them. Open an account with them and deposit the items drawn on their bank before their lobby closes or if they do a correspondent bank business deposit their own items before their evening deadlines. Some banks, however, may frown on the lobby deposit idea and not permit you to do it; but to establish a relationship with your bank some banks may permit it.

Direct Send and Package Sorting

If the drawee banks identified are out of town, compare availability and the cost of sending them a direct cash letter by an express courier. Even if you cannot clear these identified banks' items directly, most correspondent banks will charge you a reduced rate if you sort these checks by bank and do not send them mixed in with other items. It is called package sorting.

Clearing Government Checks and Postal Money Orders

You should know the volume of government checks and postal money orders processed by your bank because Federal Reserve banks will process them free of charge, and the FED will give you same day credit for these items if deposited before a mid-afternoon deadline. Correspondent banks always charge for clearing these items.

Clearing RCPC and Other Items

You should know your volume of RCPC items so you can compare cost per item fees between correspondent banks. The availability should be the same with all correspondents in your area. "All other items" consists of the other items that need not be isolated in your analysis. They will be mostly low volume checks drawn on a number of banks outside your area. If you see a concentration of these banks in or around Federal Reserve bank cities, you should compare costs, availability, and sort requirements between your correspondent bank and FED.

Return Items

The last type of item listed is "Return items." You should know the volume of these items because as of this writing, the FED does not charge for return items. They merely ask you to keep a sufficient available balance to pay for the amount of these items received.

Correspondent Bank Balance Requirements and Earnings Allowances

The "Average daily deposit" column in Figure 9–1 is determined by using the deposit total for the month provided by your correspondent bank and dividing it by the number of days during that month that you sent them a cash letter. The other columns of information in Figure 9–1 are self-explanatory except for the one entitled "Collected balance required." This balance requirement is always shown on your correspondent bank's monthly analysis billing of your account. This balance requirement is usually shown for cash letter services, as well as other services performed. It is important that you know how to equate this figure to the earnings credit your correspondent bank allows for the balances you keep with them. Every correspondent bank will quote you their earnings rate. But what is the real rate after reserve requirements or FDIC charges? It is a simple calculation. Merely divide the total price per month by the collected balance required to obtain a monthly earnings rate. Then multiply this rate by twelve to obtain an annual rate. In periods of high quoted rates, the difference between what is quoted as a rate and the real rate can be substantial. In this case you may wish to seriously consider not keeping any available balances with the correspondent bank; instead have them bill you for the total price for the month. Also, this billed amount is tax deductible.

The note in the bottom of Figure 9–1 regarding delivery deadlines is to remind you to include in your analysis the delivery deadlines for each category of items. If necessary, use a separate column. In this particular example, the delivery deadline is the same for all items sent to this correspondent bank. The reference to government checks and money orders was made to show that an option in delivery deadlines is available to receive immediate credit for these items.

When deciding whether to use a correspondent bank or the FED to clear your items, consider the following:

1. The FED will process government checks and U.S. postal money orders free, but they have to be sorted.
2. The FED does not charge a fee for return items.
3. In general, the FED's cost per item will be a little lower, but their sorting requirements are stricter.

4. Correspondents generally will not penalize you if occasionally your collected balance falls below the required level or even if you occasionally draw into the unavailable balance.
5. Many correspondents and FED will provide an end point analysis of your deposited items upon request.

OTHER WAYS TO REDUCE FLOAT AND CORRESPONDENT BANK MISCELLANEOUS COSTS

The following suggestions for reducing float and correspondent bank service costs are not related to each other or to other parts of this chapter.

1. If your bank is located near the Canadian border and either in or near a large U.S. city or near a large Canadian city and your bank receives a large dollar volume of checks drawn on Canadian banks, it may be profitable to clear these items directly with a Canadian bank for the following reasons:
   a. The per item cost (or balance requirements) will probably be lower than a U.S. bank's item cost.
   b. Availability for these items should be better—often next day availability. These items would not have to be sent for collection.
   c. If the checks deposited are drawn in Canadian funds, the exchange rate quoted may be more generous. In addition, you can add a one or two point spread which is probably what your U.S. correspondent is doing.
   d. You would be able to draw Canadian drafts yourself rather than through your U.S. correspondent bank and collect a one to two point spread in the exchange rate yourself. You would also avoid the U.S. correspondent bank's foreign draft charge.
   e. Return items would be processed faster.
2. If you're cashing a number of checks on a daily or weekly basis, which are drawn on other banks, you are providing a service of giving cash for items that you cannot collect on for at least one day. The float on these items could be substantial and you are, therefore, losing the ability to invest these funds.

3. Make sure you're not giving immediate credit to your customers who are depositing foreign items into their accounts. It could take several days, if not weeks, before your bank receives credit for these items. Your proof department can out sort these items, charge the customer's account, send the customer an advice, and send the checks in a separate cash letter to your correspondent. If you immediately credit your customer's account for large foreign items and they are lost in transit or payment is refused, upon charging these items back days or weeks later the customer may not have a sufficient balance to cover them.
4. If you are a small bank and therefore are not yet encoding the dollar amount on transit checks in MICR, consider the additional price charged for processing these items and/or the number of days lost in availability as quoted by your correspondent bank. It may be profitable for you to encode these items yourself.
5. If you are not already calculating float on every deposit made to checking and certain savings accounts, consider doing it. Some banks do not pay interest on unavailable funds deposited to business savings accounts, NOW accounts, IRA accounts, and initial funds put into large certificates of deposits. Review this practice at your bank.
6. Review your correspondent bank's charges for coin and currency orders, wire transfers, and purchase of U.S. Treasury securities and compare these charges to the FED's charges. The FED, for example, usually will charge less for the purchase of U.S. Treasury bills, bonds or notes, regardless of whether these securities are purchased for your bank's portfolio or for your customers.

SUMMARY

Analyzing your bank float and correspondent's check clearing and other fees can be a very profitable exercise for any bank. There are 23 ways described in this chapter to increase your profitability in these areas. You may be aware of some of these ways, but unless you have made an exhaustive study of this subject recently, you are probably not aware of all of them—and those you were not aware of could mean a lot of dollars lost in profitability.

The following is an itemized summary, in a question format, of the twelve ways to reduce float and the eleven ways to decrease correspondent bank fees. It will serve as a convenient checklist for you to consider if they apply to your bank's operation.

Reducing Float

1. When your lobby is closed on a particular weekday but your drive-ins or walk-up windows are open, are the items received by the tellers being processed by proof the same day?
2. Are your opened tellers processing mail deposits received that day, which in turn can be processed by proof on the same day?
3. Is the posting of your "on us" items being delayed a day?
4. Is your proof department processing on the same day the items received from tellers who are open later than normal banking hours?
5. Is your proof department processing items on Saturday when and if any tellers are accepting banking transactions on Saturday?
6. Can you take advantage of dollar sorting to meet check clearing deadlines?
7. Do you have a sufficient dollar amount of checks drawn on a certain bank in your area to deposit these checks in your account before that bank closes?
8. Do you have a sufficient volume of checks for a certain out of town drawee bank to send them a direct cash letter by courier?
9. Is your volume of Canadian checks sufficient for you to use a Canadian correspondent bank for clearing these items.
10. Have you considered the automatic float that is created by cashing large quantities of checks that are not drawn on your bank?
11. Are you giving customers immediate credit for foreign items?
12. Are you giving immediate credit to your customers for all checks deposited to accounts, particularly business checking and savings accounts, IRA accounts, and large certificates of deposit?

Reducing Correspondent Bank Fees

1. If you have a sufficient volume of checks drawn on banks in your bank's vicinity, have you considered clearing them FREE through a local clearing house?

2. Do you have a sufficient volume of government checks and/or postal money orders to clear them FREE through the nearest Federal Reserve bank?

3. Do you have a sufficient volume of checks drawn on particular out of town banks to sort these checks by bank and take advantage of the reduced correspondent bank's fees for "package sorting?"

4. Can you use the dollar sorting technique in preparing package sort items?

5. Have you compared your correspondent bank's return item fee with other bank's fees, particularly with the FED, which will process return items free?

6. When comparing earnings rates offered by competing correspondent banks (including the FED) are you considering the *real* rate being offered by these banks and not the quoted rate?

7. Have you calculated the earnings advantages of not paying correspondent bank fees with balances but rather permitting them to charge you directly for their services (remembering also, that this direct charge could be tax deductible).

8. Have you compared fees for issuing Canadian drafts and clearing Canadian checks between U.S. correspondent banks and a Canadian correspondent bank?

9. Have you compared exchange rates used by a U.S. correspondent bank versus a Canadian correspondent bank when they clear Canadian funds checks?

10. Have you considered the cost of having your correspondent bank MICR encode your checks?

11. Have you compared fees between correspondent banks (including the FED) for coin orders, wire transfers, and the purchase of U.S. Treasury bills, bonds, and notes?

PART FIVE

REDUCE OTHER MAJOR EXPENSES

Chapter 10

A Review of Data Processing Costs

After interest expense and salary expense bank data processing costs usually ranks third in dollars spent each year by banks. Since most banks in the country process their deposit, loan, and accounting functions electronically rather than manually, I will confine my comments to electronic data processing costs.

The history of electronic data processing, particularly as it relates to banks, is relatively short. It all started with the birth of the computer industry in the early fifties and in the development of magnetic ink character recognition (MICR) by the banking industry in 1959. MICR became the common language used by all banks to communicate numeric-type information to computers. By imprinting these magnetic ink characters on checks and on a variety of in-house forms, banks can communicate all necessary financial information to a computer, and the computer can then perform the calculations required to update all the bank's internal and customer related financial data.

In the sixties it was popular for banks to acquire their own computer systems and process their work in-house. This proved to be very expensive for many banks not only because of the cost of these early computers and the rapid advancements that were being made in the design and speed of this equipment, but also in the salary expense involved in operating and programming computer systems.

DATA PROCESSING ALTERNATIVES

Today there are more computer processing alternatives for a bank to consider. The in-house computer is still being used by many, particularly the larger banks. Some banks alleviate themselves of the administrative and programming headaches involved in maintaining an in-house electronic data processing system by hiring an outside firm to manage this in-house system on a day-to-day basis. Other banks do not process their work on their own computer system, but rather send it each day via messenger to a local data processing center which posts the work to the various customer accounts and bank general ledger accounts and sends the results back to the bank the following day in the form of printed reports and/or microfiche reports. For easier access to this processed work some banks have chosen to be connected on-line to their data processing center. They can inquire the status of any customer account via administrative video terminals and/or on-line teller terminals rather than take the time to search through printed reports or microfiche for the desired information.

There is still another alternative that more and more banks are using. It is called remote job entry (RJE). This is a cross between the in-house computer system alternative and the data processing center alternative. In the RJE system a bank purchases or leases a small computer system consisting of a sorter reader, a central processing unit, a disc and/or magnetic tape drive, and a printer. The bank then, rather than sending the physical documents (checks, deposit tickets, withdrawal tickets, general ledger entries) to the data processing center, captures the information from these documents with the sorter reader and sends it via telephone lines to the data center. The data center posts it to the various accounts and then sends the report information back via telephone lines to the bank's computer system which prints the reports. Banks that use RJE systems usually have a network of on-line administrative video terminals, not only for easier access to the information, but also to substantially reduce the in-house report printing that would be required if it did not have on-line terminals. Of course, with this system, the required fine sorting of the physical documents, such as for checks, is done by the bank on its sorter reader, since these documents are never sent to the data center. With the RJE system a bank can choose a remote data center to process its work. The center need not be in the same city because all information travels to and from the data center via telephone lines. In fact most data centers, regardless of their location in relation to the banks they service would prefer to eliminate processing the volumes of checks and other physical documents that are generated by banks and they price their services accordingly.

The following is a recap of the basic electronic data processing options available to banks.

1. All processing is done in-house with bank computers and bank administrative and programming personnel.
2. All processing is done in-house with bank computers but with contracted outside administrative and programming personnel.
3. All processing is done by an independent data center under a batch system (physical documents are sent to the center and reports are returned to the bank via messenger).
4. Processing is done by an independent data center with the bank using a remote job entry system (physical documents are not sent to the center all information is transmitted to and from the center via telephone lines).

When choosing one of these options consider the size of your bank, the distance from reputable data centers, costs, and the expertise of present bank personnel. These four options can be categorized into the following two basic alternatives—the use of a full scale in-house computer and the use of an outside data center.

Some banks are lured into the aura of owning and operating their own in-house full scale computer system to be used in processing all their customer account and internal accounting functions. For larger banks the cost figures are often favorable compared to the other alternatives, even after considering staffing requirements, and computer hardware and software costs. For the smaller banks the desire of being self-sufficient is attractive. There are problems, however, attached to operating a full scale computer system—and most of these are "people related." Attracting and retaining good data processing managers and programmers is a problem. These types of specialized employees have a tendency to be very mobile and can jump from bank to bank every few years, chasing better paying opportunities; or if they don't move, they could dominate the whole bank with their desires to add newer and more equipment, specialized programming, and automated unprofitable customer services or internal reporting structures.

In addition to these problems are those that are related to the programs used to operate any full scale computer system. Typically a bank will buy a set of programs to process all the bank's bookkeeping and accounting systems. These programs are sold with the understanding that periodic updates will be provided, particularly those needed to conform to changes in banking regulations, or new bank services the bank wants to offer. These updates may not come on time or may not come at all. Or, if the updates and the new programs are provided, they may not work without adding more hardware or changing the basic program package. All these problems can only be solved by purchasing more equipment and employing a sufficient number of programmers who know the particular basic programs being used in the bank's computer system.

Because of these problems a bank may decide to obtain outside administrative and programming help and actually hire a firm that specializes in running a bank's day-to-day computer operation. On the one hand the bank is still using the same computer hardware and basic software packages that it owns, but on the other hand it is now paying a higher price for the management of the computer center.

Many banks in the country use a data center to provide all their electronic data processing system needs. This data center approach can be done in two ways: remotely using an RJE system, and by using batch processing. Some data centers will offer either option, whereas others will usually only offer their services under a remote environment. The batch system (the physical documents are sent to the center for processing) is only practical if the data center is located close to the bank. With either system a bank can have on-line communications via video 'terminals and/or electronic teller terminals and ATM machines. The use of on-line video terminals is most common with banks that use an RJE system because it reduces the volume of paper reports that would have to be printed by the bank.

CHOOSE A DATA CENTER CAREFULLY

There are several considerations involved in choosing a data center. They are as follows:

Distance. How far away is the center? Do you have the option of using either the batch system or the RJE system? If you have this option, then depending on a bank's volume of accounts and transactions, the data processing fees charged by the data center might be less expensive with an RJE system (even considering the computer and video communications equipment, and telephone lines required). Data centers, through pricing, encourage banks to use an RJE system. As a note, an RJE computer system does not require especially talented people to operate or program. It is a system that is designed for this remote processing function and not for the processing of all bank internal functions. There are, however, two other specialized purposes for which RJE computer systems can be used—bulk filing and an automated proof system (Proof of Deposit called POD). In larger banks the bulk filing concept does save on salary expense for check file employees. The automated POD system allows banks of all sizes to sort transit checks into an unlimited number of categories for better availability of funds and eliminates the need for multi-pocket proof machines.

The data center itself. Is it a profitable growing enterprise and therefore not likely to go out of business? Does it keep up-to-date in offering current popular bank services? Does it conform to regulatory changes on time? Does it have emergency back-up for power and/or computer failures? Does it respond well to requests from banks for changes, or in correcting service complaints? Does it currently service banks in your size category?

The center's internal systems used/or processing bank transactions. Do they produce the customer and internal bank reports you want for all your functions DDA, savings, CDs, loan functions, general ledger, auditing, automated teller function?

Types of equipment supported by the data center. If any existing equipment in the bank or equipment the bank wishes to acquire is to be connected on-line to the data center, does the data center support (accept information from and transmit information to) that particular manufacturer's equipment? There are a number of manufacturers of bank equipment but not all data centers support all these manufacturers' equipment. For example, there may be five manufacturers of ATM equipment but data center A may support three out of these five, and data center B may only support two out of these five, and the same is true for CRTs, teller terminals, and RJE computer systems.

Costs. And now we get down to the bottom line of this presentation—costs. If you think all data processing centers charge basically the same fees, you are wrong. The expensive data centers can and do charge as much as 50% or more than the less expensive ones. This alone should indicate that you should obtain quotes from data centers each time a current data center contract is due to be renewed. And these differences in fees can amount to thousands of dollars per month in costs, depending on a bank's size. These differences could be sufficient to motivate you to incur the equipment expense of an RJE system, if you don't already have one, and update your whole bank's data communications at the same time. The key to all this is to obtain quotes from a number of data centers (at least five including your present data center) which are located in and out of your area. Don't let distance bother you if you are on an RJE system now or are contemplating one in the near future. Telephone communications (through the use of dedicated leased lines) is a reliable data link between distant places. The cost per mile is a factor but it is not the most expensive factor in a telephone communication network. The difference in cost between data centers is not related to any potential savings in your bank's staff that a data center might dangle in front of you as an advantage to signing up with their center. I'm referring to basic data processing fees. Any savings in the number of employees that may be affected is just frosting on the cake.

When comparing data centers' quotes there are several cost factors that could be involved, depending on the center. They are as follows:

Basic fees. These are the daily processing fees related to all the bank's applications to be processed. These fees are most often based on a bank's volume—i.e., the number of accounts in each application combined with the number of transactions. The data center's estimate of these fees is based on the volume statistics the bank gives them. So it is important that accurate volume statistics are given to each data center that will be submitting quotes. Once these statistics are compiled the same statistics should be given to each data center. Also, be sure you know what the basic fee does not include. There is usually an extra charge for special reports requested and for extra copies of standard reports whether these reports are to be printed on paper or reproduced on microfiche. Reviewing the data center's schedule of fees and asking a lot of questions will be helpful.

Additional fees. Equipment hook-up or support fees are sometimes charged per CRT (video screen) connected to the center, per ATM connected to the data center, and per teller terminal connected to the center. These are monthly fees not one time costs. Note: The terms video screen, administrative terminal, and CRT (Cathode Ray Tube) are synonomous. Be alert however, to any fees charged for on-line inquiries

(ATM transactions, teller terminal inquiries, CRT inquiries, CIF inquiries). The estimates for the number of inquiries that will be made if you have not been on-line up to now will probably be low. This fee will be charged on a per inquiry basis and the number of inquiries projected by the data center could be half what they really will be. This could understate the quote dramatically.

Forms costs. If you're not on an RJE system and plan to go on one, your monthly report forms cost should drop considerably, probably in half. The data centers from which you receive quotes can give you a rough estimate of this. Parallel to this, however, you may experience some immediate additional forms costs to convert your internal documents so that they will conform to an RJE system. This usually is a one time cost. In addition you should investigate the strong possibility of ordering some of your general type forms through your data center to take advantage of the volume discounts.

CIF costs. Watch out for monthly Central Information File (CIF) costs. This is an optional service many banks want but some data centers charge high for this service. These costs could be in addition to the CIF inquiry costs.

Telephone lines and modems costs. Dedicated long distance telephone lines to the data center must be leased. Modems ("boxes" connected to both ends of these lines) can be either purchased or leased. Data centers will determine the whole telephone communications equipment and telephone line network they think you need and unless you are a communications expert, which most bankers are not, then you have to rely heavily on their recommendation. The costs of the lines and the associated equipment supposedly are direct quotes from the telephone company. I was puzzled recently, however, when I compared two telephone communications quotations received from two large intrastate data centers equidistant from my location, both quoting the same equipment and the same number of long distant lines. But the quotation from one center was twice as much as the quote received from the other center—and there were thousands of dollars per month involved! I did not pursue the matter because the center quoting the higher telephone costs also quoted very high on the basic fee and had already priced themselves out of my market.

Equipment costs. If you intend to have your work processed via an RJE system with on-line CRT and teller terminals, the computer equipment and the CRT and teller equipment costs including maintenance expenses have to be factored in. Remember though, after the typical five-year write-off period (assuming that this equipment is purchased) these costs, except for maintenance, are theoretically eliminated unless you plan to up-date this equipment. Do not forget, when factoring in equipment cost, to include sales taxes, investment tax credit, basic programs supplied by the manufacturer, programming license fees, computer training classes, freight and installation charges. Also, you may need a bursting machine to separate customer statements, since these statements will be printed on your own printer in continuous form and will need to be bursted apart for mailing to your customers. The reduction of proof machine costs will offset some of this equipment cost. With the acquisition of RJE equipment, most banks will automatically convert to an automated proof system and the need for multipocket proof machines will be eliminated. Only single pocket proof machines are required. Also CRT terminals usually eliminate the need for present key punch equipment.

One time costs. Data centers charge a fee for converting a bank to their systems. This fee covers the programs they have to write to accept a bank's records and the center's costs in sending a team of employees to a bank to train the bank's employees on their system—how to read the data center's reports and CRT screens and how to input information to their computer system—which can take several weeks. Conversion fees are expensive one time costs as measured in tens of thousands of dollars depending on the size of the bank. Some centers will charge a basic conversion fee for the major bank applications and a separate fee for converting a bank to their CIF system and to an on-line ATM system. Make sure you know all the conversion fees each data center charges.

The other major one time cost is the installation charge for the telephone equipment. This cost will be included in the quotation the bank receives from the data center for the purchase or lease of the telephone equipment.

Spreading quotations. It is important to spread all quotations received on one sheet of lined paper in columns so that they can be compared easily. The first column should be used to identify the line items that will be quoted. The remaining columns will be used to record the actual dollar quotations for each data center. One of these columns should be used to record your present data center's fees so you can compare them to the quoted fees. Shown below is a suggested list of line items which includes the ones that were discussed previously.

Data Processing Fees and Forms Cost

Basic fee

CIF fee

ATM terminal support fees

CRT support fees

Teller terminal support fees

On-line inquiry fees

Forms cost

Total

Equipment Cost

CRT terminals

CRT printers

CRT controllers

CRT maintenance

RJE computer system

RJE maintenance

RJE programming license fee

Telephone lines

Telephone modems

Total

One Time Costs

Basic conversion charge

CIF conversion charge

ATM conversion charge

Total data center conversion charges

Telephone equipment installation charge

RJE training school cost

RJE programming cost

Total

For comparison purposes only, all data processing and equipment costs should be converted and listed as a monthly cost. On the equipment costs, for example, if you plan to lease some of the equipment, put in the monthly lease amount, and on the equipment you plan to purchase, put in the monthly depreciation amount. The above list may not be all inclusive but it is representative. There may be more specialized type equipment hookup or support fees such as for CRT controllers and/or CRT printers or there may be no hook-up charges. In any event, try to make the quotations as comparable as possible by listing as many special item charges as possible so that you know all the meaningful costs that you would incur by going with each data center. It could be difficult to translate the quotations received so that they can be compared easily; but it is well worth the effort because the dollars to be saved could be in the thousands per month.

Fee negotations. Believe it or not, all data center's fees are negotiable. How negotiable they are will depend on the size of your bank, whether or not your bank is located in an area in which a specific data center wants to get a foothold, how good a negotiator you are, whether or not you are obtaining a number of quotes, and probably for a lot of other reasons which will never be known. In any event, negotiating the fee is worth the effort. For a larger bank it can mean thousands of dollars per month in a direct reduction of this expense.

As I mentioned before, the key to obtaining the best price for a data center's service is to obtain a number of quotations. This, of course, is a time consuming experience but it is an education. By studying the various quotes and talking to the various centers you will learn more about data processing, the differences in the way fees are charged and which items are overpriced by which centers. You may also find that your present center is overpriced. All this information gives you bargaining power.

If you obtain four or five quotes, including one from your present center, for one reason or another you will probably narrow these quotes down to two data centers rather quickly. But even at the very outset, notify all data centers that you are obtaining several quotations and name the centers. This puts them on notice that you mean business. When you have narrowed it down to two centers, again notify both centers of their competitors' identity. You can't, of course, reveal actual quotes to competing data centers, but you can indicate that one center has some very favorable services; you can even mention the service.

Some of the methods data centers can and *do* use to become more price competitive are as follows:

1. Reduce the basic fee.
2. Reduce fees for optional service such as for CIF.
3. Reduce or eliminate monthly terminal "hook-up" charges.
4. Reduce or eliminate some or all conversion charges.
5. Give a concession (no charge) for the first month or two after conversion to their system.
6. Charge a flat fee for the life of the contract (fee is not related to fluctuations in number of accounts or number of transactions processed).
7. Freeze the maximum amount the fee will increase each year due to inflation.
8. Eliminate one time charges for future program enhancements. Data centers will often enhance a program to make it better, supposedly for the banks, but often also to make their system easier to run, and charge each bank their proportionate share of the cost of writing and testing the enhancement program.
9. Offer a good discount on RJE computer systems and CRT terminals through national contracts the center may have with certain equipment manufacturers, or through their contacts with other banks that may be trading in their equipment.

Data centers can and do make the above concessions but of course they won't if you don't negotiate. After all, if a data center is already processing hundreds of thousands of accounts for a number of banks how much can it cost them, after conversion, to process another ten or twenty thousand accounts, particularly on a remote basis? It's all done electronically anyway.

OTHER DATA PROCESSING COST CONSIDERATIONS

Depending on whether your bank's systems are processed in-house by your own computer or are processed by a data center the following additional cost savings considerations will apply.

MICR rejects. MICR encoded documents that reject from a computer are expensive items to process. The whole point of electronic data processing is to automatically and rapidly capture information from encoded documents. When a document rejects, the information on that document is not captured by the computer and the document has to be handled manually. This manual process slows up production which is expensive, and if enough documents reject, the whole purpose of electronic data processing is impaired. In addition, if your work is being processed by a data center under a batch system your center is charging you a high rate for each rejected document. It is important, therefore, to constantly monitor document rejection rates. Documents reject for a variety of reasons—poor encoding, no encoding, the document is mutilated, the reader sorter reading heads are not clean, etc. Whatever the reason, high reject rates should be investigated and corrected immediately.

MICR ribbons. MICR ribbons are used extensively by banks to encode all the documents processed by the proof department. These ribbons can be used only once, and they are expensive. There are two basic ways to buy high quality ribbons and it is about 40% less expensive to use an outside source than the more usual way of buying these ribbons. So obtain competitive quotes before purchasing this item.

Spreading data center bills. If you're currently being processed by a data center, each month the data center sends you a bill for its services. It is wise to have a clerk spread these bills on a work sheet as the bills are received. The line items can be listed once on this spread sheet in the same order they are listed on the bill. Then, each month the fee for each item can be put in by the clerk. This work sheet would have fourteen columns one to label the line item, one for each of the twelve months of the year and the fourteenth column to be used as a total column for the year for each line item. Each month's column would equal the total of that month's bill as received from the data center. By reviewing the monthly totals each month you will be able to spot any abnormal variance in the data center's fees. And this variance can then be isolated easily to specific line items. Variances can be a result of a billing error, bank related errors (such as excessive MICR rejects) or someone ordering a special report or a service without authorization.

From this spread sheet a report can be prepared each month for senior management's review. Figure 10–1 is an example of this monthly report which was prepared as of the end of June and shows a spread of six months' bills. As this report is prepared each month in the future, the current month's costs would be added to the report until all twelve months are shown. This report was prepared on a personal computer. Current year's quarterly comparison figures and percentage differences between quarters are also shown in the three right hand columns. These

Figure 10-1 Data Services Monthly Billing Report

Processing categories	*Jan 'XX*	*Feb 'XX*	*Mar 'XX*	*Apr 'XX*	*May 'XX*	*Jun 'XX*	*1st Qtr curr. yr*	*2nd Qtr curr. yr*	*% Diff*
DDA & Sav Accts.	6,739	6,324	7,254	7,184	7,353	7,479	20,317	22,016	+8%
Installment Loans	1,111	1,104	1,288	1,151	1,141	1,129	3,503	3,421	−2%
Mortgage Loans	201	169	189	188	189	217	559	594	+6%
Commercial Loans	487	487	546	539	538	538	1,520	1,615	+6%
Automated Clearing House	124	79	103	115	105	105	306	325	+6%
ATM's	1,299	1,244	1,322	1,317	1,350	1,373	3,865	4,040	+5%
Central Information File	468	450	472	461	763	772	1,390	1,996	+44%
General Ledger Accounting	870	840	890	919	901	913	2,600	2,733	+5%
Account Reconciliation	552	601	503	472	561	470	1,656	1,503	−9%
Microfiche	264	158	189	185	203	192	611	580	−5%
Misc. Charges	320	280	430	720	300	270	1,030	1,290	+25%
Telephone Communications	502	502	672	672	672	672	1,676	2,016	+20%
Grand Total	$12,937	$12,238	$13,858	$13,923	$14,076	$14,130	39,033	42,129	+8%

last three columns as well as all the computations involved in preparing this report are very simple to produce on a PC, and since the PC can retain historical data, adding the current month's costs each month to this report is a very easy task. In fact, by using the PC, the manual preparation of a spread sheet could be eliminated. At the end of each year a separate report showing last year's costs compared to this year's costs, by quarter, should be prepared. Note that Figure 10–1 is a simple report to read. Only the major processing categories are shown and each one is identified by using simple terminology. By examining a spread of many months as shown on this report, it is easy to identify potential profit improvement items or at least questions that should be answered. For example why did DDA and Savings Accounts and ATM costs start rising in March? What caused the dramatic increase in Central Information File costs in May and June? What happened to Miscellaneous Charges in April? Why did Telephone Communications increase a constant $170 per month starting in March?

Microfiche reports. Generally, it is less expensive to have your data center produce reports on microfiche than to print them on paper. The savings is even more dramatic when multiple copies of a report are required. If you haven't focused your attention on the use of microfiche in your bank, it is worth the effort not only from a cost standpoint, but also from a storage point of view. A small room filled with paper reports can be condensed to a drawer filled with microfiche.

SUMMARY

The following is a summary of those points mentioned in this chapter that could individually or in combination save your bank substantial sums of money in data processing costs.

1. For larger banks, the cost of owning and operating their own in-house computer appears favorable as compared to the data center alternative, but there are often administrative headaches attached to any in-house operation.

2. Data centers price their services more attractively to banks that have or are willing to acquire a remote job entry computer system.

3. When choosing a data center, be sure it is a profitable growing company which responds well to bank requests and problems that arise, and is on time providing updated systems that conform to bank regulatory changes.

4. All data centers do not charge the same fees. The variance in fees among data centers can be as high as 50%.

5. Quotes from competing data centers should be obtained each time a current data center's contract is due for renewal.

6. When examining a data center's quotations, be sure you know what is not included in the basic fee quoted.

7. Be alert to monthly hook-up (support) fees for all types of terminals, printers, and controllers, that might be charged as a separate fee by a data center.

8. Be alert to any separate fees charged for regular on-line inquiries and/or CIF on-line inquiries via any type of terminal (teller terminal, CRT, ATM). These separate inquiry fees are common. And the number of inquiries estimated by the data center may be low.

9. Switching from a batch system with a data center to an RJE system will reduce your forms costs dramatically.

10. Be alert to the separate Central Information File (CIF) service fee charged by most data centers.

11. Make sure you know *all* the conversion fees that a data center charges.

12. Be aware of the differences in telephone equipment, telephone line, and telephone installation costs quoted by each competing data center.

13. Spread data center quotations on one sheet of paper so that each item in the quotes can be compared easily.

14. All data centers' fees are negotiable but you have to arm yourself with a sufficient number of quotations to know which fees to negotiate, and of course, you have to be willing to negotiate.

15. Be constantly alert to your MICR items reject rate.

16. Obtain competitive quotes on the purchase of MICR ribbons.

17. Spread your current data center's bills each month so that you can monitor variations easily.

18. Investigate the use of microfiche in place of paper reports wherever possible.

Chapter 11

Reduce Interest Expense

The total interest paid on all forms of interest bearing accounts (NOWs, CDs, Money Market Accounts, Statement Savings, and Passbook Accounts) is, of course, the single largest expense item for every bank. In this age of consumerism, market competitiveness, and deregulation the methods used to compute interest have become complex and often vary even within a bank by type of interest bearing account. In any profit improvement campaign this expense, therefore, should be analyzed fully to find ways to reduce this cost. Interest expense is affected four major ways—the rate, the frequency of compounding, the balance upon which the calculation is applied, and the number of days used in the calculation.

THE RATE

Determining what rate of interest to pay on the various interest bearing accounts offered by banks is complicated and can be better addressed in a book on asset management. What should be noted here, however, is that when making decisions regarding rates or when analyzing the rates currently being paid on accounts for profit improvement purposes, the effect that any change will have on the bottom line should be known. A change of a rate on a certain group of deposit accounts by ¼%, for example, will increase or decrease this expense by $2,500 per year per $1 million of balances or $25,000 per year per $10 million of balances. The rates on certain types of deposit accounts may be tiered (i.e., the more on deposit the higher the rate paid). These tiered rates should also be reviewed for profit improvement purposes, particularly when rates are declining.

Also, when determining or changing rates for specific types of accounts, the rates being paid on other types of accounts should be reviewed to prevent chasing low balance customers into other types of accounts, since opening and closing accounts becomes a needless expense. An example of this occurred during the early days of NOW Accounts. The rate on these accounts was typically the same as passbook savings and customers would close their savings to open a new NOW Account. Banks then began to realize they were chasing low balance customers into the NOW Accounts and soon restricted the NOW Account to high minimum balance requirements. Another example of this chasing effect could occur when Money Market Accounts rates (which are normally pegged to Treasury Bill Rates) drop and go below the regular savings rate. Customers then tend to close their Money Market Accounts and open Regular Savings Accounts.

Also, when determining rates for Regular Saving Accounts a lower than normal rate should he considered for Passbook Savings in order to favor Statement Savings. This would help offset the extra expense involved for teller time in posting interest and in the updating and correcting customers' passbooks.

Finally, it should be mentioned that of all the ways shown in this chapter to reduce interest expense, reducing the interest rate is the most sensitive from a marketing point of view. Customers are accustomed to the fluctuating rates of Certificates of Deposit and Money Market Accounts. But they may resist a significant reduction in passbook or statement savings rates. Being one of the last institutions in your market area to reduce these rates would help to alleviate this problem. Also, when rates are on the rise consideration should be given to having a differentiation of rates between passbook and statement savings accounts.

THE FREQUENCY OF COMPOUNDING

The chart shown below shows a comparison interest costs for a bank per $10 million of balances for each major compounding frequency used by banks today. A simple rate of 5% is used.

Compounding Frequency	*Yield*	*Interest Cost (Per $10 MM Balances)*
Annually (No compounding)	5.00%	$500,000.00
Semi-Annually	5.0625%	$506,250.00
Quarterly	5.0944%	$509,440.00
Monthly	5.1162%	$511,620.00
Daily	5.1267%	$512,670.00
Continuously	5.1271%	$512,710.00

In the above chart a 5% rate was used to calculate the interest costs by frequency periods. For each additional 1% raise in the rate a 20% increase in each interest cost would occur. Also, of course, the interest costs would increase in the same proportion as the balances used were in excess of $10 million. In reviewing the above chart it is interesting to note two things. Once compounding is initiated the first frequency (semi-annually) creates the largest jump in costs ($6,250). From then on the jumps in costs decrease. Secondly, there are only marginal differences in costs as the frequency changes from monthly to daily to continuously. In any event, when contemplating a change in the compounding frequency always calculate the effect of the change on the bottom line for the specific account types being changed.

THE BALANCE

Significant differences in interest costs occur depending on the type of balance used to compute the interest. Since the balance in CDs remains constant, the types of balances discussed in this section refer to all types of interest bearing *accounts* to which deposits and/or withdrawals can be made (NOWs, IRA Accounts, Savings Accounts and Money Market Accounts). Interest can be calculated for the period on the average ledger balances, the average collected balances, the low balances, or under the FIFO or LIFO formulas. In today's interest sensitive environment, however, the low balance and FIFO or LIFO methods are considered archaic and even unfair depending on withdrawal activity. What should be considered, is the practice of paying interest on uncollected balances, since banks do not have the ability to invest these funds. For each $100,000 per day of deposited transit checks to an interest bearing account, a savings of $13.70 per day can be achieved assuming a rate of 5% and the funds are uncollected for one day. On an annual basis this would accumulate to $3,562 ($13.70 × 5 × 52) for each $100,000 of uncollected funds deposited per day. Parenthetically, it should be noted that some banks are not paying interest on uncollected funds deposited into certificates of deposit. In larger banks where deposits per day to savings accounts and CDs are in the millions of dollars, the interest expense saved for the uncollected portion of these deposits would amount to hundreds of thousands of dollars annually.

360 VERSUS 365 DAYS

Before deregulation banks looked for ways to increase the yield on savings accounts and certificates of deposits to compete with nonbank financial institutions. As a result the 360-day year was created which was based on a flat 30-day month for each month of the year. Banks would calculate the interest on these accounts as follows: $10,000 × 5% = $500.00 ÷ 360 days × 365 days = $506.94 and so the yield increased on a simple rate of 5% to 5.0694%. Now that deregulation has been accomplished some banks may still be using this method without having consciously considered changing it back to a 365-day basis. When analyzing this, all types of savings accounts and CDs should be reviewed to determine the method used to compute interest on each type. You could discover that the way of computing this may differ by type of account. In any event, the difference in interest expense per $10 million of balances (assuming a simple rate of 5.25%) is $7,291.65 per year. For balances of $100 million the difference would of course, be ten times this amount. Higher interest rates would also increase this difference.

The top half of Figure 11–1 summarizes in graphic form the various methods of calculating and compounding interest. It represents the only known published comparison of the yield effect of varying compounding methods coupled with varying interest calculation methods for varying days of interest. In effect it represents a total of 42 comparisons—7 comparisons for 6 different rates. To further illustrate the yield differences, the bottom half of Figure 11–1 shows the dollar amount of *additional* annual interest expense as compared to a simple 365-day basis interest calculation per $10,000,000 of deposits. For example, interest expense for a 5% rate calculated on a simple basis for a 365-day year on $10,000,000 of deposits without any compounding would be $500,000. If this 5% rate was computed on an actual over 360-day basis, the interest expense would be $506,900 resulting in an additional expense of $6,900. This is shown in the first figure in the second column of the lower half of the chart. Note that in all the headings for the columns in Figure 11–1 the word "actual" means that in calculating the interest the actual number of days in the year (365 or 366) would be used depending on the year in which the calculation was made. In all the calculations in Figure 11–1, 365 was used for all the methods labeled "actual"/365 or "actual"/360.

From reviewing Figure 11–1 the following important observations and conclusions should be made:

Observations

1. The higher the rate the greater the difference in yield in both the compounding method and in the basis days used. This is an interesting and often overlooked mathematical phenomenon that can cost a bank additional interest expense. For example, this is more dramatically shown in the column labeled "monthly compounding actual/360." Upon reviewing the yield figures in this column for a 6% interest rate, the yield is 6.255%. It would seem logical then that the yield for a 8% rate would be two percentage points higher or 8.255% but it isn't. The yield is 8.419% – 16.4 basis points higher. Similarly, when comparing 8% and 10% yields in this column (8.419% versus 10.623%), the difference is not 16.4 basis points but rather 20.4 basis points. This phenomenon appears in all columns as the basic interest rate increases.
2. Monthly compounding on a 360-day basis produces the highest expense.
3. Quarterly compounding on a 360-day basis produces a higher interest expense than continuous compounding on a 365-day basis.

Conclusions

1. As was mentioned earlier in this chapter, avoid using 360-day calculation methods.
2. Avoid compounding of any type if possible. Some banks don't even compound annually anymore on long-term certificates of deposit. This brings up another point. Although not shown on Figure 11–1, there is a definite effect of even compounding annually for long-term certificates of deposit. For example, a five-year $100,000 certificate of deposit with a 6.5% interest rate

Figure 11–1

ANNUAL YIELDS FOR VARIOUS INTEREST CALCULATION METHODS

Simple Actual/365	*Simple Actual/360*	*Quarterly Compounding Actual/365*	*Quarterly Compounding Actual/360*	*Monthly Compounding Actual/365*	*Monthly Compounding Actual/360*	*Continuous Compounding Actual/365*
5%	5.069%	5.094%	5.166%	5.116%	5.188%	5.127%
6%	6.083%	6.136%	6.224%	6.167%	6.255%	6.183%
7%	7.097%	7.186%	7.288%	7.229%	7.332%	7.250%
8%	8.111%	8.243%	8.361%	8.300%	8.419%	8.328%
9%	9.125%	9.308%	9.442%	9.380%	9.516%	9.417%
10%	10.139%	10.381%	10.531%	10.471%	10.623%	10.517%

ADDITIONAL ANNUAL INTEREST EXPENSE AS COMPARED TO SIMPLE INTEREST (365-DAY BASIS) PER $10,000,000 OF DEPOSITS

	Simple Actual/360	*Quarterly Compounding Actual/365*	*Quarterly Compounding Actual/360*	*Monthly Compounding Actual/365*	*Monthly Compounding Actual/360*	*Continuous Compounding Actual/365*
5%	$ 6,900	$ 9,400	$16,600	$11,600	$18,800	$12,700
6%	8,300	13,600	22,400	16,700	25,500	18,300
7%	9,700	18,600	28,800	22,900	33,200	25,000
8%	11,100	24,300	36,100	30,000	41,900	32,800
9%	12,500	30,800	44,200	38,000	51,600	41,700
10%	13,900	38,100	53,100	47,100	62,300	51,700

without any compounding (including annual compounding) will generate interest expense of $6,500 per year × 5 years or $32,500 for the whole term of the CD. If the simple annual interest for this CD is allowed to compound, the total interest expense for the five-year period would be $37,008.66. And the longer the term the worse it gets. If this same certificate was set up to compound more often than annually over the five-year period, the effect would be much higher than the annual compounding effect. If for marketing purposes it is difficult to avoid annual compounding, reduce the basic rate sufficiently to offset the annual compounding effect and also consider quoting (laws permitting) the overall yield effect of the annual compounding over the five-year period. In the above example of annual compounding yielding $37,008.66 of interest, the overall yield for the five-year period would be $37,008.66 ÷ 5 = $7,401.73 ÷ $100,000 = 7.4%. Another way to avoid annual compounding for long-term CDs is to automatically disburse the interest each year.

3. Do you really know what the interest calculations and compounding methods are for *all* your interest bearing type of accounts? It is suggested that you spread this information on a report format. Across the top show columns for account types, total balances by type, rate of interest, compounding frequency, basis day method, yield, and type of balances upon which the calculations made (average ledger, average collected, etc.). Then list all the types of interest bearing accounts in the bank such as NOWs, Super NOWs, passbook and statement savings, special IRA savings accounts, certificates of deposit *by maturity category* and each tier on money market savings accounts. Then when completing all the information, double check with your data processor to make sure they are computing the interest on all the account type categories the way you think they are. Reviewing a report like this is bound to produce savings in interest expense, because if you've never done this before, something to your disadvantage always surfaces.
4. When comparing your interest rates with other institutions don't assume that their high rate in one category of CDs is indicative of all CD categories. Also, inquire about their compounding frequencies and calculating methods and, therefore, their yields.

SUMMARY

This chapter introduces several ways to increase profits by reducing interest expense. All of these ways can be used separately, but for those banks that can and that choose to use many of them the combination effect can be quite dramatic in increasing profits in this area.

1. When reviewing rates know what effect any contemplated change will have on the bottom line.
2. When changing rates on specific account types, analyze those account types that are not being changed in order to avoid any possible chasing effect that might occur.
3. Always review any tiered rates particularly in a declining rate market.
4. Consider offering a lower than normal rate for Passbook Savings and offer the normal rate for Statement Savings only.
5. When reviewing the frequency of compounding for any specific account types always know the effect of any contemplated change on the bottom line.
6. Consider only paying interest on collected balances for all types of interest bearing accounts including CDs.
7. Review all account types to determine if they are on a 365-day interest calculation basis, and if they are not, change them.
8. Be aware that the higher the rate of interest to be paid the greater the difference in yield in both the compounding method and in the basis days used per Figure 11–1.
9. Avoid compounding of any type particularly on long-term CDs (including, if possible, annual compounding).
10. Avoid compounding annually on long-term CDs by disbursing the interest each year.
11. Prepare a report showing all factors regarding interest payment calculations for each account type in the bank.

Chapter 12

Profit Improvement in Purchasing

In most banks, the purchasing function is a major expense category that ranks third after interest and personnel expenses or fourth after data processing expenses, depending on the bank. Therefore it is an important area to review in every bank's profit improvement campaign. Because the purchasing function covers many areas such as capital assets (furniture, office equipment), forms, and stationery type items, these items appear as expenses in different places in a bank's general ledger. For example, capital assets appear under depreciation expense categories, and forms and stationery items appear under a stationery and supplies expense category. This general ledger segregation of costs could often hide the importance of identifying this function as a major expense area to consider in any profit improvement campaign. In many banks, the purchasing person is responsible for purchasing routine capital assets (clerical desks and chairs, file cabinets, typewriters, adding machines, and small copying machines typically costing under $1,000 per item), the hundreds of different types of forms used in the bank, and all the stationery and supply items. The person in charge of this function could easily be buying $70,000 worth of items per year for each $100 million of your bank's assets. So if your bank's assets are $200 million or $300 million, this person could be buying $140,000 and $210,000 worth of items respectively per year. Even if a concentrated effort in reducing expenses in this area only yielded a 10% to 15% reduction, this effort could reduce expenses by several thousands of dollars per year.

CENTRALIZE THE PURCHASING FUNCTION

Regardless of the size of the bank, the purchasing function should be under the control of one person. Allowing several officers and department heads, even though they may have very responsible positions, to do their own purchasing often results in lack of uniformity within the bank, unfairness, inability to obtain quantity discounts, and needless additional expense due to improper vendor selection.

The purchasing function, even though a part-time function in smaller banks, requires expertise, consistency in vendor selection and in correct buying techniques, attention to detail, and the ability to be cost conscious and to control inventory. It therefore requires one person who has these qualifications who can apply these abilities towards every type of item purchased. Fragmenting the management of this function produces needless expense and confusion.

VENDOR RELATIONSHIPS

A critical factor in the purchasing function is the development of a list of good vendors. Most vendors, although they may claim otherwise, specialize in certain products and will be very cost competitive in these products. They may carry other products, but if they do, it is only as a convenience for their customers. For example, stationery and supply vendors may be able to provide certain specialty forms or have access to furniture but their prices are higher for these items because they have difficulty competing with those vendors who specialize in printing these forms or in selling furniture. A good purchasing person will continually shop the marketplace for new vendors and not rely on the old standbys out of laziness or out of some sort of loyalty. The bidding policy of a bank often mandates the need to shop around for vendors. A good rule of thumb for bidding is if the item(s) being purchased—several typewriters, adding machines, or a large quantity of a certain form, for example—will cost more than $1,000, bids from at least two or three vendors should be obtained. For items that will cost several thousand dollars some banks require bids from four or five vendors. The bidding process not only produces the best price but also identifies which vendors can produce or supply which products at the best price. Just because one vendor looses one bid for a certain product does not mean that this vendor will not be competitive on all other types of products. Also, vendors sometimes change their emphasis on selling certain products. In any event, the bidding process, whether formal through written quotations for expensive items or by verbal quotations on the telephone, will produce a list of reliable vendors to be used depending on the item(s) to be purchased. When obtaining bids be sure each vendor is bidding on the same products or combination of products, the same quantity of these products and the freight for transporting these products to your warehouse. The bidding process also tends to keep vendors "honest." Vendors can charge whatever they think they can get away with unless there is a check. The bidding process provides that check. It requires them to "sharpen their pencil" whenever competition is present.

It is dangerous to relax professional standards and become too friendly with vendors. Vendors often like to treat buyers well with free or special deals on personal gifts, frequent free lunches and dinners, tickets to sporting or other recreational events, or personal invitations to vendors homes. Beware of these activities. There are no "free lunches." Engaging in these activities often produces laxity on the part of the recipient of these favors (the buyer) and in turn allows the vendor to develop a psychological hold over the buyer to be used in future purchases.

STORAGE

A rule of thumb for storage and obsolescence purposes, is the quantity purchased for any form should be no more than a year's supply. A year's supply of some forms for a bank such as drive-in envelopes, statement envelopes, checking and savings statements, adding machine rolls, etc., can take up a lot of space and storage space in some banks is at a minimum. Some vendors offer storage facilities for items purchased from them with release of the items from storage at regular intervals as needed. Often this service is mentioned by the vendor as a "free service," but it usually is not. Ask for prices with and without the storage. You will find that often their prices with and without storage will differ and this difference could be substantial enough to more than pay for public warehousing in your area.

INVENTORY CONTROL

Another critical factor in the purchasing function is knowing what quantity to buy of a certain item. It is easy to know how many desks or typewriters you need at a certain time, but knowing how many #10 window envelopes or #4 pencils your bank uses in a year is not easy to determine without proper records. This introduces the subject of inventory control. With hundreds of different forms and hundreds of stationery items being used in banks today, coupled with the many departments and branches that are drawing against the main supply of these items, determining yearly usage figures, which in turn determines the quantity to be purchased of a given item, can become a clerical nightmare. Basically, there are three ways banks use to determine usages—the educated guess, a manual card system, and an automated system. The educated guess system relies on the knowledge of the buyer, some research of past orders, and frequent physical inventories. The manual card system requires the posting of the quantity of each item ordered by each branch and department, each time it is ordered, to a card specifically designated for each type of item in storage. Considering the hundreds of items, the hundreds of cards required, and hundreds of times each item is ordered by the branches and departments each year, this can become a very labor intensive system and subject to a multitude of clerical errors. Because the educated guess system is highly unreliable and the manual card system is labor intensive and subject to a high degree of clerical error, banks are looking more and more toward automating their inventory control system, particularly for forms, through the use of the personal computer. There are PC programs available in the marketplace which will enable a bank to control the inventory of items and more reliably determine when items will run out of supply, and therefore know what quantities should be purchased. Moreover these automated systems allow a bank to easily group forms together into size categories so that they can be ordered at the same time which substantially reduces the cost of each type of form ordered. The subject of grouping forms is covered in more detail later in this chapter. Other advantages of an automated system include—reducing the risk of running out of forms, reducing the frequency of physical inventories, and providing usage reports by cost centers (branches and departments). There are some initial costs involved in automating a system, however, such as the cost of the program, the cost of the PC and the weeks of preparation time required to convert from a manual system. For banks, particularly those over $300 million in asset size, a good automated system will pay for itself in a few years by providing the bottom line advantages shown above.

STOCKLESS INVENTORY

To further reduce the clerical effort in either an automated system or a manual system, some national vendors and even some local vendors located in large metropolitan areas offer stockless inventory systems for stationery and supply type items (pencils, pads of paper, staples, rubber bands, etc.). These stockless inventory systems offer direct ordering from a branch or department (through the purchasing department) directly to the vendor. The vendor in turn fills the order each week or biweekly and will often deliver the order directly to the cost center (branch or department). Also, as a by-product of this system the vendor provides the bank with printed reports of usages and costs of items by cost center. This system eliminates the need for purchasing to determine quantities to be bought and stored because the cost centers order directly from the vendor. The purchasing department, however, controls the ordering by reviewing the orders before they are sent to the vendor and by reviewing the periodic cost center reports received from the vendor. Vendors charge for this service but these charges are usually less than the costs of tying up the bank's funds in inventory, storing items, preparing and delivering orders, and internally determining usages for these hundreds of items. Other advantages are that it is almost impossible to run out of supplies, and branches and departments can be easily limited to certain types of items that can be ordered through the use of a limited catalog which reduces the possibility of ordering expensive specialty items.

REDUCING THE COST OF BANK FORMS

Banks traditionally purchase a multitude of different forms, some are used each month by the thousands, and some are only used occasionally during the month. In the larger banks, forms purchasing is done by a specialist who knows the best ways to cost effectively purchase forms. In the thousands of smaller banks, however, this function is usually delegated to an employee who has little training in this area, and this function is only a part of this employee's many daily duties. This section will cover several ways to reduce this expense which can be used easily by any employee in any bank regardless of his or her expertise in this area. Although this section is titled forms cost, the word "forms" relates to all printed matter that a bank may purchase including marketing brochures and annual reports. Also, even though this section is devoted to the purchasing of paper related products, some of the principles mentioned will apply to non-paper supplies such as pens, pencils, paper clips, etc.

The cost of forms is directly related to a number of different factors. These factors are for the most part separate from one another in the sense that they each provide ways to reduce this expense, but when they are considered together the savings can even be more dramatic.

The cost of forms are related to the following basic factors:

1. Quality
2. Quantity
3. Design
4. Source

Quality. Basically this refers to two areas—type of paper being used and the use of color. Paper comes in a variety of thicknesses. The thicker the paper the more expensive the form. Thickness of paper in the printing business is measured by weight (pounds per 1,000 sheets of paper) 20 lb. paper means that 1,000 8½" × 11" sheets of this paper weighs 20 lbs. To use paper three times the weight of 20 lb. paper (60 lb. paper) does not increase the cost three times. The difference in cost is only about 25% not 300%. Paper thickness (weight), therefore is only a significant cost factor when many thousands of pieces of paper are involved. If heavy paper stock is to be used on a mail out form (statement stuffer, special marketing brochure, or annual report) care should be used not to use paper stock that is too heavy. This increases the postage on the piece to be mailed. Even though only a few thousand of these forms are printed and the cost of the paper is insignificant, the cost of the postage could skyrocket the overall cost of using the form.

Introducing a color other than black on a printed piece is always more expensive. Colored paper or the use of colored ink on white paper could increase the cost of a form 10% to 20%, and using four color processing could increase the cost of printing by 400%! So when discussing with your printer the use of color on a form to be ordered, always obtain the differences in cost for the use of color compared to using black. An alternative and inexpensive use of color is a process known as tinting.

Any color (including black) can be printed in shades. Thus a basic form or a marketing piece can be made more attractive by shading part of the form. Black can be shaded in a number of degrees from jet black to a light gray on one piece of paper. And this shading process adds little if anything to the cost of printing the form.

Quantity. Forms printers will charge a flat charge for setting up a new form and a running charge for the actual printing of the form. The flat charge includes the costs for design, typesetting, plates, die cuts, carbons, perforations, and collating. The running charge includes the actual printing and the paper costs. Upon reordering this same form from the same printer the cost is reduced because some of the flat charges are not required.

The aforementioned explains why it costs less per form printed to order forms in larger quantities. The flat charges usually cost the same whether you order 1,000 or 1,000,000 of the same form. And there are also some economies in the actual printing (running) of a larger quantity of the same form at one time. Costs for forms are quoted at a price per thousand pieces, and this price usually includes both the flat and running charges. This price per thousand is reduced for each 5,000 pieces printed. The larger the quantity ordered, therefore, the less expensive the cost per thousand forms and therefore the cost per form.

Even though you can save money ordering larger quantities of a form, it is important to consider the use of a form. Obviously if a bank only uses 5,000 of one form per year, it is foolish to order 25,000 copies just for the quantity price break. As mentioned before the rule of thumb is never order more than a year's supply of a particular form. There are four basic reasons for this: obsolescence, deterioration, cost of money, and storage. Because of the changes in banking regulations and data processing techniques many bank forms become obsolete, often in a matter of months. There is no point, therefore, in obtaining a good quantity price for a form and then throwing away half the forms because they can no longer be used!

Forms can physically deteriorate when they get too old. For example, the glue on envelopes can deteriorate and become less effective, and/or if they become damp can begin to stick to one another. Paper could yellow when it is stored too long thus making it useless. Another example of deterioration, related to the purchasing of supplies, is the true story of a banker who once purchased 30,000 ball point pens at a very low cost per pen. The only problem was that the bank only used 1,000 of these pens per year and the pens dried up in two years! Also, the cost of money has to be considered in purchasing larger quantities of forms, particularly if the quantity will last more than a year. To tie up funds in a large forms inventory can be expensive.

Design. Clerical productivity and size should be two interrelated cost considerations when deciding on design. In these days of high salary expenses it pays to make sure that forms are designed to minimize the time it takes for a clerk to complete and handle these forms. For example, most forms used in a bank are completed by a typist, but how many of them were designed to be used in a typewriter? The principal weakness of many of these forms is that the printing is not line-spaced for use in a typewriter and so the typist has to continually adjust the roller to conform to the printed lines in order to complete the blanks. Hundreds of these forms are typed each day and the time wasted adjusting the typewriter repeatedly for each form, form after form, day after day, can mean thousands of wasted clerical hours per year. Many customer forms are not designed to fit into window envelopes and so additional time is required to type an envelope. Other forms designed for a window envelope require folding to fit it into the envelope—another clerical operation—and/or are designed to fit into an odd-size window envelope thus creating an additional envelope expense. Some notifications to customers are prepared on letter size paper in letter form (usually duplicated on copying machines) and the blanks are typed (usually on a typewriter that is different in type style from the type on the letter itself. It would be better and more professional if the letter was changed to the right size printed form for insertion (without folding) into a window envelope.

Multiplicity should also be considered when choosing a design for a form. How many functions in a bank require the completion of many forms when one multipart form would suffice? The new account signature card is an example of an inefficient form. Banks often require the completion of more than one signature card when a person opens a new account. And the clerk or the customer has to complete two or three of these cards for one account. It would be much easier to have a multipart form for signature cards with carbons and thus eliminate the need for either the customer or the bank employee to complete more than one card for the account opening. Allied to the use of a multipart signature card is the use of a general signature card for all accounts rather than use a distinctive card for each type of account opened. Many banks still use a different signature card for each type of savings and checking account. And often these cards are different sizes. This can be expensive because of the printing plates required, the nonconforming sizes, and the resultant loss of economies in quantity purchases.

The way a multipart form is designed to issue certificates of deposit can reduce labor costs. A CD can be designed in multiparts to incorporate the CD, the maturity notice, advices of debits and credits, and the bank's copy of the CD. Such a form may be designed in a way that only requires typing the CD information once and this information is recorded in its proper place on each copy of the form through the use of carbons. Each copy of this form is designed differently to show only pertinent information with regard to that copy. All of the information is typed on the first copy but through design only some of the information is visible on the other parts. The result of this type of design is the elimination of typing five or six separate forms for each CD. In most banks today issuing and reissuing CDs, paying interest, and advising customers about CD transactions are time consuming clerical functions.

The above suggestions introduced the use of multipart forms to reduce clerical typing costs. Multipart forms are, of course, more expensive than one part forms but they are not more expensive in direct relationship to the number of parts—i.e., a two part form does not cost twice as much as a one part form, and a three part form does not cost three times as much as a one part form (a single form without carbons). The reason for this is that the flat charge, which is the most expensive cost of the form, does not increase in the same proportion as the number of parts increase. The following example will make this clearer. Suppose you are ordering a 3½" × 8½" multipart form with carbons. The cost per thousand (if one thousand of these forms are ordered) for this form for the number of parts ordered could be as follows:

Number of Parts Ordered (one thousand forms)

	1 Part	*2 Part*	*3 Part*	*4 Part*	*5 Part*	*6 Part*
Flat charge	$300.00	$345.00	$375.00	$405.00	$435.00	$465.00
Running charge	3.00	8.50	12.75	17.25	22.00	26.50
Total price	$303.00	$353.50	$387.75	$422.25	$457.00	$491.50
OR						
The cost per form (÷ 1,000)=	$ .30	$ .35	$ .39	$ .42	$ .46	$ .49

To carry the above example a step further and to illustrate why one obtains a price break when more than one thousand of the same form are ordered at the same time, the figures shown below show the price per thousand if five thousand forms are ordered.

Number of Parts Ordered (five thousand forms)

	1 Part	*2 Part*	*3 Part*	*4 Part*	*5 Part*	*6 Part*
Flat charge	$300.00	$345.00	$375.00	$405.00	$435.00	$465.00
Running charge for 5M	15.00	42.50	63.75	86.25	110.00	132.50
Total price for 5M forms	$315.00	$387.50	$438.75	$491.25	$545.00	$597.50
OR						
The price per M (÷ 5)=	$ 63.00	$ 77.50	$ 87.75	$ 98.25	$109.00	$119.50
OR						

Number of Parts Ordered (five thousand forms)

	1 Part	*2 Part*	*3 Part*	*4 Part*	*5 Part*	*6 Part*
The price per form (÷ 1000)	$ .06	$ .08	$ .09	$ .10	$ .11	$ .12

Note that in computing the above costs, the flat charge remains the same and only the running charge is five times the amount shown in the 1000 quantity example. The bottom line in all this is that the cost per thousand forms if five thousand forms are ordered is substantially lower than if only one thousand forms are ordered. For example, if you ordered five thousand three part forms the cost per thousand forms would be $87.75 compared to $387.75 for ordering only one thousand forms. To put it another way, the total cost to your bank for ordering five thousand of these three part forms would be $438.75 compared to $387.75 if only one thousand of these three part forms were ordered. Can you imagine the price per thousand if 100,000 of these three part forms were ordered!

The other major consideration regarding the design of a form is its size. For printing purposes paper is manufactured in large rolls and in sheets. Any form you design should conform to standard sizes that have been developed by the printing industry. This reduces the possibility of wasting paper and the need for additional press runs during the actual printing process—both of which would add considerable cost to the overall printing of the forms. There are many standard sizes (both in the width and length of the form) from which to choose. Your printer will gladly advise you about which standard size is appropriate for the type of form to be printed.

There is another size factor that is very important. In fact it is so important from a cost perspective that it overshadows any other factor so far mentioned. This factor is called grouping. Grouping is that process whereby a bank will manage its inventory of a variety of forms of *the same size* in such a way so they all can be grouped together to be printed at the same time. Each form may have a different design, color, printed matter, number of parts, etc., but they are all *the same size.* There are several types of forms used in banking that easily can be grouped together. One type of form to group is official checks: cashiers checks, money orders, expense checks, trust checks, dividend checks. Other groups of forms by size could be cash in and cash out tickets grouped with deposit receipts, general ledger debits and credits grouped with various multipart customer debit and credit advices *and* savings withdrawal tickets; and certain computer forms. Remember it doesn't matter for what purpose the form is to be used or what is printed on it or even whether or not it has multiparts. All that matters is that each form in the group is *the same size.* How cost effective is the printing of several forms of the same size at the same time? It is extremely cost effective as the following example will indicate.

Let us assume that a particular bank's use of official checks per year is as follows:

Cashier's checks – 25,000
Money orders – 50,000
Expense checks – 5,000
Dividend checks – 5,000

Also assume this bank orders these checks from a printer once a year (a year's supply) and all of these checks are the same size. If this bank ordered each of the above types of checks at a different time during the year, the costs for having these checks printed separately would be as follows. For simplicity it is assumed that all checks are 3½" × 8½" and all checks are to be printed in 3 parts.

	Flat charge	*Running charge*	*Total cost*
Cashier's checks (25M)	$375.00	$318.75	$683.75
Money orders (50M)	$375.00	$637.50	$1,012.50
Expense checks (5M)	$375.00	$63.75	$438.75
Dividend checks (5M)	$375.00	$63.75	$438.75
Total quantity 85M		*Total cost*	$2,573.75

Aggregate cost per M = $30.28
($2,573.75 ÷ 85)

Now if this same bank managed its official check inventory so that all of the different types of official checks came due for reorder at the same time and all of the checks were ordered at the same time, the costs would be:

	Flat charge	*Running charge*	*Total cost*
Cashier's checks (25M)	$375.00	$318.75	$ 683.75
Money orders (50M)	0	637.50	637.50
Expense checks (5M)	0	63.75	63.75
Dividend checks (5M)	0	63.75	63.75
Total quantity 85M		*Total cost*	$1,448.75
		Minus 10% quantity discount	144.87
		Net cost	$1,903.88

Aggregate cost per M = $15.34
($1,303.88 ÷ 85)

Note that in the second example the flat charge was only charged once. The result is a total cost savings of $1,125.00 (3 × $375.00 or $2,573.75 – $1,448.75). The 10% quantity discount shown is an added cost savings for the total quantities shown, because printers will usually give this percentage (or more) discount on 200,000 or more pieces of paper printed at the same time. In this one order there were 255,000 pieces of paper printed (85,000 forms × 3 parts to a form). Adding the flat charge savings of $1,125 to the quantity discount savings of $144.87, the total savings for ordering all these forms at the same time was $1,269.87—and this savings was just for ordering all official checks at the same time. The savings multiplies, of course, as other forms are group ordered. The bottom line to all this is that it is possible, by using this method of group ordering, to reduce your forms cost by almost 50%! It pays, therefore, to design as many forms as possible into only a few basic sizes, manage their inventory, and group order them. Unfortunately many printers, and particularly the salesmen representing printers, will not mention this method of ordering forms because it means decreases in their sales and commissions, and so many bankers are not familiar with this type of ordering.

Source. The final factor regarding the cost of forms is the choice of a printer. All printers do not charge the same price. There are many reasons for this: some do not do a quantity business, some only want to print certain specialized forms, their overhead costs are different, or their printing equipment is designed to handle only certain size or types of forms efficiently. Quotes from several printers should be obtained on any large orders. How you define large will depend on the size of your bank but $1,000 or more is a place to start.

Some banks, particularly those located in a small community like to use the services of their local printer; and for forms ordered in quantities of 1,000 or less, there is usually little or no cost savings associated with using an "outsider." But for larger orders one should at least obtain quotes and know if the local printer is reasonably competitive. When you are going to order new forms from a local printer, however, be sure you have designed the form as simply as possible. It should be easy for a typesetter to understand, because these printers charge by the hour (as high as $50.00 per hour) for typesetting the form and a complex form can take several hours to typeset. There may be an additional small flat or setup charge and the total cost of the form could be very expensive.

Some forms used in a bank, particularly those not used very often, can be designed and typed on a standard sheet of paper (8½" × 11" or other standard size) and brought to a printer or better yet to a speedy printer, for duplication. Since there is no typesetting involved the cost of reproducing is minimal. The form may even be small enough to be typed two or three times on the same standard size paper thereby reducing paper costs. Also, if you only need a few hundred copies of a form don't be afraid of duplicating them on your own copying machine at a cost of $.02 or $.03 per copy. On 100 or 200 forms no printer can match that price.

SUMMARY

The purchasing function in banks is a major expense category and therefore an important function to investigate in any profit improvement campaign. This chapter identified 20 ways to improve profits in the purchasing function.

1. Make the purchasing function one person's responsibility. Do not allow other department heads, branch managers, officers or employees to purchase items.
2. Develop lists of vendors to be used for items to be purchased. Do not rely on one or two vendors for all types of items.
3. Require bids for all orders of $1,000 or more.

4. Remember that vendors do specialize in the products they offer.

5. Beware of vendors who offer frequent "free" gifts, lunches, outings, etc.

6. Do not order more than a year's supply of any product.

7. If storage space is at a premium, investigate a local public warehouse before using the storage facilities of a vendor.

8. Consider using an automated inventory control system.

9. If available in your area, consider using a vendor's stockless inventory system for stationery and supply type items.

10. Although the cost of using heavyweight paper for forms or brochures is not significant if the form is printed in small quantities, the possible increase in postage cost could skyrocket the overall cost.

11. Know the cost of using color on a form (other than black on white).

12. Substitute tinting for the extensive use of color.

13. The price per thousand forms ordered reduces substantially as the quantity of forms ordered is increased.

14. Design forms so that they will line up properly in a typewriter and will fit without folding into a standard size window envelope.

15. Use multipart carbonized forms rather than a number of single parts which require individual typing.

16. Design forms to conform to standard sizes.

17. Order all forms of the same size at the same time.

18. Obtain quotes for large form orders. All printers do not charge the same prices.

19. When ordering forms from a local printer keep the form uncomplicated to minimize typesetting costs.

20. Forms used in small quantities are often less expensive to produce if designed and typed by a bank typist and duplicated by a speedy printer or with your own copying machine.

Chapter 13

Reduce Postage and Telephone Expenses

This chapter covers two major categories of costs—communicating by mail and via the telephone. Both of these expenses are growing, not only because of the rising basic costs charged by the U.S. Postal Department and the telephone utility companies, but also because of the increased use of these communication tools due to the expanding range of financial services offered by banks and the increases in the level of sophistication of banks' internal communication networks. As new types of savings, checking, investment, loan, and automated teller-type services are offered by banks a variety of marketing brochures, advices, statements, and plastic cards are mailed to customers. Telephone inquiries about these services are increasing and the banks' internal communications networks are being improved to answer these questions more efficiently. This is being made easier by a variety of in-bank communication terminals connected on-line via telephone lines and modems to centralized computer systems. All this only accents the need for bankers to be more alert to ways of reducing these expenses.

POSTAGE EXPENSE

As we all know, postage in banks today is a sizable expense item. Banks mail out monthly checking account statements, quarterly savings account statements, a multitude of advices, marketing pieces, and at the end of the year thousands of 1099s—all in addition to the normal type of business mail. And about 97% of this mail is sent first class. How much mail is sent out by a bank depends on the size of the bank. If you do not know how much your bank sends out each year, you should find out. You will be amazed at the quantity. As a very rough rule of thumb, a bank sends out approximately 3,000 pieces of mail per million dollars of assets per year! So if your bank has assets of $100 million you probably sent out 300,000 pieces of mail each year and 97% of that goes out first class. If you are sending all of this mail at the regular current rate of $.25 per piece for less than one ounce, you're spending approximately $75,000 a year—or $750 per million dollars of assets.

The following is a description of eleven ways that are currently being used by banks to reduce postage expense. You will note that almost all of these ways are centered upon two major concepts—to reduce the postage per piece of mail sent out and to reduce the number of pieces mailed.

1. *Presorting mail by zip code.* Many banks are sorting their first class mail by zip code before delivering it to the post office because of the current $.04 reduction in postage allowed per presorted piece ($.21 rather than $.25). The mail still goes out first class and often arrives at its destination sooner because it can be processed faster through the post office. If you read the posting regulations and requirements about presorting, you could get discouraged because it appears complicated, but it really is not once you get used to it. The best way to start this project is to ask your postmaster to explain the presorting procedures to your mail department employees. The post office will be very helpful because they would prefer to receive the mail presorted, particularly from a bank, because of its volume, and because it is less mail the postal employees will have to sort. As mentioned before, there are regulations regarding presorting that must be followed. There are two volume regulations that could restrict a smaller bank from presorting on an everyday basis: each mailing (defined as each time you go to the post office to deliver mail) must have at least 500 presorted pieces total; and each zip code sort must

have 10 or more presorted pieces. A zip code sort means that all the 10 or more pieces of mail in the sort must have the exact same five digit zip code. For example, if most of your bank's mail is addressed to four different zip codes in your area, and you presort, each of the four sorts must have 10 pieces of mail in the bundle and all the pieces in all four bundles must total 500 pieces or more. Smaller banks may not have 500 pieces of mail each day and could not presort except on heavy statement mailing days. How profitable is presorting? To use our $100 million bank example, with 300,000 pieces of mail each year and considering 97% of this mail is first class, then 291,000 pieces are sent first class. But how much of this can be realistically presorted? Conservatively speaking a bank should be able to sort about 65% of its first class pieces or, in our example, 189,150 (.65 × 291,000). At a savings of $.04 per piece, the annual savings in postage would be $7,566.

2. *Odd size mailings.* Beware of special mailings of odd size envelopes designed by advertising agencies for marketing mailing pieces. The odd size could not only increase the first class postage but also preclude each piece from being presorted (there are some size limitations to the pieces to be presorted) resulting in a twofold waste of postage.
3. *Bulk rate.* Consider sending some of those marketing pieces at a bulk rate, particularly if you are sending out a massive mailing, and the exact timing of their delivery is not critical. The bulk mail rate is almost half the normal first class rate. Note that the post office will not forward or "return to sender" any bulk mail with an incorrect address.
4. *Mailing of advices.* Each year a bank mails out thousands of advices of debits and credits to customer's accounts. Many of these advices are generated because of customers' requests for routine debit and credit transactions to their accounts such as crediting CD interest to an account, crediting direct deposits to an account (Social Security payments, payroll deposits), debiting utility bill insurance premiums and loan payments, or preauthorized scheduled transfer of funds from a checking account to a savings account (money market savings, regular savings, IRA). Many banks have discontinued the practice of mailing out several of these advices, particularly if the customer receives a statement each month for the account being automatically debited

or credited. Considering the thousands of these forms prepared each year by a bank, and the associated postage, envelope cost, and the data processing or labor cost to prepare the form, the potential savings by not mailing these forms or even mailing fewer of them is substantial. Some banks do not send out advices on direct deposit of Social Security payments, for example, which is a major savings to these banks. It is worth while for the bank to provide a guarantee of payment which permits customers to draw on these funds on the third of the month regardless of whether or not the payment has been automatically credited to the account. Note: Federal Reserve Bank's Regulation E, concerning notices to customers for transactions to accounts made by means of electronic funds transfer such as Social Security payments, payroll deposits, utility bill, and insurance premium payments, requires other forms of communication to customers if notices are not mailed. Any bank seriously considering ways to reduce its postage expense should carefully review each type of notice mentioned above to see what notices could be eliminated. Remember that the total savings of all expenses for the preparation and mailing of any form is probably about twice the amount of the postage saved.

5. *Mail deposit postage.* For some banks paying postage for mail deposits is very expensive. Bankers are often reluctant to discontinue the practice of providing postage paid envelopes because they don't want to alienate any customer who is using them to deposit money—deposits being the basic reason why banks exist. And mail deposits can be easier and less expensive to process than deposits made directly to a lobby teller. But even considering all this, some banks have eliminated this expense. After much discussion we decided to do this in a $50 million bank several years ago. The consequences were about five customer complaints, no noticeable reduction in the use of this service, and a savings of $10,000 per year in postage expense—and this was at a time when postal rates were almost half the present rates.
6. *Combined statements.* Encourage customers to open or to switch to a statement savings account rather than use a passbook account, and then encourage them to accept a savings account statement combined with a checking account statement. You will

save all that postage for mailing out the quarterly savings statements and you will be encouraging customers to use multiple services. You will also reduce the teller staffing expense required to maintain passbook accounts.

7. *Forwarding addresses.* Check to see if your bank has requested the post office to return the mail that has a forwarding address to your bank with a notation of the new address rather than forward it. This is done by banks in an effort to have correct addresses on their files. The problem with this procedure is that you pay double postage on the piece — once for the original mailing and a second time when mailing out the piece with the new address — and in addition, the post office charges you a $.30 fee for supplying you with the new address. Considering how mobile customers are today, this can be a very expensive procedure.
8. *Multiple 1099 mailings.* If your bank is on an automated central information file, your data processing company (or department) should be able to provide you with 1099 interest information for multiple same name savings accounts on one form for mailing to customers at the end of the year. Since many customers have more than one savings account and/or CD, this procedure would save you thousands of dollars each year in 1099 postage — let alone the labor savings.
9. *Stuffer weight.* Watch the weight of those marketing stuffers that are sent out with your DDA statements each month. It doesn't take much additional weight to put the majority of DDA statements over the one ounce postal rate — thereby increasing the postage on each piece 85%! The *additional* postage expense on 5,000 DDA statements, that normally weigh less than one ounce, but weigh over one ounce when a heavy stuffer is added, is $850.00 per month. And if this is done each month the annual additional expense multiples up to $10,200.
10. *Electronic mailing scale.* Although, in the introduction of this book I mentioned that I would not advocate the purchase of equipment to save money, the electronic mailing scale is a piece of equipment that should at least be mentioned because the payback period, particularly for larger banks, could be about twelve months, and it is so much more efficient than weighing mail on the more traditional type weighing scales. The advantages of an electronic weighing scale are as follows:

a. The digital readout of postage required eliminates the decision-making process mail clerks have to make on borderline pieces. On borderline packages, mail clerks will often put the higher postage amount on the piece to ensure that the mail will not be returned for insufficient postage or forwarded with postage to be collected from the addressee—either circumstance has a negative effect on the mail clerk's job performance.
b. These scales will usually take weights up to 10 pounds. This eliminates the need for additional scales for heavier pieces.
c. These scales have many of the postage rates built into the machine. This eliminates the need to refer to postal charts and manuals.
d. New postal rates are easily programmed into the scale which eliminates the need to have a service man install new rate charts as could be required on mechanical scales.

An electronic mailing scale can be purchased, currently for about $1,500.00, from those manufacturers who supply you with your other mail machines (postage meter, folding, and inserting machines). These companies will probably allow you to try out a demo for a few days before you decide to purchase.

11. Don't mail heavy statements. Some corporate customers issue hundreds of checks per month, and the postage expense of mailing out these DDA statements can be prohibitive. Alternate means of delivering these statements to customers should be used. Encourage customers to pick up the statements at a branch office, or deliver them by a bank messenger or a local commercial delivery service.

TELEPHONE EXPENSE

Telecommunications in banking today has become a very complex and costly item, particularly in those banks that have extensive networks of ATM machines, on-line teller machines, and/or administrative terminals (CRTs). The lines and modems that interconnect all these networks to a main computer are in addition to the traditional telephone line and equipment costs that provide basic communications between bank departments and branch offices and the public. In this section of this book we will confine our remarks to traditional phone equipment and its corresponding

Figure 13–1 Analysis of Telephone Expenses—Month of May, 19xx

Type of Service	*Main Office*	*North Branch*	*South Branch*	*East Branch*	*Operations Center*	*Total*	*% of Grand Total*
Equipment Lease							
Local & Zone Calls							
Long Distance Calls							
Trunk Lines							
Special Lines							
Alarm Lines							
Directory Advertising							
Miscellaneous							
Taxes							
Total							

costs. The more complex computer related telecommunications equipment and costs were covered in Chapter 10.

The following are six ways to decrease telephone expense.

1. Analyze your telephone bills. You do not have to be an expert in telephone communications to spread these costs (even if only for a one month period) as billed to you by your regional telephone company. Spreading a month's costs should be done by each location by type of service. Your telephone company most likely bills you for each phone number used, and the phone number is a key to help you identify the location and corresponding costs for that location, be it a branch office or a large department. Types of service would include several broad categories such as charges for monthly equipment (lease and/or maintenance costs); local and zone calls; long distance calls; trunk lines; special lines for ATMs, CRTs, teller equipment; alarm lines; directory advertising; miscellaneous charges; and taxes. If your bank is a unit bank, or your telephone system consists of only one basic phone number for all locations, separating costs by location could be difficult. But in any event it is important to at least spread the bill by types of service.

   Figure 13–1 is a sample format that can be used to spread monthly phone bills by type of service, by location. Note the percentage of grand total column (the last right hand column). This represents what percentage of the total monthly telephone expense each particular service costs. So, for example, if after completing this analysis you find that long distance calls represent 50% of your total monthly telephone expense, you would certainly want to take measures to substantially reduce this cost. The whole purpose of this analysis is to identify where the money is currently being spent. This is the first major step in pinpointing specific areas where costs can be reduced.
2. There are still many banks that have the traditional mechanical equipment (as contrasted to modern electronic equipment) that was installed 20 or more years ago. This equipment may still be operative, but most of it was acquired on a lease basis and part of this lease includes maintenance. The maintenance costs have been increasing dramatically on this old equipment because of the unavailability of parts and the difficulty of finding trained

personnel to repair this equipment. New electronic equipment can be either leased or purchased from a variety of companies, including the telephone company. Quotes should be obtained from several suppliers. These quotes will be for the equipment to be located in your bank – i.e., the small computer to operate your internal system, the switchboard, telephone instruments, and the internal wiring. Telephone lines used to communicate with your branch offices, your customers, and everybody else inside or outside your local area, are always leased from the telephone company.

You will find that acquiring this new equipment will not be more expensive than leasing and maintaining your present old mechanical equipment; and as time goes on, it will be less expensive because of rising maintenance costs on the old equipment. In addition, the newer equipment automatically gives you more features because it is electronic. Some of these features are labor saving, such as switchboard operation, and some are direct cost savings such as the decreased need for call directories and multibutton phone instruments, the ability to restrict phone use by location, and the ability to report long distance calls by phone extension.

3. When considering the acquisition of new telephone equipment, consider purchasing it rather than leasing it. The cost of purchasing (including maintenance charges) may be about the same as leasing for the first five years. But after that, when the purchased equipment has been written off on your books, the cost dramatically reduces by thousands of dollars per year. The main argument proposed against the purchase of this equipment is that the electronic equipment is being continually updated in design, efficiency, and in its uses as a communications vehicle (its ability to be linked with other electronic gear such as word processing equipment and micro computers). This may be true but how many bankers really look at updating their internal telephone equipment that often. In smaller banks it is often only reviewed out of necessity rather than a desire to have the most up-to-date system. After all, when was the last time you really looked at your system? If you have mechanical equipment, it was probably 20 years ago. Even if you have electronic equipment now, you probably have no immediate intention to acquire newer equipment (if your

present equipment is giving you good service). To be realistic, bankers probably view basic internal telephone communications in the same light that they view plumbing! Both are necessary but as long as they are doing the job, there are other more important areas that need attention. The point of all this is, that whatever equipment you acquire now, you will probably keep for ten years or more, and so it is considerably less expensive to purchase this equipment than to lease it.

When purchasing this equipment, however, be sure that you investigate the vendor's maintenance support and have it verified by several other present users of the equipment you plan to purchase. Telephone communications is vital to a bank. It is a bank's main link to its customers and it is important that it is operating at all times.

4. Review those special lines that you installed years ago. These would include the number of trunk lines, lines to branch locations, lines to private phones in the bank, long distance lines, ATM and CRT lines. Many of these may not be needed now or less expensive alternatives may now be available. Your local telephone utility company can help you with this.
5. If you're located in a large metropolitan area, review your directory advertising costs, which can be very expensive, particularly if your branches are located in a number of communities. Extensive advertising in the yellow pages of a number of directories is costly. I know of one bank that analyzed their phone bills using the format shown in Figure 13–1, and discovered that 20% of their monthly telephone expense was being spent for directory advertising! This was quickly addressed and resulted in a savings of $15,000 per year for this bank.
6. Shop the larger long distance service companies for the least expensive rates in relation to the cities they service and your individual bank's needs. Rates vary considerably between companies. But if you decide to change companies obtain a reference from a comparable size institution in your area.

SUMMARY

The seventeen ways of reducing postage and telephone expenses described in this chapter are summarized as follows:

1. Presort mail by zip code.
2. Be alert to the increased postage expense for odd-sized mailing envelopes.
3. Consider sending marketing mail at the bulk rate.
4. Stop mailing routine debit and credit advices.
5. Discontinue the practice of paying postage for mail deposits.
6. Promote combined statements to save postage.
7. Discontinue the practice of not having mail forwarded.
8. Combine 1099 mailings.
9. Watch the weight of marketing stuffers.
10. Consider acquiring an electronic weighing scale.
11. Hand deliver or encourage customers to pick-up large checking account statements.
12. Analyze telephone bills.
13. Convert old mechanical telephone equipment to new electronic equipment.
14. Purchase rather than lease new telephone equipment.
15. Review the need for special lines installed years ago.
16. Review directory advertising costs.
17. Shop the larger long distance service companies.

Chapter 14

Reduce Costs in Several Miscellaneous Expense Categories

This chapter lists several ways to reduce costs in other expense categories not covered in previous chapters. They are presented in capsule form because only a minimum of explanation is required. All of these ways however, are important to consider in a bank's overall profit improvement campaign. In combination these ways can save thousands of dollars per year in unnecessary expenses.

LEASED EQUIPMENT

List *all* the equipment your bank is now leasing. This list should include teller terminals, proof machines, posting machines, encoding machines, mail equipment, copying machines, typewriters, and calculators. It is important to make the list complete. The purpose of making this list is to force you to reexamine your reasons for leasing each piece of equipment. You will probably discover some leased equipment that you no longer use or which was originally to be leased for a short period of time due to some temporary need. We all know of stories about equipment that was leased for a specific purpose at one time but through the months and years this purpose was long forgotten. Meanwhile the money spent for the lease could have paid for the equipment two or three times over, if it had been purchased. The classic example of this is leasing copying equipment. Hundreds of dollars a month can be wasted by leasing copying equipment, particularly if this equipment is used in multiple locations. The lease amount for some of this equipment is outrageous. The cost of leasing for 18 months could pay for the equipment. And watch out for the cancellation clause. Some lease contracts, particularly with copying machines, have stiff penalties for breaking the contract before the term of the lease expires.

SMALL EQUIPMENT MAINTENANCE CONTRACTS

As each maintenance contract comes up for renewal, review the need for it. Some maintenance contracts tout monthly or quarterly inspections and cleanings for adding machines, check protectors, mechanical teller machines, etc., but this maintenance is never done as often as quoted in the maintenance contract. Also, you may be paying for maintenance contracts on equipment you've stopped using. It is wise to resist the temptation to sign a maintenance contract when purchasing new equipment of this type at least for the first year or two. Most of this equipment will not need to be serviced and after this period, if it needs repair, it may be less expensive in the long run to have it repaired on a when-needed basis, rather than putting it under a maintenance contract. Banks use a variety and a quantity of small equipment and it is well worth the effort to closely monitor the need for maintenance contracts. I suspect manufacturers of this equipment get rich on these contracts.

ENERGY COSTS

In this day and age the cost of energy in the forms of petroleum products, electricity, and natural gas, has become a major expense item for banks, particularly those banks that operate a number of branch facilities. A long conversation with your heating and cooling contractor could save you thousands of dollars per year in energy costs. The contractor will suggest updating or replacing antiquated energy wasting furnaces, air conditioners and thermostats, and the use of timers for each location to turn energy on and off as needed. Also consult with your local power company for energy conservation ideas. It could suggest ways to insulate your buildings better. If you own or lease automobiles switch to smaller cars, particularly those with four cylinder engines. Four cylinder engines will stand up under wear and tear as well as six and eight cylinder engines and probably you will save half the gasoline expense, and maintenance on these engines is less expensive.

OFFICE SPACE

Office space today is very expensive. Think twice before you build a new building or add on to an existing one. Consider the cost of the new structure itself, and also the cost of architects, conforming to new fire codes (sprinkler systems, for example), new codes to accommodate handicapped people (ramps, larger rest room facilities, larger doors), the additional energy costs, the additional maintenance costs, the additional furniture costs, the cost of providing parking, and last but not least, the loss of income that could be earned on all the above costs. So take another look at your present facility. Remodel it, rearrange departments, combine departments, use space saving furniture, space saving files, space saving storage units. Use your lower level for office space rather than for storage and rent additional storage space if necessary.

GROUNDS MAINTENANCE

Examine your contracts for lawn and garden care and snow removal. These contracts can be expensive. Perhaps a high school student on vacation, or your own maintenance man could take care of any lawn mowing and minor gardening that is required rather than hiring a contractor for the season. Snow removal could be done on a call basis rather than on a contract basis. And trash removal could be done by your janitor rather than by an outside firm.

MICROFILMING

Try to eliminate the expense of purchasing and maintaining microfilming equipment in each branch. If you can't avoid microfilming in a branch office at least don't develop the film until it is needed. This should eliminate about half your overall film cost. As a safety precaution transport the film in a fireproof box.

ATTORNEY'S FEES

Avoid the practice of retaining an attorney. Only call them when necessary and don't permit employees, including junior officers, to call an attorney without authorization. Employees will often use an attorney as a crutch to avoid researching a problem themselves.

DIRECTOR'S FEES

Only pay directors for meetings they attend, and limit the number of special subcommittees. Director's meetings should be held no more than once a month.

PERIODICALS

List your bank's subscriptions to newspapers, magazines, newsletters, reports, and bank directories. The list of these subscriptions will astound you. It is possible that there are many duplicate subscriptions that have been ordered over the years by managers and officers who did not know that someone else in the bank had already subscribed to these same periodicals. Assign a more senior officer to review this list of subscriptions with those employees who are receiving the periodicals, and then cancel those that are duplicated or unnecessary.

DONATIONS

All calls requesting donations should be directed to one officer in the bank who can coordinate this function. Donation seekers like to call several officers within a bank hoping that their cause will attract the attention of at least one of the officers. If all calls are directed to one experienced officer, that officer is better able to decide which causes are worthy of the bank's contribution.

TRAVEL EXPENSES

Travel expenses can get out of hand particularly for attendance at out of town conventions and seminars. Some national conventions, for example, are often held thousands of miles from the bank and attendance requires considerable amounts of time and money. There are the expenses for airline fares, taxis, parking, meals, hotel accommodations, and the cost of attending the convention. If a number of employees in the bank are permitted to go to their favorite conventions, the costs can escalate dramatically. Also, annual conventions need not be attended every year. Once every three years is sufficient. As a substitute, these employees should be encouraged to go to local or regional conventions that do not require any travel expense.

It is certainly advantageous to encourage developing employees to seek and obtain additional education, but much of this is available locally through AIB and correspondent bank seminars or local community colleges. The one-to-three day seminars held in distant places are expensive to attend for the same reasons mentioned in relation to conventions. When long distance travel is required always enlist the services of a good travel agent. Travel agents are the only reliable source for getting the best airline, hotel, and car rental rates.

SUMMARY

The following is a summary of the cost saving points made in this chapter.

1. When possible, purchase equipment don't lease it.
2. Make sure you still use whatever equipment you are leasing.
3. Make an effort to eliminate the expense of leasing copying equipment.
4. Maintenance contracts for small equipment are usually not worth the expense, especially during the first two years after the equipment is purchased.
5. Contact your local heating and air conditioning contractor and your local power company to determine ways to conserve energy in all your locations.
6. Consider purchasing only bank automobiles that are equipped with four cylinder engines to save up to 50% in gasoline and engine maintenance expenses.

7. Think of all the costs involved in building new office space and then, before building, explore space conservation methods that can be used in your present space.

8. Use alternate, less expensive means for grounds maintenance and snow and trash removal.

9. Reduce or eliminate the microfilming function in your branch system or at least don't develop this film.

10. Avoid using attorneys on a retainer basis. Restrict employees calls to attorneys.

11. Pay directors only for meetings attended. Eliminate unnecessary meetings.

12. Eliminate unneeded and duplicate subscriptions to periodicals.

13. Direct all requests for donations to one officer in the bank in order to control bank contributions.

14. Restrict officers from traveling to distant conventions and seminars.

15. When long distance travel is necessary enlist the services of a good travel agent.

PART SIX

REDUCE OPERATING LOSSES

Chapter 15

Three Major Operating Loss Categories and How to Reduce and Control Them

There are three operations-type losses that have plagued bankers for years because there is no ironclad way to eliminate them completely. Even keeping them under control can be difficult depending on the bank's location, the type of customers it services and its internal operating procedures. These three loss categories are teller differences, bad check losses, and losses from kiting operations. This chapter will address these three types of losses by describing effective internal procedures that a bank can adopt to minimize them. Not every bank experiences heavy losses in each of these three areas, but many banks from time to time have problems in at least one of these areas. These problems can have a significant effect on overall bank income. The procedures that are described in this chapter have been tried and have been proven to be very effective in controlling these losses. Even if you don't have problems in any of these areas now, these procedures will ensure your continued success.

TELLER DIFFERENCES

There have been many studies made in relation to the causes of teller differences. The results of these studies indicate that good management procedures in hiring, training and day-to-day supervision of tellers always lead to a low rate of teller differences. And, of course, the converse of this is true—poor management leads to a high rate of differences.

The term teller differences as used in this section refers to cash differences and does not include losses that tellers might have in cashing bad checks, allowing improper savings withdrawals, etc.

When you examine the subject of teller differences, two factors come to mind: the frequency of differences and the amount of the differences. Both of these are interrelated to some extent. A record of an exorbitant number of differences per month indicates carelessness, and carelessness in general can lead to increased losses for a teller. Since this book is devoted to describing ways to increase profits, our concentration will be in the amounts of teller differences, and to be even more specific the amount of shortages. But even by addressing just these problems, the number of overall differences should reduce, because of the close relationship between these two factors.

First of all, does your bank have a teller difference loss problem? As a general rule, if your tellers are averaging a net shortage of more than $12 to $15 per month, your bank has a problem. Twelve dollars per month in net shortages is a good general goal for banks with about a 50/50 mix of urban and suburban transactions. Some banks of course will be below this because of their location and the type of customers they service. And some banks may have losses higher than $12 per month, but if they are higher than $15 per month, regardless of their location and type of customer, then their losses are undoubtedly excessive.

The above general rule is very interesting, but how does a specific bank determine its own acceptable levels of net teller shortages? The procedure is simple. Take the total of *net* shortages for last year or the recent twelve month period and divide this by the average number of tellers employed during the same period, and then divide this sum by twelve to obtain a monthly average. It is important to use a net shortages figure (the difference between the total overages and the total shortages). The theory behind this is that many normal overages are offset by shortages even though the offsets cannot be pinpointed; but both the shortages and the overages involved are considered unfounded and have to be written off. Also, in this computation part-time tellers should be calculated as half a teller. So, for example, if a bank shows the following statistics for a twelve-month period the average net shortages per teller per month is $11.89 ($5,420 ÷ 38 = $142.63 ÷ 12 = $11.885).

Total shortages	$8,230
Total overages	$2,810
Net shortages	$5,420

Average number of full-time tellers	26
Average number of part-time tellers	24
Total number of full-time equivalents	38 [26 + (24 ÷ 2)]

So for this bank, during this period, each teller on average had $11.89 worth of net shortages per month. Note that in computing this average, if a bank had two or three large unfounded shortages (over $500) during this period and no corresponding large charged-off overages, then these shortages should be subtracted from the total net shortages for the period in order to produce a better average with which to develop norms for tellers. To further refine this procedure, net tellers' shortages by branch location can be computed using the same calculations shown above. In a bank with several branch offices comparison can be made of the averages between branches in similar locations to determine acceptable levels for all branches within these locations.

Once you have performed the above calculations you would know how each teller is doing in relation to the average, and those tellers who are doing poorly can now be identified and counseled accordingly. This counseling should produce results that will automatically reduce the overall bank average in the next twelve-month period.

But how does a bank with a high average dollar amount of net shortages per teller per month attack this problem? As mentioned earlier, teller differences are directly related to the type of overall teller management provided by the bank. This includes not only the quality of the day-to-day supervision of tellers, but also the hiring and training of new tellers. Before new tellers are hired care should be given to make sure that they have basic simple arithmetic abilities and that they are comfortable working with numbers. There are tests on the market that can determine this. The American Bankers Association has done a lot of research in this area with particular attention to the legal aspects developing a test that conforms to EEOC standards.

Training new tellers is the second factor affecting teller differences. Research has shown that to rely only on classroom-type training, where a number of new tellers are being trained at once, is not as effective as one-on-one training. Larger banks which hire a number of teller trainees per year cannot realistically provide one trainer per trainee and so a training class environment is more practical. Smaller banks that don't have a formalized teller training program use the buddy system which is in effect one-on-one training, but the trainer often doesn't approach the training of a new teller in any organized fashion. If several trainers are involved in the occasional training of new tellers, there might be a problem of consistency—all trainees may not be trained the same way. A possible solution for the larger banks would be to continue to use the training classroom environment for the usual two-to-three-week period and cover the basics of teller work. This should include some training in how banks operate, the services that banks offer, customer service, and the overall check collection system. This should be followed up, however, with another three weeks of one-on-one training in the branch where the trainee is to be assigned—i.e., the use of the buddy system. These individual trainers in the branches could be designated as sponsor tellers, and, of course, in this type of training, the trainee is working live with the customer while the sponsor teller is watching over each transaction. These sponsor tellers should be trained to reinforce the teller methods taught in the training class and not to teach the trainee alternate ways of handling cash and customer transactions. It is important that the trainee receive consistent training throughout the whole training program.

Smaller banks should use the buddy system for the whole period of training. But management should select a senior teller in every branch as the training teller in that branch with the understanding that that teller is to perform the training function for each new trainee assigned to that branch. These training tellers, of course, must be instructed by management in how to train new tellers. This instruction should include a list of topics to be covered with the trainee and an understanding between management and the training tellers that all the trainers will teach trainees the same procedures for handling cash and customer transactions.

The third and final factor affecting teller differences is the quality of supervision of the tellers. Whether this supervision is performed by a designated supervisor of tellers, an assistant branch manager, or a branch manager, tellers should be supervised. They should have someone available to them to answer questions, to resolve conflicts and to take an interest in their well-being and growth within the bank. Supervision of tellers also includes performance counseling, not only in the overall performance of each teller, but more specifically in teller difference counseling. And now we are back to the central theme of reducing teller shortages. When a bank is having teller shortage problems, individual counseling is a key to reducing shortages. Tellers must know what their individual record of shortages has been and what is expected of them in relation to the bank's averages of shortages per teller, or whatever norms a bank chooses to use. Teller's difference records should be reviewed with each teller at least quarterly. And for tellers who have problems, their records should be reviewed with them monthly.

Banks have many options for establishing norms for teller shortages and for the action to take when these norms are exceeded by certain tellers. The simplest way to establish norms is to use the bank's averages of net shortages for all tellers or for all tellers within those branches in a specific geographical region. And then tellers' performances can be measured against these norms on a cumulative quarterly basis. So, for example, if a norm, based on a bank's average of net shortages for all tellers is set at no more than $10.00 worth of net shortages per month, then, for a quarter, the cumulative net shortages should not exceed $30.00. The supervisor, upon reviewing the teller difference records with all tellers each quarter, should mention to each teller the norm, show each teller his or her own record of differences, compliment the teller if his or her record is below this norm, and counsel the teller if his or her record is above the norm. The counseling process should include questions such as: why do you think you have trouble keeping within the norm? Are there parts of the teller function you don't understand? Do you have trouble concentrating on your work? Why? Do you enjoy doing teller work? How can I (as the supervisor) help you? Answers to these questions should help resolve any problems a particular teller may be having. But there are always some tellers who won't respond to this type of counseling, for whatever reason, and will respond better to more formal actions on the part of management such as warning letters, probation, transferring the teller to another position in the bank, or dismissal. Banks that employ a number of tellers generally follow the dismissal route as a final course of action and transfer a teller to another position only in special circumstances.

A bank should have a definite policy for warning employees before dismissing them. This policy should outline the tiers or levels of disciplinary actions and depend on the amounts of the cumulative net shortages. The first level of action should be a warning letter to any teller who has exceeded the norm by a certain cumulative amount. This letter states the norm, that the teller has exceeded the norm and must take the necessary steps to reverse the cumulative net shortages during the next three-month period. If this does not help, and a teller continues to have shortages that accumulate up to a second tiered amount, the bank could either issue a second warning letter or put the employee on probation. When putting an employee on probation, proper written notice of the probation must be given to the teller describing the reason for it, its duration (usually 90 days), and notification that the employee will be dismissed from the bank, if during the probation the rate of teller shortages does not return to the original norm for all tellers. The teller and the teller's supervisor should sign all warning letters and notices of probation, and a copy of these letters and notices should be given to the employee and a copy should be retained in the employee's personnel file.

The above procedures may seem elaborate for a bank to go through in order to try to reverse a teller's poor difference record, but the procedure has two advantages. It does motivate many tellers to do better in reducing their shortages, and for those tellers who cannot or will not respond, it paves the way for a bank to dismiss nonperforming employees without incurring a multitude of legal liabilities.

In conclusion, therefore, in order to substantially reduce abnormal losses due to teller cash shortages a bank has to develop a norm for all tellers. This norm is based on the bank's averages. And tellers who cannot or do not conform should first be counseled, then warned, then put on probation, and finally, when all hope is lost, dismissed. Management does have a duty, in fairness to tellers, to screen applicants properly before they are hired as tellers, and once they are hired, to train them well and provide them with adequate day-to-day supervision.

BAD CHECK LOSSES

Losses from bad checks are a problem that banks have lived with, with much consternation, for years. Every time a series of bad checks is cashed the whole bank is in an uproar. Senior managers come out of their offices and pounce on teller supervisors, branch managers, and often, disregarding the chain of command, interview the teller themselves. As a result all the tellers are on guard and obtain approvals for everything—even for checks they have been cashing for the same customers for years. Gradually through the weeks fewer and fewer items are referred by the tellers for approval and the tellers return to their normal "modus operandi" until the next time there is a series of bad check losses. Meanwhile throughout the year the bank has lost thousands of dollars to the bad check passer. What *is* the answer?

The answer is to analyze the problem. I will not try to define the ways someone can pass a bad check to a teller, but I will try to define the basic way a ring of bad check passers operates because it is from these rings that a bank suffers most of its bad check losses.

There are only four different check cashing situations that a teller will face. They are:

Check Being Presented Is:	*Check Is Presented By:*
1. Drawn on us	A customer of the bank
2. Drawn on us	A non-customer of the bank
3. Drawn on another bank	A customer of the bank
4. Drawn on another bank	A non-customer of the bank

First of all, bad check passers do not use checks drawn on your bank. They will always use checks drawn on another bank because the checks they use are always stolen. And they assume that the customers from whom these checks were stolen have already notified their banks. This eliminates situations 1 and 2. Bad check passers know that banks do not cash checks drawn on another bank for non-customers. Considering this, therefore, there is only one way a check passer operates situation 3. He or she presents a check drawn on another bank and either is a customer of the bank or assumes the identity of a real customer. If she or he is a customer of the bank, he or she is a new customer and not well known to the tellers. If the bad check passer assumes an identity of a real customer (by stealing or borrowing a checking account statement from the mails to obtain an account number, balance, and sample signatures from the cancelled checks enclosed in the statement), he or she is not known by the tellers. It is also known that the check passer will not risk discovery for small amounts of cash, and so the cash received is usually in excess of $200 (and usually not more than $500 so as not to arouse suspicion or go beyond a teller's check cashing limits). Check passing rings deal in volumes of checks and will hit a bank with several of these same checks in a one-to-three day period, and then go on to the next bank. Also, of course, a check passer rather than attempting to cash the check outright, will often deposit part of the check and request cash back (but the amount of the cash back is almost always in excess of $200). Checks used by check passers are almost always stolen from small companies and from companies that are not in the immediate trading area of the bank where they attempt to pass the check. These checks will be drawn on banks within the same metropolitan area in which that bank is located.

The known facts about bad check passing situations can be summarized as follows:

1. The amount of cash received is more than $200.
2. The check is drawn on another bank.
3. The maker of the check is not well known.
4. The endorser (the person receiving the cash) is not well known.

All of these four facts are always present in fraudulent check passing transactions. In other words if any of the four facts are not present in the transaction, the person receiving the money is not a professional check passer. We all know of some exceptions to number 3 such as the stolen U.S. government check (the maker is well known the U.S. government), and the occasional large well-known company's payroll checks which are stolen from the recipient. Stolen government checks are a separate type of bad check loss which can be stopped if tellers obtain positive identification from the endorser(s) before cashing these checks. Fortunately with the advent of direct deposit, losses from stolen government checks are diminishing. Check thefts from large well-known companies occasionally stolen from the recipient but very rarely stolen from the company itself, are not common occurrences and are not part of a bad check passing ring's mode of operation. What we are describing here are ways to stop the big check cashing losses and not those related to government checks, or to those losses that occur from an occasional stolen check drawn on a well-known company.

Now that we know the four characteristics that are always present in combination when a check passer is attempting to fraudulently cash a check, we can train tellers to be on the watch when all four of these characteristics are present in a transaction. The key to this whole presentation is that there is real danger only when all four of these characteristics are present in the transaction. At first glance, when tellers are exposed to these characteristics they always key in on the first one and think that they are in danger if they don't obtain approval for every check over $200! So tellers have to be educated to the importance of all four characteristics being present in one transaction.

The first step in training the tellers is to develop a simple written procedure, and if the problem has been acute, add a warning to the procedure. A sample written procedure with a warning is shown below.

WARNING
IN CHECK CASHING OR
LESS CASH TRANSACTIONS
IF:

1. The amount of cash involved exceeds $200 *AND*
2. The check is drawn on another bank *AND*
3. The maker of the check is not well known *AND*
4. The endorser (the person receiving the money) is not well known

(All four in combination)
OBTAIN AN APPROVAL
OR if there is a loss, the teller
will be subject to IMMEDIATE DISMISSAL

____
Teller Signature

____
Date

This procedure could be printed on card stock (on bright red colored stock) and tacked up in each teller's window as a constant reminder. Also, a copy of this procedure should be signed by each teller and placed in the teller's personnel file. Some variations to the warning could be to change the word "warning" to "danger" and to change the words "subject to immediate dismissal" to "placed on immediate probation" or "will be dismissed from the bank." In any event, this procedure would have to be explained to the tellers by covering the following points:

1. An explanation for the reason for the procedure such as: in the last six months tellers in the bank have cashed or have given cash back on a total number of thirteen bad checks and the total loss to the bank has amounted to $4,253, and for the past twelve months these losses have amounted to $7,325. Then show the tellers the thirteen checks.

2. The "subject to immediate dismissal" phrase only applies if all four of the factors shown exist for the specific transaction incurring the loss. If the amount of cash received is $200 or less, or the check is drawn on our bank, or the check is drawn on another bank but it is a common payroll check often cashed by tellers in your branch, or the person receiving the cash is well known to you because you have waited on him or her many times in the past, then this warning does not apply, even if there is a loss.
3. The key to this procedure is that all factors have to be present at the same time in order for this procedure to be effective.
4. The instances when all four factors will be present in combination will be rare because most of the checks that tellers cash or that are deposited with cash back, are either drawn on the bank, or are cashed often in your branch (are well known), or the person receiving the money is well known.
5. Tellers are to be reminded that this procedure does not replace all other check cashing procedures such as checking balances, checking signatures, placing holds, obtaining approvals for certain dollar amounts, but it is an additional procedure. And therefore, when all four factors are present in combination tellers are not required to check anything but are required to obtain an approval. Tellers must not use their own judgment in this particular circumstance no matter how much checking they do or how many years of experience they have.

Teller supervisory personnel, of course, have to be aware of the dangers involved when these transactions are presented for approval. If the tellers there just are not that many in the first place. But some tellers will be scared and will present items for approval that need not be presented and this new procedure will have to be reviewed with them again on an individual basis. But if a bona fide transaction is presented for approval teller supervisory personnel should be on guard and verify everything, particularly that there is a sufficient collected balance in the account to cover the check in the event it is returned; to place a hold on the account for the appropriate number of days; and to positively identify the customer presenting the item.

It was mentioned earlier that the check passer will either assume the identity of a real customer, or will have opened an account under a false name a few days or weeks before attempting to pass the check. By requiring positive identification, preferably two pieces of good I.D., supervisory personnel will stop the check passer cold, because he or she obviously doesn't want his or her real identity known. Remember there will be very few instances where all four factors will be in combination so you won't be bothering very many, if any, of your bona fide customers. Finally, to help thwart check passing rings from attempting to open accounts in your bank, new account personnel should be trained to get positive I.D. before opening any account, and if your bank is located in an area that is serviced by a company that offers a new account verification service, it is strongly suggested that the bank join this service and insist that new account personnel contact this service before any checking or savings account is opened. Independent companies that offer a new account verification service to banks store adverse information about bank customers on their computers, such as those accounts closed by banks for cause (excessive overdrafts, for example) and those names on accounts opened by members of check passing rings which use false I.D. and/or on which check cashing losses have been reported. Banks belonging to this service call in the new account information (name, address, driver's license number) to be verified before the account is opened and if a negative report is obtained the account is not opened. If the customer wants further information on why the bank refused to open the account the customer is referred by the bank to the company. This whole procedure is another weapon for bankers to use in the war against those who are determined to defraud banking institutions.

KITING LOSSES

Check kiting is that illegal procedure whereby a bank customer will take advantage of the time required by banks to clear checks to build up false balances in a checking account. It is potentially the most dangerous type of loss situation a bank may encounter. There are two reasons for this. First of all, the losses involved even from one check kiter can amount to thousands of dollars, and secondly, most insurance companies do not cover losses due to kiting operations.

To start a kiting operation a customer will open an account in more than one bank. The customer then proceeds to draw checks on one bank and deposit them in the other banks and vice versa. This creates fictitious balances on which to issue checks to creditors or to cash checks. By continually drawing checks on one bank and depositing them into other banks a kiting operation can exist for several months without detection as long as all banks involved are willing to pay these checks against uncollected funds. The first bank in the chain that detects the kite and starts returning checks because they are drawn against uncollected funds, stops the kite and usually does not suffer any losses. The other banks, however, suffer losses equal to those recent deposits that are not yet collected. One kiting operation can involve many banks because one customer can and will open accounts in a number of banks. The number of banks involved in a kite is only limited by a kiter's ability to keep track of the ongoing deposits that must be made every few days to each bank account connected to the kite.

The best way to stop potential kiting operations is for a bank to refuse to pay checks drawn against uncollected funds. Unfortunately most banks will pay these checks as a service to their customers. And this practice is good as long as customers do not attempt to take advantage of this practice and start a kiting operation. There are ways, however, for a bank to detect and guard against losses from kites, even though they generally permit customers to draw checks against uncollected funds.

How to Detect and Guard Against Kiting

1. Review accounts that are drawing against uncollected funds. Since most banks' checking accounts are processed by computers, computer programs have been designed to provide reports on those customers who are drawing checks against uncollected balances. The computer receives this information as a by-product of the proof operation. So as each deposit slip with its corresponding deposited items is processed in proof, the dollar amounts for not on us checks being deposited are captured and assigned a certain number of days for which the funds are considered uncollected. The number of uncollected fund days assigned for each deposited item is determined by the location of the drawee bank. The sophistication of this assignment is limited by the sophistication of the proof operation itself. In an automated proof environment, for example, deposited checks can be assigned uncollected fund days according to a number of drawee bank locations. If the proof department is not automated only two or three uncollected fund-day assignments can be made, and all not on us checks deposited have to be categorized into these two or three slots. The reason for this is that in a nonautomated proof environment the dollar amounts of not on us deposited checks have to be encoded in magnetic ink on the bottom of each deposit

slip, and there is only enough room on a deposit slip for two or three fields of this uncollected fund information. In an automated proof operation, however, this uncollected fund information is captured by a sorter reader which has considerably more capacity for storing this information. In any event, regardless of the sophistication of the proof operation, the amount of not on us deposited items is eventually recorded as part of a customer's main account record and reported each day on what is usually called an uncollected funds report. It is important to note here that when a bank first establishes its uncollected fund reports with a computer system, it selects the number of uncollected fund days to be assigned to each category of not on us deposited items (for example, five days for deposited checks drawn on Chicago, seven days for Los Angeles, three days for local checks). If a bank has not looked at this assignment in a number of years however, it is important that it be reviewed to make sure that it is accurate and truly reflects the number of days it physically takes for an item designated into a location category to travel to that location and to return; because that is what uncollected funds are all about. If all checks drawn on all accounts were always paid and never returned as unpaid, there would be no uncollected funds reports, or no possibility of kiting.

Since many customers deposit items drawn on banks located outside their area, the uncollected funds report for checking accounts as produced by a bank's computer system will be voluminous. So to review each and every account that shows uncollected funds would be too time consuming. Accordingly, to establish a dollar limit for the amount of uncollected funds in an account that would be subject for review would be more practical. Separate dollar limits for personal and business accounts would also be advantageous. These dollar limits should be high enough to eliminate the review of the massive number of accounts, but low enough to conform to the amount a bank can absorb if a loss did occur due to a kite. Depending on the size of the bank and therefore the number of accounts to be reviewed, the dollar limits would be higher for larger banks than they would be for smaller banks. But remember, when setting these limits for both business and personal accounts it is the dollar amount of a loss that a bank could afford to write off due to one or two kiting operations that must be considered, and not the aggregate amount of losses due to a number of kites. Excessive losses due to kiting are not due to the number of customers operating a kiting scheme but rather to the high amounts involved with only a few customers. Kiting losses are not like overdraft losses. There are only a very few customers, if any, who are engaged in a kiting operation which could subject a bank to a real loss, but there are many customers overdrawing accounts that could cause write-offs.

Once these dollar limits are set, a report could be manually prepared each day showing those personal accounts and business accounts that exceed these uncollected fund limits. This report should show the current balance (after all activity is posted), the uncollected fund balance, and the total amounts of checks paid and deposited credited on the account to date.

The following is an example of what four business accounts would look like on this report:

Uncollected Fund Report
as of March 23, 19xx
Business Accounts ($5,000 and over)

Name of Company	*A/C Number*	*Ledger Balance*	*Uncollected Balance*	*Today's Withdrawals*	*Today's Deposit*
ABC Printing Co.	027-5555	$ 2,537.57	$ 7,373.00	$1,750.00	-0-
XYZ Bakery Co.	037-6223	3,470.00(OD)	10,500.00	4,007.12	-0-
DDC Manufacturing Co.	047-6237	3,000.00	15,000.00	5,000.00	$5,000.00
AAA Food Processing Co.	047-7235	30,725.83	12,750.00	8,372.57	6,322.00

Theoretically all four of these companies could be involved in a kiting operation or none of them could. One day's report is not conclusive but it could show signs. ABC Printing Company's statistics are somewhat typical of many accounts that would show up on this type of report. AAA Food Processing appears to be no problem today because the ledger balance is more than sufficient to cover any or all the deposited checks if they were returned. XYZ Bakery is suspect because of the large overdraft and the large uncollected funds position. DDC Manufacturing is suspect because of the large uncollected funds balance in relation to the ledger balance and because of the same large amount showing in the withdrawal and the deposit columns. Anyone who reviews this type of report would have to become familiar with analyzing it, and would have to review it in relation to previous and subsequent daily uncollected funds reports to identify patterns within an account. Also, those who review this report should have a good knowledge of the business accounts in the bank to help them interpret the information shown. Copies of this report should be distributed daily to those who approve overdrafts so that a more complete potential loss picture is presented before an overdraft is paid. The decision to pay a $2,000 overdraft on a customer with a zero uncollected balance is different from paying the same overdraft for a customer who has a $15,000 uncollected balance! This report helps guard against any losses that result from the return of deposited checks regardless of whether or not there is a kite involved.

In any event, the information shown on this report is not the only information required to totally protect a bank against kites. It only provides danger signals which have to be viewed in combination with other factors.

2. Review checks paid on accounts. Checks paid on checking accounts (over a certain dollar limit) should be reviewed each day by a supervisor to determine if the maker, for example the DDC Manufacturing Co., or the one who signs the check for the company is related in any way to the payee and/or endorser. If the DDC Manufacturing Co. is the maker of the check and the DDC Manufacturing Co. is the payee/endorser, then the DDC Manufacturing Co. has more than one account and the location of that account can be determined from the bank endorsements shown on the reverse side of the check. This information about the DDC Manufacturing Co. combined with the information shown on the sample uncollected fund report would be highly suspicious.
3. Review returned deposited checks. These charge backs should be reviewed each day by someone in management in the same way that paid checks are to be reviewed. I have seen more kites detected and potential losses stopped from reviewing charge backs than from any other single source. Charge backs are to be reviewed as soon as they enter the bank, even before they are processed, so corrective action can be taken to avoid a loss on the

account as soon as possible. Here again the loss does not have to be related to a kite, it can simply be that there are not sufficient funds in the account to pay for the charge back.

4. Review deposited checks. This can be done in the teller area or in the proof area. Tellers or proof operators should show large dollar amount deposited checks to their supervisor. The supervisor then can review relationships between the maker and the payee and/or endorser, and if an item is suspicious, bring it to the attention of that officer who is reviewing the uncollected funds report.

   It should be noted here that those employees reviewing checks paid, returned deposited checks, and deposited checks, should report anything suspicious to the officer in charge of reviewing the uncollected funds report who ideally should be the same officer who approves overdrafts. Funneling all this information to one officer's attention gives that officer a complete picture of any potential losses that could be imminent. That one officer could then consult with any other officer to determine the appropriate action. It does not matter how many officers know *all* the facts, but funneling all information to at least one person should be done to prevent important information from getting lost.

5. Holding funds on deposited items. Tellers in some banks are instructed to place holds on accounts for certain items that are deposited by customers. The object of this procedure is to prevent customers from cashing checks against these funds until the deposited checks have cleared. In a computer processing environment these holds can be placed for any number of days depending on the item being held. This procedure may not be related to the computer generated uncollected funds report mentioned earlier because the source from which information for this report is obtained is from the proof operation and not from holds placed by tellers. But there is an advantage to this procedure as related to kiting.

   One of the ways kiters will try to obtain money is to try to cash their own checks on the fictitious balances that they have generated through their kiting operation. If tellers have been dutifully putting holds on the kiter's account for deposited items, then tellers will not cash a check if the held amounts are equal to or greater than the ledger balance. Also, if a customer knows of a bank's procedure of requiring tellers to put holds on deposited items the kiter will be discouraged from using his or her account in that bank as part of the kiting scheme.

6. Other telltale signs. There are other ways to spot a potential kiting operation.
   a. A check is paid and a deposit is made both for approximately the same amount and the balance in the account does not change substantially.
   b. Large transactions are posted to an account that has been traditionally a small account.
   c. The average balance in the account is less than the size of a transaction.
   d. Repeated requests from a customer to verify balance information on his or her account and/or to determine whether or not a large check has been paid.
7. Other safeguards. To make it more difficult for the potential check kiter and therefore to protect the bank better, the following normal type of banking procedures should be enforced.
   a. Checks should not be certified against uncollected funds
   b. Uncollected funds should not be transferred between accounts, or by wire to another bank, without an officer's approval.
   c. If checks to be cashed or savings withdrawals are presented against uncollected balances (beyond a certain dollar limit), they should require an approval.
   d. Cashier's checks should not be issued against uncollected funds without an approval.
   e. The personnel department and/or the auditing department should periodically review all employee checking account statements for signs of a kiting operation.

SUMMARY

Throughout this chapter several ways were explored to substantially reduce losses attributed to teller differences, cashing bad checks, and illegal kiting operations. These ways, mostly in the form of procedures which are summarized below, will not only help the bank that is having a problem in any of these areas to correct this problem, but also will help any bank to avoid any future problems in these areas.

1. Calculate the average net shortage per teller per month amount for your bank.

2. Develop teller difference norms using this average, and notify tellers how well they are doing in relation to these norms. Tellers doing poorly in relation to these norms should be counseled.

3. Banks with definite teller difference problems should examine their screening practices for hiring new tellers, their new teller training methods, and the effectiveness of their teller supervisors, and they should develop a system for formally warning tellers with poor difference records.

4. Know how rings of bad check passers operate.

5. Train tellers in the importance of knowing the four characteristics always present in a bad check cashing transaction and to be on the watch for these four characteristics when they occur in combination.

6. If the problem is acute in your bank develop a simple written procedure for tellers to follow with a warning attached.

7. Train new account personnel to obtain positive I.D. before opening an account, and to use the new account verification service to which the bank subscribes.

8. A loss from one kiting operation can be larger than most other types of losses combined. It is the most dangerous type of a loss involving a customer.

9. Examine accounts that show uncollected funds beyond a bank defined limit.

10. Review, for possible kiting schemes, checks paid on accounts, returned deposited checks, and deposited checks.

11. All suspicious information gathered as a result of reviewing the items mentioned in numbers 9 and 10 above should be shown to one officer, preferably to the officer in charge of paying overdrafts.

12. If not already a procedure in your bank, consider requiring tellers to place holds on accounts for deposited not on us items.

13. Be aware of the other telltale signs of a potential kiting operation.

PART SEVEN

MANAGEMENT CONCEPTS FOR IMPROVING PROFITS

Chapter 16

Compress the Organizational Structure

As an organization grows so does its management structure. Some of this structure growth is obviously necessary, but unfortunately in many banks much of it is often unnecessary and extremely expensive. This unnecessary structure growth can appear in all levels of management and is often due to what is commonly, and often jokingly, called "empire building." Empire building, in turn, is caused by either or both of two basic human needs within a manager's psychological makeup: the need to keep his or her job (a survival need) and the need to be viewed by superiors, peers, and subordinates as important (a self-worth need). If the satisfaction of these needs, however, is allowed to continue without control, it can become expensive to the organization.

As mentioned before, empire building can occur at all levels of management. Senior officers, therefore, should analyze whether the satisfaction of either of these needs has become extreme either in their own way of managing or in the way their subordinate managers manage their departments.

In reviewing the organizational structure of a bank, the goal is to increase profits by compressing the structure. This in turn will produce the time management spends in managing the bank and ultimately will reduce the number of employees (both management and nonmanagement) needed to operate various functions within the bank.

The first step in analyzing a bank's organizational structure is to know the structure. A detailed organization chart should, therefore, be developed showing all levels of management, the managers' names, the names of their functions or departments, and their main areas of responsibilities (including a listing of their bank related committee memberships). Typically, the organization chart should start at the top with senior officers, followed by middle level officers, and finally by more junior officers. Once the organization structure is known, the analysis of the structure for compression possibilities (and, therefore, profit improvement) can begin. The following is a listing of thought-provoking questions, ideas, and comments that should be considered when reviewing the various levels of management and their responsibilities:

1. Do the functions of two or more of the senior officers overlap? If so, this can cause confusion and redundancy between the senior officers involved and, therefore, wasted time.
2. Can the functions of two or more of the senior officers be combined? For example, can the senior officer in charge of branch administration also take on the overall responsibility for back room operation, personnel function, and/or marketing? It is surprising what additional responsibilities a senior officer can absorb if challenged. Remember that the elimination of just one senior officer can produce $50,000 to $100,000 or more of annual profit improvement!
3. Can a senior officer's support staff be reduced? How many, for example, administrative assistants are really needed?
4. Do your regional branch managers also manage a branch? If not, could they? A regional branch manager who is also a branch manager can effectively supervise from two to four other non-regional branch managers depending on the size of the other branches to be supervised.
5. If your regional branch managers are not branch managers and you wish to retain this type of structure, could you increase the number of branches for each region? The suggestions mentioned in #4 above and in this section would obviously eliminate some regional managers and/or branch manager salaries.
6. Some banks have branch managers that supervise more than one smaller size branch and the assistant managers in these branches

take care of the day-to-day supervisory duties. Could this concept be adopted in your bank?

7. Can any of your department managers be responsible for more than one department? Proof, bookkeeping, central file data entry, mailroom, item research, record retention, purchasing, building maintenance, and ATM and telephone equipment servicing are typical departmental functions that could be centralized in various combinations under one manager.
8. Do the functions in two or more departments extensively overlap to the point where departments should be combined or that some whole departments could even be eliminated? This overlapping is more common in larger banks where management has created a department to perhaps fill a temporary need long ago and allowed the department to continue to exist even after the original need slowly disappeared. Identifying the functions of departments, as mentioned earlier, will uncover this overlapping.
9. Identifying department functions will also uncover policies and procedures within a department that are no longer necessary. This will provide an opportunity for substantial profit improvement through the reduction in staffing requirements.
10. During the last few years banks have been investigating, with considerable profit oriented success, the using of outside sources (called outsourcing) for certain either highly technical or labor intensive functions now performed by employees of the bank. Considering the savings in salary, fringe benefits, space requirements, equipment, and utility expenses, the cost of using an outside source to perform a function could be much lower than performing the function within the bank. Typical bank functions outsourced by banks include data processing functions, legal services, food service, intra-branch office messenger services, daily transportation of checks for clearing, warehousing of forms, record retention, record destruction, grounds maintenance, lobby and parking lot security service, security equipment servicing, mail services for special mailings, and bulk cash handling and shipping services. More specific profit improvement information regarding the outsourcing of data processing functions is presented in Chapter 10, "A Review of Data Processing Costs."
11. How many in-bank committees are your officers involved in? From examining your detailed organizational structure you will

be able to first chart all the numbers of committees in your bank and then the number of committees in which each officer is a member. In general, because belonging to committees can be time consuming, committees should be few in number, be comprised of as few officers as possible, and meetings should not last longer than two hours. Ancillary to the existence of committees is the subject of meetings, which are also time consuming. The principles mentioned above concerning committees also apply to meetings. Both committees and meetings take officers away from their normal duties, and unless these meetings are controlled they can be nonproductive.

SUMMARY

This chapter explores ways to increase profits by compressing the organizational structure. To accomplish this one must first know, in detail, the structure of the bank and then analyze that structure for compression possibilities. Such possibilities should include the combining of functional responsibilities of officers and manager of all levels, combining or eliminating departments, eliminating unnecessary or redundant procedures within departments, and investigating the possibility of outsourcing certain functions currently performed within the bank. The structure of a bank also includes the use of committees and other types of general meetings which should be analyzed for their usefulness.

Chapter 17

Motivate for Profits

Improving profits in a bank cannot be done by the president alone. It requires the cooperation of all levels of management within the bank. This cooperation can be obtained if one understands basic concepts about people and how they are motivated. The purpose of this chapter is to identify those factors which can be used by all members of management from the president on down to motivate their subordinates towards improving profits not only in their day-to-day duties but also in their role in any profit improvement project that is currently in place.

The first step in identifying those factors that motivate people toward accomplishing profit improvement objectives is to understand what is commonly known about human nature, particularly as it relates to the subject of motivation. People have a variety of needs such as food, rest, shelter, and protection from physical and emotional harm. They need to feel important, to respect themselves, and to be self-fulfilled. People have intelligence and, therefore, are curious; people can think, analyze, imagine, judge, and decide. People are emotional and, therefore, perceive love, anxiety, disappointment, inadequacy, joy, peace, boredom, etc. People are social and, therefore, need to be with other people. They communicate with and are influenced by other people.

These needs and characteristics are influenced in varying degrees depending on the individual and a by a person's heredity, rearing, culture, social relationships, knowledge, experiences, and independent thinking. In addition, people often change to some degree in their attitudes and interests as they live through the decades from youth to old age.

Because people are obviously complex, a motivational principle has to be used with the overall understanding that its degree of effectiveness is more often than not directly related to the person to be motivated. In other words, no principle is equally effective to all people or to all people at the same time. Applying these principles, therefore, can become highly individualized and consequently could be considered to be more an art than a science.

In addition to the above mentioned concepts about people in relation to motivation, other considerations and assumptions were made in the process of identifying the specific motivating factors that will be discussed. These considerations and assumptions are as follows:

1. The employer (both management and nonmanagement personnel) work in a bank.
2. The employees are engaged in a direct profit improvement assignment. Motivational factors related to discipline problems, work ethic problems, training problems, etc., are not mentioned.
3. It is assumed that the employees to be motivated are currently managed well. It is difficult to motivate employees at any level who are poorly managed. Poorly managed employees are very difficult to motivate toward any goal beyond just getting the job done well enough to get a paycheck. That's why excessive turnover within a department or branch can usually be traced back to just plain poor management. Any manager who does not organize the work efforts of his or her department, does not communicate well with subordinates, or does not make good decisions and act upon them is not a good manager and is incapable of effectively motivating people.
4. The factors are discussed conceptually. Their relationship to profit improvement assignments is discussed more fully at the end of this chapter.

PRAISE AND RECOGNITION

Even though each person possesses all the needs and characteristics mentioned earlier, it is important to understand that each person is uniquely different. No two people are exactly the same. Because of the individuality of people, each person recognizes their own individuality more fully than that of others and takes a very natural interest in themselves. For this reason each person likes to be called by name and likes to talk about his or her own ideas, family, car, house, vacation, experiences, and achievements.

The most obvious motivators related to individuality are praise and recognition. Through sincere and honest praise and recognition a manager can motivate employees literally to move mountains. Unfortunately, these motivators are often not used to their full potential by the bank department manager. Employees are more often reprimanded for what they do wrong, rather than praised for what they do right.

Praise and recognition can take many forms, ranging from verbal compliments to increased salary, promotions, titles, job enrichment, etc. Often a simple unexpected verbal compliment such as, "I'm glad you're working in this department. You have an outstanding way of dealing with customers," or "You're doing a super job in this department. Keep up the good work" will go a long way toward motivating an employee to continue his or her good work in the weeks to come. Money, titles, and promotions show recognition of a job well done and are also effective for motivating future performance if the employee is a good performer and the recognition is well deserved. But dangling these prizes in front of a poor performer in the hopes of improving performance has mixed motivational results and is highly dependent on the individual involved.

To use money as an example, the poor performer who is confronted with the alternative of performing better on the job or forfeiting a salary increase may improve his or her performance long enough to obtain the salary increase, and then regress to former poor performance habits. Generally speaking, money, titles, promotions, and the like are better motivators of future performance if they are used to recognize an already good worker rather than to bribe a poor worker. Conversely, withholding these tangible forms of recognition from the well-deserved can be very devastating to their morale and can cause demotivation. The subject of using money as a motivator is discussed further in the section on incentives.

To illustrate the motivating power of praise and recognition, a true story should be told of what happened years ago in the proof and transit department of a medium-sized, multibranch eastern bank. The manager of the department at that time was intrigued with the subject of how to motivate the proof operators to process more items per day through the machines.

In those days the multipocket proof machines were constructed in such a way that, as the checks were added, the operator would press one of twenty buttons to activate a flap which covered the particular pocket into which the checks were to be placed. There were twenty of these pockets surrounding the keyboard and as the operator's right hand would index the amount of each check and activate the flap over the pocket, the left hand was used to physically place the check in the pocket. Since there were twenty pockets, the location of many of them were almost beyond the reach of the operator's left arm and hand. The reaching involved in placing these checks into the correct pocket was at times physically strenuous.

There was a counter on each machine that automatically registered the number of items as they were being processed. The counter which was reset to zero each morning could register up to 9,999 and then would role over to 0,000 indicating that the operator had processed 10,000 items that day. Added to the speed factor of processing 10,000 items was an accuracy factor. The checks were added in batches, and each batch had to be balanced to the penny. If the operator was inaccurate in indexing the amount of the checks, thus causing an out of balance condition, the operator would have to stop the machine, look for the differences, and correct it before continuing, A fast but inaccurate operator, therefore, would waste too much time looking for differences and could never reach the 10,000 item mark. Consequently, because of the physical layout of the machine and the combined speed and accuracy factors, processing 10,000 items in a single day was a difficult accomplishment. It wasn't very often that any of the eleven proof operators in this department accomplished this feat.

There was one veteran operator, however, who on occasion would roll over the machine thus signifying the processing of 10,000 items. When this happened the manager and the other employees in the department would notice and marvel at the skill of this employee.

The manager of the department, having assigned himself the project of devising a way to motivate all the proof operators to process more items through the machines, focused his thoughts on the magic of the 10,000 item mark—an ambitious motivational goal! The manager thought of the more traditional ways of recognizing efforts with money, gift awards, lists of names on the bulletin board, etc., but he discarded them as being too cumbersome and possibly ineffective. Finally, the manager decided to keep the whole thing simple, and remembering his grade school days, went out to the ten-cent store on his lunch hour one day and bought one package each of green and black construction paper and a box of large gold stars. After work that day, when all they employees had gone home, he cut out from the green paper three by nine inch placards, and from the black paper, two by eight inch placards. The black placards were pasted on to the green ones thus creating a green border around the black. In the middle of the black field one large gold star was pasted. Several of these signs were made, placed in an envelope, and put in the manager's desk for safekeeping.

The object of making these signs was that the next time an operator reached 10,000 items, the manager would take one of them from his drawer and attach it to the operator's machine for all to see—a sort of "badge of skill." No one knew what the manager had in mind. There was no announcement, no fanfare. Several days went by. Then one Friday the work was heavy, and the veteran operator was running fast. By noon she had approached 6,000 items, by 2:30 she reached 8,000 items, and finally at 4:30 she rolled over her machine—10,000 items. It was time for the gold star. The manager was fearful. Was this too simple, too childish an idea? Would it backfire? Was this the right type of praise and recognition? Mustering his courage, he took a sign out of his desk, walked over to the operator, and attached it on her machine. The operator looked up quizzically and wanted to know what it was. The manager merely said, "It's a gold star for rolling over your machine. Congratulations!" The operator smiled a little, and then the manager walked away. At the end of the day some of the other operators happened to walk by her machine and, noticing the gold star, asked the operator what it was. The seeds of motivation had been sown.

The very next business day the same operator rolled over her machine again. The manager went over to her machine with his box of gold stars and pasted another one next to the first. The sign had been designed to hold a maximum of five gold stars in a line on the field of black. Within two weeks there were five gold stars on that operator's sign. Also during this time, something magical was happening. Production was up among the other operators. Within a month three other operators received their first gold stars. At the end of six months the veteran operator had been awarded over fifty gold stars; the whole side of her machine was decorated with signs each filled with gold stars. During this period everyone in the bank became aware of the gold star awards and would come into the department to see them and praise the operators. The manager was pleased. The motivator of praise and recognition had worked. In fact it had "moved mountains."

The motivators of praise and recognition relate to fundamental needs within each person—the need for self-esteem to be self-confident and the need for self-respect. Again, these needs relate directly to the individuality of people.

GOAL SETTING

The story about the gold stars introduces another motivator that is related to individuality—goal setting. Employees will be motivated to perform a function better if they know what is expected of them. Performance standards should be determined for each job and explained to the employee. The manager then should watch to see that these standards are met by the employees. Without goals, employees will vary widely in their performance from day to day, or will set their own goals which often do not in any way correspond to those that management would perceive as challenging or even adequate. The concept of the individuality of each person suggests that goal setting be individualized. It is fine to have overall departmental goals, but it is each individual, as part of the whole, who is going to fulfill these goals. The manager must relate an overall goal to individual shares. This fixes responsibility upon the individual. In reality, overall goals are accomplished by individual efforts.

In the previous paragraph the subject of monitoring performance in relation to the goals was mentioned. This monitoring should always be done in the concrete—reported in writing. There is an old adage that states, "What gets tracked gets done." The process of monitoring or tracking performance in relation to goals is in itself a motivator. The employee responsible for the goal is being watched and, furthermore, this watching or monitoring is put on paper in the form of a report for all to see. It is not just tucked away in a manager's mind to be soon forgotten. Once employees realize they are being "tracked" they will almost always perform better and some will excel almost beyond imagination. Tracking results is a powerful motivator because it shows in the concrete the abilities of the performer (a self-esteem need). Good performers will excel. Poor performers will do better. Remember the gold star story? The posting of the stars was the tracking mechanism.

INCENTIVES

The individuality of each person suggests that to get results, reward the individual. In the gold star story, the stars themselves were the incentive or the reward. This was a simple reward but a powerful motivator because it dramatically satisfied the basic self-esteem need with each person. Any incentive that builds one's self-worth is probably the most effective of all motivators. And this incentive is even more effective in that everybody knows about it because not only are the employees who excel the most motivated but also other employees are motivated through the competitive environment in the group.

Earlier in this chapter the subject of using money as a reward was introduced. In any psychological survey conducted concerning motivational factors, money usually ranks in the middle of these motivators mentioned. High on the list are the self-esteem type motivators like verbal or written praise. However, money will attract a few employees to excel, particularly those who either need the extra money or need to satisfy a self-fulfillment need by earning money. To some people the more money a person earns the more successful the person is. In recent years money incentives have been used extensively by banks in order to develop and sustain a sales culture within the bank. Money incentives are used for those who cross sell and who open (sell) accounts beyond certain goals. Because these incentives are usually paid at sales meetings where all are present, it is unclear whether it is the recognition the employee receives when accepting the reward or the reward itself that is the motivator. In any event, in a sales environment the ultimate goal is to develop the money reward principle toward a commission type pay system, thus placing less emphasis in the salary type of pay system. The money incentive, therefore, becomes part of the employee's paycheck and is relied on for sustaining his or her standard of living. Considering all this, one should not conclude that because money incentives are used in a sales environment that they also should be used as an incentive in relation to a specific profit improvement project.

Other type incentives used are extra free holidays or weeks of vacation, plaques, jewelry, employee of the week awards, etc. Whatever is decided upon for an incentive, the element of self-esteem should be a part of awarding the incentive, i.e., awarded in front of others or the name of the employee is placed on a plaque or published in a newsletter. And the reward should be given as a result of a published tracking system which shows without question who really deserves the reward. In other words, the reward was truly earned not merely based on the opinion of a manager.

ANXIETY

Anxiety as it relates to being a motivator in the modern workplace is defined as a mild form of apprehension that can be used by a manager to motivate an employee to perform up to a standard. Those who manage other people have a certain degree of influence over those being managed because of their position. It is assumed, however, that the manager is a good manager and therefore is respected by the employees. Respect doesn't automatically come with the manager's position. It has to be earned. As was mentioned before, a poor manager will have difficulty applying any motivator. The influence that a manager has comes from the manager's ability to effect a change (either positive or negative) in an employee's well-being as it relates to working in the bank. More specifically, a manager can change an employee's salary, promotional possibilities, standing within the department, and even ultimately decide whether or not the employee will continue to work in the department. The employee instinctively knows that the manager has these abilities. And the manager also knows that the employee knows this.

When a manager attempts to influence an employee toward a goal by producing apprehension in the employee's mind, it can and should be subtle by merely explaining to the employee that the goal is now part of the employee's overall assignment and that it is expected of him or her. The veiled apprehension introduced to the employee is that because the added job goal is like all the other parts of the employee's job, it must be done or the employee will be subject to the same negative possibilities as if the other parts of the employee's job were not performed in a satisfactory way, i.e., reduced or no salary increase, transfer to a different job assignment, or, in the worst case, possible termination. These negative possibilities are not stated to the employee. It's just that they exist when a manager asks an employee to do a job in a way that the employee knows that the manager is serious about the request.

Another form of apprehension that can be used to motivate an employee toward a goal is in the form of a challenge. The goal is presented as a challenge. Is the employee up to the challenge? If not, why not? Others are doing it. Why can't the employee? This challenge is always presented to an employee on an individual basis—never in front of others. By singling out the person and counseling him or her, apprehension is automatically introduced and usually will produce positive results.

UNDERSTANDING THE PROFIT MOTIVE

When trying to motivate, particularly a member of management toward a profit oriented goal, it is important that the manager fully understands why the bank exists, which is to make a profit. All noncharitable organizations (including banks) exist primarily to make a profit. Without a profit, the organization will cease to exist. With meager profits, the organization will not grow, and the employees in the organization cannot grow in regards to compensation, increased responsibilities, and promotion.

An important part of being a manager of a department or a branch is being able to contribute to the bank's profits. It is a major function of everyone in management. In many organizations, increased compensation and promotional opportunities are granted to management personnel in direct relation to the individual manager's contribution to the organization's profits during the preceding year. Therefore, the sooner a lower level manager becomes more profit oriented, the sooner a lower level manager will become a senior level manager.

Once this motivation concept is instilled and understood by a manager it becomes a continuous internal motivator. The manager will perform profit oriented assignments to the best of his or her ability because it is ultimately in his or her own best interest.

SUPPORT FROM THE TOP

The final factor to be identified as a motivator in a profit oriented project is the degree of support that senior management gives to the project. The more support that senior management gives in announcing and explaining the project to those involved in the beginning, versus the interest shown as the project progresses, the better the results. This concept is used in Chapter 1, "The Profit Improvement Campaign." It should also be used in any major profit oriented project, and the more senior the officer is that is supporting the project, the better.

HOW TO USE THE MOTIVATORS TO IMPROVE PROFITS

This chapter has identified the following factors that should be used to motivate employees to perform well when they are a part of a profit oriented project.

Praise and Recognition
Goal Setting
Incentives
Anxiety
Understanding the Profit Motive
Support from the Top

All the motivators described above should be used to some degree in all profit improvement projects implemented within a bank. Three of these motivators—praise and recognition, goal setting, and support from the top—must be used to a high degree. Without these motivators, little will be accomplished. The gold star story is a classic example of the power of praise and recognition. Examples of goal setting are shown in detail in Chapter 2, "How to Reduce Teller Staffing Effectively," in chapter 5, "NSF Charges," and in Chapter 8, "How Much Cash Do You Really Need?" In most profit improvement projects the developing of statistics, which represent several months of past history, will provide goals for the future. Then continuing on with those statistics and publishing them for all to see will provide the motivator for attaining goals. If any manager is not consistently meeting these goals then a "nudge" (introducing anxiety) including possibly a reminder of the "profit motive" from the manager's superior should be done.

In all the subjects relating to profit improvements described in this book, a senior member of management both developed and supported the project—and they all produced excellent results. For the types of profit improvement subjects presented in this book, symbolic type of rewards such as a gold pen or a silver cup would be appropriate. A substantial incentive would not be necessary.

SUMMARY

This chapter identified and discussed six motivators relating to profit improvement. Three of these should be used in all profit improvement projects: praise and recognition, goal setting, and support from the top.

Anxiety and understanding the profit motive should be used on an "as needed" basis. The incentives motivator was identified more to be discussed than to be used. With the exception of using symbolic rewards, major incentives are not needed to produce results in the profit improvement projects typified in this book.

Chapter 18

Revisit Branch Profitability

Anytime the subject of branch profitability is discussed, the first thing that comes to mind is how to determine the net income derived from a branch. Invariably, this leads to discussions about ways of determining income for a branch relating to the branch's deposits (by type of deposit) and about allocating indirect expenses, such as for salaries and operating expenses relating to administrative, loan, personnel, and marketing departments. This often results in a multitude of conceptual conflicts about allocation formulas none of which are perfect and many of which are often too complex to be practical in application.

This chapter defines branch profitability as how to make branches more profitable. Consequently, the concern of this chapter is not to determine the net income of a particular branch but rather how to increase controllable income and decrease controllable expenses in a branch.

The key element in increasing the profits of a branch is in the use of statistics. This principle, discussed in the first chapter, emphasized their importance in conducting a bankwide profit improvement campaign. In addition, various statistical formats were used throughout this book. In the previous chapter the use of statistics was discussed as a motivator

("What gets tracked gets done"). In this final chapter it will be discussed again in relation to increasing branch profits.

THE POWER OF STATISTICS

To dramatically illustrate the power of using statistics in managing a function, a true story should be told about a bank manager many years ago. The story is not specifically about a branch manager but about a bookkeeping department manger in a unit bank whose function was similar, concerning income, to a branch manager in a bank with several branches.

The bank was located in an urban area and had about 15,000 checking accounts—many of which had a low average monthly balance but high activity. The bank had just begun what was to be a year-long drive to increase profits. The president directed the senior officers in the various divisions to generate and implement ideas that either increased income or decreased expense.

One day the senior operations manager was describing the bank's profit improvement campaign to the manager of the bookkeeping department in an effort to solicit his help. As the discussion progressed, it centered around what the manager of the bookkeeping department could do to increase profits. A brief discussion about decreasing expenses in the department (which yielded few ideas) was followed by a discussion about income. Both the senior operations manager and the department manager began asking each other about income items related to checking accounts. There were a lot of questions asked such as: "I wonder what the monthly service charge income is for the different types of accounts, for overdraft charge, for returned deposited checks, etc." Neither manager had any statistics available and, therefore, no answers.

At the next meeting a few days later, the two managers analyzed readily available service charge income statistics which had been obtained from the control department. In reviewing these statistics they found that the income from checking account related service charges of all types seemed low in relation to the number of accounts maintained and to the volume of checks processed. The manager of the bookkeeping department, who also had the daily responsibility of reviewing overdrawn checking accounts, knew that there was a high volume of checks returned for "insufficient funds" each day. During the meeting he happened to remark, "You know, if we increased our return check charge for overdrawn accounts by only one dollar per check we could probably increase our income a lot per month." The senior manager asked, "By how much?" After thinking a moment the bookkeeping manager answered, "Well, we return probably sixty or seventy checks per working day times twenty-two working days—that's about $1,300 to $1,500 per month." Both managers looked at each other in amazement.

This simple piece of statistical information about overdraft charge provided a spark that literally ignited something in the bookkeeping manager's mind. This manager, who was good at his job mainly because he was highly people oriented, had shown no interest in or aptitude for numbers up to this point in his career. For some reason, he became intrigued with the idea of increasing income through checking account related service charges.

He began by keeping detailed income records for his department. No source of income was left unaccounted—business-account service charges, personal-check charges, stop payment and returned deposited-check charges; income lost from waived or rebated charges were all meticulously recorded. This statistical recordkeeping motivated him to think of ways to increase income. He recommended and obtained approval to raise service charge rates to a level more in keeping with industrywide rates. He lobbied and was successful in having other officers in the bank charge those accounts which for years had been on a service charge waive basis. He charged customers a per hour rate for special services performed. Month after month he recorded and reviewed his income statistics and watched the income grow and grow. The result of this one man's efforts, with the aid of statistics, increased income in this bank from checking account related charges over $10,000 per month—$120,000 per year! This remarkable performance could not have been accomplished without the accumulation and review of statistics.

STATISTICS FOR IMPROVING BRANCH PROFITS

The following is a product of twenty-five years of experience in developing meaningful statistical information for the purpose of either increasing income or decreasing expenses in a branch. You will note that for the most part it is a departure from the usual type of statistics shown in relation to branch operations, because it identifies what is not done rather than what is being done as it relates to increasing profitability. Figure 18–1 shows a listing of items for which statistical data should be compiled for each branch in the system. Each item relates to a branch activity that is directly controlled by a branch. Note that there is only one expense item identified—the number of employees in a branch, thereby indicating a possible potential savings by decreasing personnel expense. Many of the other expenses associated with a branch such as forms, supplies, utilities, postage, depreciation, FDIC insurance, interest expense, etc., are either not highly controllable by the branch manager or are not usually major enough to warrant detailed investigation. There is plenty of profit improvement opportunities available in investigating the many income (fees waived) items shown. And these income items, once researched, will show what is not being done in dollars and the direct potential profit improvement. The items shown in Figure 18–1 are arranged into three categories—basic branch statistics, fees waived statistics, and other income related statistics.

COMPILING AND FORMATTING STATISTICS

Many of the branch statistics mentioned can be found from existing computer reports and reports generated by the accounting department. If certain fee waived information cannot be found broken down specifically by item as shown in the listing, totals of groups of items ("all teller fees waived" for example) would have to be used first and then broken down by hand later if an analysis of the total statistics warranted more investigation.

After the statistical information for each category for each branch has been obtained, a meaningful report of branch statistics can be prepared for each and all branches. The best time period for this type of report is a specific point in time for the basic branch statistics, and a month's activity for all other statistics. The report doesn't necessarily have to be compiled monthly but the report itself should cover a month's time period. Figure 18–1 shows a sample format for reporting these statistics for the five branches of a hypothetical bank. Note that only examples of basic branch statistics are shown in Figure 18–1. Note that the percentage of total bank information is shown. This statistic is an appropriate analysis tool for basic statistics but may not be appropriate for some of the other categories of items. The calculations shown regarding staffing in Figure 18–1 are an example of how to analyze basic branch statistical information and are explained more fully in the next section. Finally, note that in compiling these statistics start with basic branch statistics, then, as explained in the next section, compile and analyze items in the fees waived section one at a time.

Figure 18-1 Branch Statistics Report

	Main Office	% of Bank Total	North Branch	% of Bank Total	West Branch	% of Bank Total	East Branch	% of Bank Total	South Branch	% of Bank Total	Bank Totals
Basic Branch Statistics	3.537	42.1	1,903	22.6	1,272	15.1	987	11.7	710	8.4	8,409
Number of personal DDA accounts	571	38.0	450	29.9	233	15.5	124	8.3	125	8.3	1,503
Number of commercial DDA accounts	4,108	41.4	2,353	23.7	1,505	15.2	1,111	11.2	835	8.4	9,912
Total of DDA accounts	7,810	31.8	9,626	39.2	2,861	11.7	2,270	9.3	1,952	8.0	24,519
Number of savings accounts											
(passbook and statement)	11,918	34.6	11,979	34.8	4,366	12.7	3,381	9.8	2,787	8.1	34,431
Grand total number of accounts											
Total Deposits (in thousands)	$88,321		$86,157		$32,347		$18,200		$12,132		$237,158
Number of FTE employees	10	31.6	11.7	37.0	4.7	14.9	2.7	8.5	2.5	7.9	31.6
Total number of FTE employees	14	29.4	16.7	35.0	7.7	16.2	4.7	9.9	4.5	9.4	47.6
Ratio of number of FTE tellers to											
total number of DDA accounts	410:1		201:1		320:1		411:1		334:1		314:1
Fees Waived Statistics											
Number of accounts and amounts of fees waived for:											
Personal DDA accounts											
Commercial DDA accounts											
Totals for DDA accounts											
Savings accounts											
Grand total for all accounts											
NSF fees not collected											
Dollar amount of fees waived for:											
Money orders sold											
Cashier's checks sold											
Traveler's checks sold											
Collection items handled											
Utility payments received											
Other Income Related Branch Statistics											
Number of installment loans originated in branch											
Dollar amount of installment loans originated in branch											
Number of mortgage loans originated in branch											
Dollar amount of mortgage loans originated in branch											

ANALYZING BRANCH STATISTICS FOR PROFIT IMPROVEMENT

The purpose of putting all the statistics for each branch on one report is so that each type of statistic for each branch could easily be compared with the other branches. The basic statistics about each branch are shown first on the report so that other categories of statistics can be easily compared to the basic information. If, for example, through research, it was found that money order fees waived for the north branch totaled $1,000 in a month and the money order fees waived at the main office totaled only $250.00 during a month, and knowing from reviewing the account statistics that both branches are approximately the same size, it would be obvious that the tellers are not collecting money order fees properly at the north branch. Since we are reviewing the north branch's statistics, note the ratio of FTE (full-time equivalent) tellers to the total number of DDA accounts at the north branch. There are 201 DDA accounts per FTE teller, quite low compared to the other branches. Note that the ratio of FTE tellers is calculated on the number of DDA accounts. DDA accounts traditionally generate more teller activity than savings accounts, making them a better factor to use. The 201 DDA accounts per FTE teller ratio would strongly indicate overstaffing of tellers at the north branch. The use of ratios more dramatically illustrates possible problem areas within a branch. From comparing basic statistics in relation to staffing it appears that the north branch is overstaffing by approximately three FTE employees—two of which are tellers. Parenthetically, the total deposit amounts for each branch are shown mainly for reference purposes. Bankers traditionally relate the size of a branch with deposit totals. For profit improvement purposes, however, the other basic information shown is more useful.

With regard to the listing of other items shown, Figure 18–1, note that each item in the fees waived section relates directly to profit improvement. The statistics for each of these items for each branch should be developed and analyzed one at a time, and if your bank has not recently investigated the amount of NSF fees waived by branch personnel, this should be the first item researched. It is usually the easiest item for which to develop statistics and it is a very lucrative profit improvement project. Developing statistics by branch for fees waived can be laborious, depending on the data processing system in your bank. Starting with NSF fees waived, however, should be easier than most of the items, and with proper tracking will produce instantaneous results. In developing these NSF statistics, as mentioned before, a monthly time period should be used. After reviewing these NSF statistics the amount of profit improvement potential will be obvious, and when comparing these statistics to the number of DDA accounts in each branch, the branches needing improvement in this area will also be apparent. Most larger banks are now using a 10% waived tolerance as a goal. So, for example, if the NSF activity in a bank should produce $10,000 per month if all fees were charged, then $1,000 per month is the maximum amount allowed to be waived in the bank as a whole.

After the statistics mentioned for NSF fees waived have been tabulated and it is determined that collecting these fees should be improved, a separate monthly report just for NSF fees waived should be produced using the format shown in Figure 18–1, with names of the branches spread horizontally across the top of each column and the months of the year listed vertically. This then becomes an ongoing tracking report which should be published monthly and sent to all branch managers. This report should then be reviewed by the managers and the branch administrator in a meeting each month. This process continues each month until the increase in income in this area rises to an acceptable level as determined by senior management. Remember, what gets tracked gets done!

The same analysis described for NSF fees waived can be used for all the other fees waived items. After NSF fees, the other fee waived items should be researched in the following approximate order—commercial DDA accounts, savings accounts, and then the various teller-related fees starting with money orders and cashier's checks. As mentioned earlier, it is best not to try to develop statistics for all the items at once. Start with the basic statistics and then continue on through each of the waived items, one at a time. Projects for increasing income for each fee waived item should be also started one at a time and tracked. These projects can overlap, but usually three is the maximum number both the branch managers and the branch administrator can handle at one time.

When developing statistics for fees waived for checking and savings accounts, you will find other subjects that may have to be addressed, such as revisiting current policies on the types of accounts that have been traditionally waived (i.e., estate accounts, bowling league accounts, club accounts, and even municipal and quasi-charitable organization accounts). In addition, a mechanism for combining the profit or loss for multiple accounts of each commercial DDA customer may have to be developed.

Finally, the listing of items to be researched in Figure 18–1 includes a section called "other income related branch statistics." This section was added to the list to show efforts being made by each branch to develop income via the loan functions. This information prevents the branch administrator and others in senior management from obtaining a lopsided view of the efforts of a particular branch and its manager. If, for example, the income lost from waived fees is high for a particular branch but the volume of loans for that branch is also high, the lost fee income information is mitigated by the high loan volume. The income derived from loans—both from the interest and from related loan fees—is substantial. Although it may be difficult to obtain the actual dollar amount of the income generated from loans in each branch it is relatively easy to obtain the number and amount of loans generated in a given month and, then, if advisable, tracked monthly via a separate report. The mere tracking of this information and publishing it monthly should help produce more loans.

In conclusion, addressing the profitability of the branches in a bank by using the concepts described in this chapter is a major project, but the rewards can be substantial. You can expect a 20% to 50% increase in total bank fee income. But always remember—track it.

SUMMARY

In this chapter a nontraditional approach to branch profitability is discussed. The emphasis is placed on how to increase the profits of branches—and not on how to try to determine the specific net income of a branch. The key element in increasing profits in a branch is through the use of statistics developed for each branch and then compared again to the statistics of the other branches in the bank. The power of statistics cannot be overemphasized in this nontraditional approach to branch profitability. It gets results. Most of the items shown, for which statistics are to be obtained for each branch, related to what is not being done by a branch, rather than what is being done. These items are categorized into three major areas—basic branch statistics, fees waived statistics, and other income related branch statistics. Statistics for each waived fee item should be compared and analyzed one at a time, starting with NSF fees waived and proceeding with waived fees for commercial DDA accounts, personal DDA accounts, savings accounts, and finally teller-related fees. Each fee waived category needing improvement should then be tracked individually on a separate ongoing monthly published report. "What gets tracked, gets done."

The labor involved in compiling the fee waived statistics can, in some instances, be substantial but the results can be staggering.

Index

About the Publisher

PROBUS PUBLISHING COMPANY

Probus Publishing Company fills the informational needs of today's business professional by publishing authoritative, quality books on timely and relevant topics, including:

- Investing
- Futures/Options Trading
- Banking
- Finance
- Marketing and Sales
- Manufacturing and Project Management
- Personal Finance, Real Estate, Insurance and Estate Planning
- Entrepreneurship
- Management

Probus books are available at quantity discounts when purchased for business, educational or sales promotional use. For more information, please call the Director, Corporate/Institutional Sales at 1-800-PROBUS-1, or write:

Director, Corporate/Institutional Sales
Probus Publishing Company
1925 N. Clybourn Avenue
Chicago, Illinois 60614
FAX (312) 868-6250